DATE DUE

DEMCO 38-296

Historical Dictionary
of Political Communication
in the United States

Historical Dictionary
of Political Communication
in the United States

Edited by
Guido H. Stempel III
and
Jacqueline Nash Gifford

Greenwood Press
Westport, Connecticut • London

Historical dictionary of
political communication in

Library of Congress Cataloging-in-Publication Data

Historical dictionary of political communication in the United States
/ edited by Guido H. Stempel III and Jacqueline Nash Gifford.
p.   cm.
Includes bibliographical references (p.   ) and index.
ISBN 0–313–29545–X (alk. paper)
1. Communication in politics—United States—History Dictionaries.
I. Stempel, Guido Hermann, 1928–   . II. Gifford, Jacqueline Nash.
JA85.2.U6H57   1999
324.7'0973'03—dc21   99–21818

British Library Cataloguing in Publication Data is available.

Library of Congress Catalog Card Number: 99–21818
ISBN: 0–313–29545–X

First published in 1999

Greenwood Press, 88 Post Road West, Westport, CT 06881
An imprint of Greenwood Publishing Group, Inc.
www.greenwood.com

Printed in the United States of America

The paper used in this book complies with the
Permanent Paper Standard issued by the National
Information Standards Organization (Z39.48–1984).

10 9 8 7 6 5 4 3 2 1

Contents

Introduction   vii

**Historical Dictionary of Political Communication in
the United States**   1

Selected Bibliography   157

Index   163

About the Editors and Contributors   169

Introduction

This dictionary includes the people, organizations, events, and ideas that have been significant in the slightly more than two centuries of political communication in the United States.

This requires that we define political communication, something that even unabridged dictionaries do not do. They offer definitions of such things as political arithmetic, political economics, and political geography, but not political communication.

Political communication is communication about politics and government, about or within political campaigns, and about or by politicians. It covers such varied things as political speeches, televised debates, newspaper editorials of endorsement, media exposés of politicians, media coverage of governmental activity, photo ops, and publicity generated by the staff of politicians. These aspects of political communication and many others are covered in this dictionary.

Our emphasis is on the significance of each person, organization, event, or idea for political communication. We believe that everything that is included is important for those who are interested in political communication. The material presented here rises above the routine because the more than two dozen scholars who have written entries have consulted significant sources of information about the various topics. The result is new insights on some familiar people and events.

Political communication is as old as our republic. A piece of political communication—the Declaration of Independence—started this country. Thomas Jefferson began the Declaration by saying that we were separating ourselves from Great Britain. He also provided a long list of grievances of the colonies against the British.

Before that, though, comes a statement of political philosophy that remains our credo today. Most recall these ringing words from the second paragraph:

We hold these Truths to be self evident, that all Men are created equal, that they are endowed by their Creator with certain inalienable Rights, that among these rights are Life, Liberty, and the Pursuit of Happiness.

But the next sentence shaped the political destiny of the United States.

That to secure these Rights, Governments are instituted among Men, deriving their just Powers from the Consent of the Governed.

Strong words. A government rules by the consent of the people. There is no divine right of kings, emperors, or presidents. The people will decide, and that means they must be informed, that there must be political communication. Eleven years later, as the Constitution was being written, Jefferson wrote:

The way to prevent these irregular interpositions of the people is to give them full information of their affairs thro' the channels of the public papers & to contrive that those papers should penetrate the whole mass of the people. The basis of our government being the opinions of the people, the very first object should be to keep that right; and were it left to me to decide whether we should have a government without newspapers or newspapers without a government, I should not hesitate a moment to prefer the latter— but I should mean that every man should receive those papers and be capable of reading them.[1]

What Jefferson proposed, the First Amendment attempted to ensure. It read:

Congress shall make no law respecting an establishment of religion, or prohibiting the free exercise thereof; or abridging the freedom of speech or of the press; or the right of people to peaceably assemble, and to petition the Government for a redress of grievances.

Yet, only seven years later, freedom of the press was threatened with the passage of the Alien and Sedition Acts of 1798. They were used to suppress criticism of government, and they became the central issue of the presidential election of 1800. Jefferson's victory in that election meant that the Alien and Sedition Acts would not be renewed. The way was opened for political communication.

It was, however, a kind of political communication far different from what we know today. Newspapers represented political factions and promoted those factions. Truth was a lesser concern. It was an elitist press, but it served an elitist electorate. In 1824, the first presidential election for which there are records of the votes cast for each candidate, only 400,000 of the 10 million people (4 percent) in the United States voted. Three times that many voted in the next election, and participation in the political process has continued to expand.

The 1830s brought a press for the masses—the penny press of Ben Day and James Gordon Bennett. It was a sensational press that was less political. In response, Henry Raymond started the *New York Times* in 1851 with a goal of providing objective coverage. There would be two more bursts of sensationalism—the yellow journalism of the 1890s and the tabloids of the 1920s. Yet while the emphasis on politics was less, the newspaper remained the major means for politicians to reach the masses. The only other way was to go on a speech-making tour.

That changed with the advent of radio in the 1920s, although it wasn't until the 1930s that we saw a politician make widespread use of radio. President Franklin D. Roosevelt understood what could be done and had a radio voice unmatched by his political rivals. Then, after World War II, television came on the scene and became indispensable for politicians. Dwight Eisenhower used television more effectively than his opponents in the 1950s, and it is widely thought that John Kennedy defeated Richard Nixon for the presidency in 1960 because he looked so much better on television. Some wondered whether a tall, somewhat awkward, stern-faced person like Abraham Lincoln could have been elected president in the era of television.

With television there clearly was an emphasis on images in political communication, and yet that wasn't really anything new. Images have always played a major role in American politics. George Washington was the "father of his country." He could not tell a lie, as the legend of the cherry tree illustrates, and much is made of the story that he threw a dollar across the Potomac. James Monroe presided over the Era of Good Feeling, so called to this date by some historians, although bitter sectional factionalism was soon apparent.

William Henry Harrison was elected president on a slogan of "Tippecanoe and Tyler Too." What it meant was that Harrison had defeated the Indians at the Battle of Tippecanoe, and Tyler was his running mate. What that had to do with being president is anybody's guess. Lincoln was "Honest Abe" and "the rail splitter." The former is commendable for a president, but the latter has nothing to do with the duties of the office.

We began the twentieth century with Theodore Roosevelt, the "Rough Rider." The story was that the Rough Riders had stormed up San Juan Hill in Cuba during the Spanish-American War. Now historians doubt that they went up the hill, and if they did, it was on foot because it is well documented that the horses were mistakenly left in Florida.[2] President Franklin Roosevelt offered us the "New Deal," and President Harry Truman made it the "Fair Deal." President John F. Kennedy talked of a "New Frontier," and President Gerald Ford, the former Michigan football player, offered us "WIN" for Whip Inflation Now.

All of this is image with little substance. It continues today. Perhaps contemporary political consultants do it more and better. Clearly, they have been quick to make use of emerging technology such as videotape and the Internet.

While political communication has been with us as long as we have been a country, the study of political communication really hasn't. Its origins can properly be traced to the work of Walter Lippmann and Paul Lazarsfeld in the years between World War I and World War II.

Since then the study of political communication has expanded for two major reasons. One is the expansion of media and the related expansion of political communication. The other is the initiation of doctoral programs in mass communication and the growth in political science doctoral programs since World War II.

There has been more to study and more people to study it. Consequently, we know a great deal more about political communication. The conventional wisdom of politicians has given way, to some extent, to the knowledge of researchers who have studied various aspects of political communication.

It is difficult to chart a trend in that research. We are still pursuing some of the issues that Lazarsfeld and his colleagues studied. This is, in part, because political communication is a complex process. Harold Lasswell reduced political communication to who says what to whom with what effect. That seems easy enough until you realize that each of the four parts interacts with the other three, and in some instances combinations of the three interact to produce a result with the fourth one.

Yet, if we do not have all the answers, it probably is because we have not asked all the questions. Unquestionably, we have more answers than we used to have. It has been said that knowledge is tentative and always expanding, and there are few fields in which that is more true than the field of political communication changes. This dictionary is a benchmark for where the field is, which we hope will be helpful to those who will do the research that expands our knowledge of political communication.

NOTES

1. Leonard W. Levy, ed., *Freedom of the Press from Zenger to Jefferson* (Indianapolis: Bobbs-Merrill, 1966), p. 333.

2. Richard Shenkman, *Legends, Lies and Cherished Myths of American History* (New York: Harper & Row, 1988), pp. 88–89.

Historical Dictionary
of Political Communication
in the United States

A

ABRAMS v. UNITED STATES. Freedom of expression case in which Justice Oliver Wendell Holmes departed from the restrictive doctrine of "clear and present danger" to a more liberal view concerned with the actual impact of expression on the national welfare. On August 23, 1918, Jacob Abrams was arrested in New York City for distributing two leaflets that condemned President Woodrow Wilson for sending American troops to Russia and called for a general strike to protest. Abrams was arrested for violating the Sedition Act of 1917. While Abrams was out on bail, the Supreme Court upheld two convictions of antiwar socialists, Charles T. Schenck and Eugene V. Debs. Both unanimous decisions were written by Holmes. In the Schenck case, he wrote:

The question in every case is whether the words are used in such circumstances and are of such a nature as to create a clear and present danger that they will bring about the substantive evils that Congress has a right to prevent.

Abrams was convicted, and the case went to the U.S. Supreme Court, which upheld the conviction, 7–2. Justice John Clarke wrote the majority opinion, following Holmes' reasoning in *Schenck* closely. Holmes, however, sought to refine the doctrine. He denied that "the surreptitious publishing of a silly leaflet by an unknown man" met the clear and present danger test. He went on to say that the First Amendment protects the expression of all opinions, "unless they so imminently threaten immediate interference with the lawful and pressing purposes of the law that an immediate check is required to save the country."

SOURCES: *Abrams v. U.S.*, 250 U.S. 616, 1919; *Schenck v. U.S.*, 249 U.S. 47, 1919.

Larry L. Burriss

ADAMS, SAMUEL (1722–1803) is often called the "Father of the American Revolution." Adams, who grew up in Boston and was educated at Harvard, began his political career as a clerk of the Massachusetts General Assembly. In that role, he wrote many letters to the other colonies informing them of various acts and measures passed by the General Assembly. He is credited for inciting action against the Stamp Act and was one of those who incited the Boston Tea Party. He barred the doors of the General Assembly when British soldiers attempted to interrupt a meeting at which the assembly determined whom to send as delegates to the First Continental Congress.

SOURCES: Daniel J. Elazar and Ellis Katz, eds., *American Models of Revolutionary Leadership*, 1992; Frank Magill, *Great Lives from History: American Series*, 1987.

Jacqueline Nash Gifford

AGENDA SETTING is the theory that the media don't tell people what to think, but rather what to think about. In other words, the media define what the issues are. The concept traces back at least to Walter Lippmann's *Public Opinion*, but the first research data come from a study by Maxwell McCombs and Donald Shaw.

Agenda-setting studies compare the ranking of issues by the public, the media, and the politicians. They usually are highly correlated. McCombs and Shaw concluded in their study that the media had set the public agenda for the presidential election of 1968. Subsequent studies have suggested that, in some instances, the agenda is set by the politicians and picked up by the media. Other studies have suggested that, in some instances, the public sets the agenda.

So, while it is clear that the agendas of the politicians, the media, and the public often are very similar, it often is not clear which of the three originated the agenda. (*See also* Maxwell McCombs; Donald Shaw.)

SOURCE: Werner J. Severin and James W. Tankard, Jr., *Communication Theories*, fourth edition, 1997.

Guido H. Stempel III

AGNEW, SPIRO T. (1918–1996) became vice president of the United States on January 20, 1969, and was reelected in 1972. However, he resigned in disgrace on October 10, 1973, after pleading nolo contendere (no contest) to tax evasion. In return for his plea, government prosecutors agreed not to prosecute him on charges of extortion and bribery.

A labor lawyer, Agnew was elected Baltimore County chief executive in November 1962 and was elected governor of Maryland four years later. As vice president, Agnew became known for his colorful language and combative style. He described critics of President Richard Nixon's Vietnam War policy as "nattering nabobs of negativism" and "pusillanimous pussyfooters." He denouced "hopeless, hysterical, hypochondriacs of history" and "ideological Eunuchs." He led the attack of the Nixon administration against the media, opposing "instant analysis" by television commentators and complaining of "liberal bias" in the media.

SOURCES: Jim G. Lucas, *Agnew: Profile in Conflict*, 1970; "Vice-President Agnew Resigns, Fined for Income Tax Evasion," *New York Times*, October 11, 1973, p. 1.

Michael W. Singletary

AILES, ROGER (1940–) is a political communications consultant turned broadcaster—or perhaps it is the other way around. He began his broadcasting career as a student at Ohio University by doing an early morning radio show. Upon graduation in 1962, he went to work for KYW-TV in Cleveland. At KYW, he worked on the Mike Douglas Show, one of the first television talk shows. In three years he was promoted to producer.

While at KYW in 1968, Ailes met Richard Nixon, then a candidate for president. Nixon was upset that he had to resort to television to get elected. Ailes convinced Nixon that television was here to stay and that Nixon would lose if he didn't learn how to use it. Nixon hired Ailes as his media adviser. Ailes proposed a series of media events to shape Nixon's image as a serious, yet caring person. One of these media events was a television program called "Man in the Arena," featuring Nixon going head-to-head with a group of inquiring citizens in spontaneous give-and-take. The participants had, in fact, been hand-picked, and the programs were, to a large extent, staged.

Nixon won the election, and Ailes found himself in demand as a political consultant, but he kept his hand in television. In the 1980s, he was executive director of a show featuring Tom Snyder and Rona Barrett. He assisted presidential candidates Ronald Reagan and George Bush. For Reagan, he developed strategies to get voters to see past Reagan's age. He helped Bush shed his wimpy image and reportedly urged Bush to counterattack in his interview with Dan Rather about Iran-Contra. Ailes denied any connection with the Willie Horton ad, perhaps the most controversial ad of a highly negative campaign. It was, in fact, done by a political action committee, and by law Ailes, as a member of the Bush campaign staff, could not have been involved.

Ailes refused to help Bush with his reelection campaign in 1992. Instead, he sought to help Rush Limbaugh turn his radio talk show into a television program. In 1993 he became president of CNBC, NBC's cable venture. He left that job in 1996, when the cable channel merged with Microsoft to start MSNBC.

SOURCES: "Ailes Out at CNBC," *Broadcasting and Cable*, January 22, 1996; *New York Times Magazine*, January 2, 1995; *1989 Current Biography Yearbook*.

Jacqueline Nash Gifford

ALIEN AND SEDITION ACTS OF 1798. These acts restricted naturalization of aliens and public criticism of the federal government. Conflict with France over blocking passage of U.S. ships set the stage for these acts. French government officials demanded bribes from American representatives to let ships pass. The press reported this but withheld the names of the French officials, identifying them only as "X, Y, and Z." This fueled the Federalist Party's contempt for the Republican Party and led to the passage of the acts. The acts were used largely to prosecute journalists who criticized the Federalists and President John Adams. There were 14 such prosecutions, and all resulted in convictions. The acts became a major issue of the presidential election of 1800. With the defeat of Adams by Thomas Jefferson, the acts were allowed to lapse.

SOURCE: Jack P. Green, *Encyclopedia of American Political History*, 1984.

Jacqueline Nash Gifford

ALSOP, JOSEPH (1910–1989) **AND STEWART** (1914–1974). These brother columnists were among Washington's most prominent, influential, and controversial post–World War II journalists. Joe got his start in the newspaper business in 1932, right out of Harvard, because his grandmother was a friend of the *New York Herald-Tribune*'s publisher. He was soon transferred to Washington and began writing a column in 1937 with veteran newsman Robert Kintner called "Capital Parade." After war service, despite Stewart's total lack of news experience, the brothers teamed up on a column called "Matter of Fact." The pair quickly became known for their well-researched blend of gossip and opinion. They were strident cold warriors, nicknamed "Doom and Gloom," but made their mark opposing the communist witch-hunt of Senator Joseph McCarthy. The collaboration lasted 12 years, until Stewart asked out of the arrangement, in which he was subservient to his overbearing older brother. Stewart Alsop went on to be a contributing editor for *Saturday Evening Post* and died of leukemia in 1974. Joseph Alsop continued writing the column until 1975 and became increasingly influential in the Kennedy and Johnson presidencies. In the early 1960s, he left the faltering *Herald-Tribune* for the *Washington Post* and was ultimately syndicated in almost 200 papers. He died at 78 of lung cancer in 1989.

SOURCES: Leann Grabavoy Almquist, *Joseph Alsop and American Foreign Policy*, 1993; Richard Kluger, *The Paper, the Life and Death of the New York Herald Tribune*, 1986; Robert W. Merry, *Taking on the World: Joseph and Stewart Alsop—Guardians of the American Century*, 1996.

Marc Edge

AMERICAN ASSOCIATION OF RETIRED PERSONS (AARP) is one of the largest special interest groups, with more than 30 million members. Its goal is to protect the rights and advance the causes of citizens over the age of 50. Its main focus has been Social Security and health care. It publishes the magazine *Modern Maturity*, which is distributed to members. Its circulation of more than 21 million is the second highest of any magazine in the United States.

SOURCES: Allan J. Cigler and Burdett A. Loomis, *Interest Group Politics*, 1995; Kathleen Thompson Hill and Gerald N. Hill, *Real Life Dictionary of American Politics*, 1994.

Jacqueline Nash Gifford

AMERICAN CIVIL LIBERTIES UNION (ACLU). A group whose primary goal is to protect constitutionally guaranteed freedoms, especially freedom of expression. Founded in 1920, ACLU has a quarter of a million members. It has had considerable impact on political communication through supporting court tests of laws that promote censorship or restrict speech. It gained early fame through the Scopes "Monkey" trial, which tested the constitutionality of a Tennessee law that forbade teaching Darwin's theory of evolution.

SOURCES: Allan J. Cigler and Burdett A. Loomis, *Interest Group Politics*, fourth edition, 1995; Leon Hurwitz, *Historical Dictionary of Censorship in the U.S.*, 1995.

Jacqueline Nash Gifford

AMERICAN FEDERATION OF LABOR–CONGRESS OF INDUSTRIAL ORGANIZATIONS (AFL–CIO) is the collective group of organizations that work to protect the rights of labor. The AFL–CIO represents 13 million workers. Union locals retain their individual identities and manage their own business. However, when issues arise affecting rights of unions and their members, the national organization takes charge. The AFL–CIO is a major lobbying force and also a major political action group that contributes millions of dollars in presidential and congressional election campaigns.

SOURCES: Jay M. Shafritz, *The HarperCollins Dictionary of American Government and Politics*, 1992; Kathleen Thompson Hill and Gerald N. Hill, *Real Life Dictionary of American Politics*, 1994.

Jacqueline Nash Gifford

ANDERSON, JACK (1922–) is considered one of America's muckrakers. He has been covering Washington since 1947 as a newspaper and magazine columnist. While attending the University of Utah, Anderson became a reporter for the *Salt Lake City Tribune*. One of his earliest investigative reports—an exposé on Mormon polygamy—got him in trouble, and he left school to become a missionary. He then became a reporter for the *Deseret News*. He was drafted into the army during World War II and was assigned to *Stars and Stripes*.

After the war, he went to Washington to write for columnist Drew Pearson, who wrote a syndicated column called "Washington Merry-Go-Round." Anderson took over that column when Pearson died in 1969. In 1954, he became Washington correspondent for the Sunday supplement *Parade*.

Anderson received the Pulitzer Prize in 1972 for his reporting on the Security Action Group papers that showed the Nixon administration's favoritism of Pakistan in a war between that country and India.

SOURCE: Neil A. Grauer, *Wits and Sages*, 1984.

Jacqueline Nash Gifford

ARMSTRONG, BESS FURMAN (1894–1969), a member of the women's press corps who covered Eleanor Roosevelt, was introduced to newspapering by her father, Archie, who ran a weekly newspaper in southwestern Nebraska. Furman was a member of the inner circle that enjoyed the good graces of the First Lady. Mrs. Roosevelt discussed the press conference idea with her before the 1933 inauguration. Her decision to conduct press conferences made history because she was the first president's wife to do so.

Only women could attend Mrs. Roosevelt's conferences. They worked as reporters at a time when newspaper city rooms were "as sacred to men as a stag club or pre-Volstead saloon," according to journalism historian Ishbell Ross. While more than 10,000 women worked for newspapers at this time, only a handful worked as reporters, known as front-page girls.

The Associated Press in Washington hired Furman in 1929. She came there from the *Omaha Bee-News*, where she had been since 1920. She had covered Democrat Al Smith's stump speech in Omaha in 1928 and also covered Herbert Hoover's visit to his Iowa hometown. In 1927 she filed front-page stories on President and Mrs. Calvin Coolidge's vacation in South Dakota. The stories were accompanied by her photo, indicating her front-page-girl status.

SOURCES: Maurine H. Beasley, ed., *The White House Press Conferences of Eleanor Roosevelt*, 1983; Ishbell Ross, *The Ladies of the Press*, 1974.

Liz Watts

ARNETT, PETER (1934–) is recognized as one of America's greatest war correspondents. He is actually a New Zealander by birth. There he dropped out of high school and headed for a career in journalism at a daily newspaper called the *Southland Times*. Over the course of the 1950s, he worked for a variety of Australian papers, and finally, in 1961, he became an Associated Press (AP) stringer.

In the 1960s, Arnett covered Southeast Asia and eventually South Vietnam. In South Vietnam, he worked hard to cover every angle of the war, which sometimes included reporting on discrepancies between what the U.S. government reported publicly and his own investigative reporting from the scene. This type of journalism style earned him fans and foes: fans who welcomed the fresh, honest reporting style and foes who labeled him a Vietnamese sympathizer, a title he rejected. In 1966, he received a Pulitzer Prize for his reports from Vietnam, where he reported on the war and related events for 11 years.

Arnett's reporting skills and international reputation helped launch CNN in its endeavors to cover news events live no matter where they occurred. In the 1980s, he covered the Middle East, including the TWA hijacking in 1985. But it wasn't until 1991 and the Gulf War that CNN was put on the map for its ability to cover the war instantly—with help from Arnett. When the war started, Arnett, other CNN staffers, and other Western journalists were in Baghdad, the main city hit by rockets from the multinational collaborative effort to drive Iraqi leader Saddam Hussein from Kuwait. When full war broke out, the Iraqi government permitted only one Western news agency to remain in Baghdad—Arnett and CNN—but only if the information they used was "approved" and thus censored by the government.

It was his interview with Saddam Hussein, however, that lead to criticism by other journalists. Arnett justified his position as he had during Vietnam: the public had the right to know as much as possible, and under the First Amendment he was permitted to tell it as he saw it. When he left Iraq in mid-1991 (he and the Iraqi government had disagreements over what news would be censored), he was praised by several news organizations for his stellar work as a war correspondent.

SOURCES: Peter Arnett, *Live from the Battlefield*, 1994; *Current Biography*, 1991.

Jacqueline Nash Gifford

B

BACKLASH. A term used by political scholars and journalists to define the phenomenon of the white "countermovement" against civil rights laws and acts that protect the rights of minorities, such as African Americans and women. The term is often used to describe such social trends as "reverse discrimination" and the rise of hate groups. Although the term was coined in the 1960s, it still is applicable today and has been the source of many modern articles and books, including Susan Faludi's *Backlash*, which looks at the political setbacks women have faced since the Civil Rights movement.

SOURCES: William Safire, *Safire's New Political Dictionary*, 1993; Jay M. Shafritz, *The HarperCollins Dictionary of American Government and Politics*, 1992.

Jacqueline Nash Gifford

BENNETT, JAMES GORDON founded the *New York Herald* in 1835. He revolutionized news coverage. He made it clear at the outset that he intended his paper to be politically nonpartisan. He pioneered coverage of Wall Street, high society, religion, police, and sports. His influence on coverage of those areas is still evident in the media today. His approach to news succeeded in making the *Herald* the daily newspaper with the largest circulation. More important for our purposes, Bennett's notions of news included coverage of Congress. He found that while reporters were permitted to attend House sessions, only reporters from Washington newspapers were permitted at Senate sessions. He waged a two-month campaign in 1841, with a number of editorials denouncing the exclusion, and in July 1841 the Senate changed its rules to permit all bona fide reporters in its meetings. The change was permanent. Bennett's campaign had established the right of media to cover the Senate, and other media were to follow the *Herald*'s lead.

SOURCES: Edwin and Michael Emery, *The Press and America*, sixth edition, 1988; Sidney Kobre, *Development of American Journalism*, 1969; Fred Marbut, ''The United States Senate and the Press, 1838–41,'' *Journalism Quarterly*, Summer 1951.

Guido H. Stempel III

BLACK, HUGO (1886–1971) was a U.S. Supreme Court justice selected by President Franklin Roosevelt in 1937. He is known for his strict interpretation of the First Amendment, thus believing that the federal government should not make any laws impeding free speech.

Black did not have a formal law degree, but rather a degree from a junior college in Alabama, his boyhood home. He did manage to run a small, but unsuccessful, law firm. He also had ties to the Ku Klux Klan to help his social standing among those in his community. Despite this, he was elected to the U.S. Senate for two terms before becoming a justice, a position he held for 34 years. He was, with the possible exception of his colleague Justice William Douglas, the strongest supporter of the First Amendment in the history of the Court.

SOURCES: Leonard W. Levy, *Encyclopedia of the American Constitution*, 1994; *The Oxford Companion to the Supreme Court of the United States*, 1992; Melvin Urofsky, *The Supreme Court Justices, a Biographical Dictionary*, 1994.

Jacqueline Nash Gifford

BLACK PANTHERS is considered to be the most militant black power movement in the United States. Known for its violence, the group sought to bring the issues of black America to the nation's mind during the 1960s and 1970s through a show of force against white bureaucracy. Memorable skirmishes took place between the Panthers and the police in California, New York, New Jersey, and Illinois.

In 1966, the Black Panther Party, on which the Black Panthers is founded, was created by Huey Newton and Bobby Seale. The group's philosophy was based on improving housing, jobs, and education and insisting upon fairer treatment in the judicial system. The Federal Bureau of Investigation (FBI), then headed by J. Edgar Hoover, followed the activities of the group to curtail their violent tendencies.

Eventually, the group split into two subgroups, one on the East Coast and the other on the West Coast. The more militant branch (East Coast) was lead by Eldridge Cleaver, and the other by Newton and Seale. The latter group continued the efforts of the original Black Panthers minus the violence.

SOURCE: John W. Smith, *The Urban Politics Dictionary*, 1990.

Jacqueline Nash Gifford

BLACK POWER is an expression created by black militant leader Stokely Carmichael during the 1960s Civil Rights movement. Carmichael, then president of the Student Nonviolent Coordinating Committee (SNCC), created the phrase to describe the activities of ''the political left who became frustrated by the moderate approach of the more traditional civil rights movement.'' To many civil rights supporters, both black and white, the phrase exemplified the growing violent tendencies of young blacks. Carmichael went on to use the phrase during his association with the Black Panthers. (*See also* Stokely Carmichael.)

SOURCE: John W. Smith, *The Urban Politics Dictionary*, 1990.

Jacqueline Nash Gifford

BLACK PRESS. The first black newspaper, *Freedom's Journal*, was established in 1827. An abolitionist publication, *Freedom's Journal* advocated for black rights. Frederick Douglass, the well-known abolitionist, began publishing his newspaper, *North Star*, in 1847. The first black female journalist was Ida B. Wells, who championed human rights and wrote for both the black and Anglo media in the late nineteenth century. The black press flourished early in the twentieth century but by 1970 was struggling to maintain its readership. Circulation of even the most successful papers, such as the *Chicago Defender*, had plummeted. Rising production costs and competition from other media are reasons most often cited for the decline. Today, the total number of black newspapers is close to 200. Some of these are free publications, but others maintain paid circulations.

The oldest circulating African-American newspaper is the *Philadelphia Tribune*, founded in 1884. It is published three times a week and established a Web site in 1996. The oldest daily newspaper is the *Chicago Daily Defender*, which began as a weekly in 1905. The black press of the 1990s has attracted nonblack investors, a trend that has met with mixed reaction because these publications survive, while many smaller, community-based papers do not. Although contemporary black newspapers struggle to compete for advertising dollars, surveys show that black newspapers are the primary source of news for their readers. (*See also* Frederick Douglass; William Lloyd Garrison.)

SOURCE: Clint C. Wilson, *Black Journalists in Paradox: Historical and Current Perspectives*, 1991.

Carol M. Liebler and B. Carol Eaton

BLUMLER, JAY (1924–) is a British political communication researcher. He has been director of the Centre for Television Research and professor of sociology and political aspects of broadcasting at the University of Leeds in England. He also was a lecturer at Oxford College and finally at the University of Maryland, from where he retired in 1989.

Blumler's contributions to political communication lie in the realm of the effects of television in the process, particularly in books he either coauthored or wrote. Some of his more influential books are *Television in Politics: Its Uses and Influence* (1968), *The Challenge of Election Broadcasting* (1978), and a coauthored book, *The Formation of Campaign Agendas* (1991). In the latter book, he uses British and U.S. election data to analyze messages and communication strategies. For example, he studies the gatekeeping process, agenda setting, and journalism's role in the political communication process. At the crux of the work is an attempt to discover who really influences political communication—spin doctors (working on behalf of their clients, politicians), the media, or the public. He also compares British and U.S. political coverage.

SOURCES: *Directory of European Political Scientists*, 1985; *Political Communication: Issues and Strategies for Research*, 1975.

Jacqueline Nash Gifford

BOORSTIN, DANIEL (1914–) is an author who comments on American history. Boorstin studied at Harvard, Oxford, and Yale. He taught history at the University of Chicago for 25 years. He has written many books on American politics, including *The Genius of American Politics* (1959), *The Americans: The National Experience* (1965), *The Americans: The Democratic Experience* (1975), and *The Image* (1962).

The Image was a departure, in a sense, from his other works, as he examined the failing qualities of the American Dream over the country's lifetime. Specifically, he pointed to the superficiality of the modern world and how it fuels the inability of modern Americans to understand their political system.

He was openly critical of the process of political communications, where, in his view, phony events (he coined the term "pseudo events") are created by public relations people to attract journalists who, without analysis of the events, act as a sleeping funnel for the information to an even more apathetic American audience. The implication, wrote Boorstin, is that these events perpetuate responses that create more pseudo events or information, and thus a cycle is created.

In addition to his writing, Boorstin served as the 12th librarian of Congress. Since his retirement in 1987, he has continued to write insightful essays and books on American history and politics.

SOURCES: *Current Biography*, 1988; *Who's Who in America*, 1997–1998.

Jacqueline Nash Gifford

BRANDEIS, LOUIS (1865–1941). U.S. Supreme Court justice appointed by President Woodrow Wilson to replace Joseph R. Lamar in January 1916. Brandeis, born in Kentucky to Jewish parents, attended Harvard Law School and had his own practice in Boston before joining the Court. During his private practice days, he built a reputation for being a "people's attorney" who was out to protect the rights of the common man. With such a background, it is no wonder that, as a Supreme Court justice, Brandeis often favored individual rights in cases regarding the First Amendment and privacy.

In *Schenck v. U.S.*, for example, he initially agreed with the majority opinion that speech against the government should be restricted during times of war or in light of "clear and present danger," a litmus test proposed by Justice Oliver Wendell Holmes. However, Brandeis later changed his mind and did not agree with this "test" as applicable to all speech against the government. In *Whitney v. California* eight years later, he delivered this ringing endorsement of free speech:

Those who won our independence were not cowards. They did not fear political change. They did not exalt order at the cost of liberty. To courageous, self-reliant men, with confidence in the power of free and fearless reasoning applied through the processes of popular government, no danger flowing from speech can be clear and present, unless the incidence of the evil apprehended is so imminent that it may befall before there is opportunity for full discussion. If there be time to expose through discussion the falsehood and fallacies, to avert the evil by the processes of education, the remedy to be applied is more speech, not enforced silence.

Brandeis also is known for his interest in the right to privacy, a right he believed was justified in the First Amendment. This included limiting the ways in which the government or press could obtain evidence by using new technology, such as wiretapping, to violate one's privacy.

SOURCES: Philippa Strum, *Louis D. Brandeis, Justice for the People*, 1984; Melvin Urofsky, *The Supreme Court Justices: A Biographical Dictionary*, 1994; *Whitney v. California*, 274 U.S. 357 (1927).

Guido H. Stempel III

BRENNAN, WILLIAM J., JR. (1906–1997) was a U.S. Supreme Court justice appointed by President Dwight D. Eisenhower in January 1957 to succeed Associate Justice Sherman Minton. He served on the Court for 33 years.

Brennan grew up in New Jersey and, after completing law school, set up a practice there. After serving in the army in World War II, he returned to law and served in many judicial posts in New Jersey.

During his years on the Court, Brennan was viewed as a liberal with a strong adherence to the literal interpretation of the First Amendment. Because of this, he often favored the rights of the press in legal matters. The best-known example of this is *New York Times v. Sullivan*, in which he authored the majority opinion, which put burden of proof on public officials to prove actual malice or reckless disregard of the truth when they sue for libel. (*See also New York Times v. Sullivan.*)

SOURCES: Steven W. Colford, "Ad Industry Loses Hero in Brennan," *Advertising Age*, July 30, 1990; Dennis Hale, "Justice Brennan's Record on Speech and Press Cases," *Editor & Publisher*, February 3, 1990.

Jacqueline Nash Gifford

BRINKLEY, DAVID (1920–) describes himself as doing the news longer than anyone else on Earth, and with good reason. His career spans 53 years and, according to the title of his autobiography, "11 presidents, 4 wars, 22 political conventions, 1 moon landing, 3 assassinations, 2,000 weeks of news and other stuff on TV and 18 years of growing up in North Carolina."

He was the youngest of five children, whose father died when he was eight. He dropped out of high school because of lack of interest, except for English, and through that passion a teacher encouraged him to go into journalism. He became a reporter for the hometown paper, the *Wilmington Morning Star*, and later became a special student in English at the University of North Carolina at Chapel Hill.

Following World War II, when he worked for the United Press, he went to a job interview that changed his life. CBS offered him a job in Washington as a radio broadcaster, but upon returning there he found there wasn't a position. He walked across the street and got a job at NBC. At NBC, he got his first taste of political writing as a White House and Capitol Hill correspondent.

With the advent of television, he was offered an opportunity to air stories he had researched and written. In 1951, he joined the network's early evening news program called *The Camel News Caravan* and appeared on the talk show *Commentary*. Viewers took a liking to Brinkley's style—a blend of objectivity, intelligence, precise language, dry tone with wit to match, and thoughtfulness.

In 1956, NBC took a gamble and placed him and Chet Huntley together to cover the presidential nominating conventions. That pairing lead to a bigger gamble: using the pair as the anchors for a nightly news program, later called *The Huntley-Brinkley Report*. With advances in television technology, Huntley appeared in New York, and Brinkley in Washington. It ranked as the top news program for 14 years and won many professional broadcasting awards, including the George Foster Peabody Award and an Emmy. He has won three Peabody and ten Emmy Awards.

In 1976, Brinkley became coanchor with John Chancellor, and then Brinkley became a commentator. In 1981, he moved to ABC and his own program, *This Week with David Brinkley*, in which he and other ABC reporters and newscasters discussed weekly political happenings.

SOURCES: David Brinkley, *11 Presidents, 4 Wars, 22 Political Conventions, 1 Moon Landing, 3 Assassinations, 2,000 Weeks of News and Other Stuff on TV and 18 Years of Growing Up in North Carolina*, 1995; *Current Biography*, 1987.

Jacqueline Nash Gifford

BROWN, HUBERT GEROLD (Jamil Abdullah Al-Amin) (1943–) penned the autobiographical book *Die Nigger Die* as a member of the Black Power movement in the 1960s.

Brown grew up in Baton Rouge and attended Southern University, a black college. His generation was fed up with the slowness and lack of response to Dr. Martin Luther King's Civil Rights movement. Instead, Brown and his peers advocated a "violence for violence" approach to make social changes.

Oddly, Brown did become chairman of the Student Nonviolent Coordinating Committee (SNCC). However, in this position, he still advocated violence when met with violence by police officers, coining the statement "violence is as

American as cherry pie.'' His talks are said to have incited riots throughout America, including ones in Cambridge, Maryland. There he was reported to have started an incident that resulted in arson, and consequently he was sought for this crime. He was even put on the Federal Bureau of Investigation's (FBI) Ten Most Wanted List, which Brown argued was in response to his political speech. He went into hiding and later was caught near the scene of a robbery. Although no evidence was uncovered, he was found guilty and plea-bargained for reduced time if he admitted he was connected with the arson charges in Maryland. In jail, he changed his name to Jamil Abdullah Al-Amin and converted to the Muslim faith. He now lives in Atlanta, where he works within the Muslim community as an educator.

SOURCES: *Current Biography*, 1994; Jack Salzman, David Lionel Smith, and Cornel West, *Encyclopedia of African-American Culture and History*, 1990.

Jacqueline Nash Gifford

BURGER, WARREN (1907–1995) was the chief justice of the U.S. Supreme Court from May 1969 to July 1986. He was appointed by President Richard M. Nixon.

He was born in St. Paul, Minnesota, to Swiss-German parents. He graduated from law school with highest honors and worked as a lawyer with a local firm. His work with the Republican candidates' campaigns, including that of Dwight Eisenhower, fueled his national judicial career, including a position on the U.S. Court of Appeals.

The Burger Court ruled in favor of the media and the First Amendment less often than the Warren Court had. It ruled against confidential privilege for newspeople and took away some of the gains for the media made in *New York Times v. Sullivan* and subsequent decisions of the Warren Court. Yet decisions of the Burger Court in a series of cases beginning with *Nebraska Press Association v. Stuart* (427 U.S. 53, 1976) clearly established the right of the media to report on court cases. In *Miami Herald v. Tornillo* (418 U.S. 241, 1974) the Court rejected the concept of a right of reply for persons criticized by newspapers.

Burger was not a fan of the press. He resented television cameras in the courtroom and did not permit them in the Supreme Court. However, in *Chandler v. Florida* (449 U.S. 560, 1980), he did vote to give states the right to permit cameras in their courtrooms if they choose.

SOURCES: Leon Friedman, *The Burger Court*, 1978; *The Oxford Companion to the Supreme Court of the United States*, 1992.

Guido H. Stempel III

BUSH-RATHER INTERVIEW. On January 25, 1988, CBS Evening News anchor Dan Rather interviewed George Bush, vice president and presidential candidate. The nine-minute interview followed a five-minute, videotaped feature that Rather narrated. Bush watched the feature from his location for the live interview—his desk at his Capitol Hill office.

The interview was controversial, confrontational, and, in the end, consequential. One in a series of interviews and profiles of the 13 candidates, this interview ran longer than scheduled. Both participants interrupted each other and talked over the other's talk uncountable times. The men raised their voices and accused each other of less than noble intent and of less than professional behavior.

The videotaped feature voiced doubts about Bush's role in the Iran-Contra affair. Rather's interview questioning centered on those issues. Bush voiced displeasure over this line of questioning, insisting that he, instead, be allowed to articulate his positions on issues of his choice.

Public and media response to the interchange was extensive and varied. Some accused Rather of overstepping the bounds of objective reporting, indicating that he had badgered Bush in a partisan fashion. Others praised Rather's insistence that Bush answer questions that Bush preferred to finesse. Some said the interview "dewimpified" the vice president by showing he could stand up to powerful opponents. The interview foreshadowed future use of high-profile television interviews as important forums in presidential election politics.

SOURCES: "Special Section: The Dan Rather/George Bush Episode on CBS News," *Research on Language and Social Interaction*, 22, 1988; Transcript of the program (Tape of the program is available from the Vanderbilt Television News Archive).

Edward Lee Lamoureux

C

CABLE NEWS NETWORK (CNN). Atlanta broadcaster Ted Turner took advantage of satellite technology when he dedicated "America's News Channel" in 1980. By delivering his programming directly to cable operators by satellite, Turner avoided having to build a conventional network of affiliates to rebroadcast his news. Turner's gamble was a money loser for the first five years, and the red ink flowed faster when he launched a second network—CNN Headline News—in late 1981 to stave off a bid by ABC and Westinghouse to create a competing news channel. In its first five years, CNN lost more than $70 million, but the financial picture improved as cable channels grew in popularity and increased their market penetration. In 1985, CNN made a profit of $18.8 million, compared to a loss of $15.3 million the year before. That year, CNN reached 33 million households—80 percent of U.S. cable homes and almost 40 percent of U.S. television homes. Also in 1985, Turner created CNN International and went worldwide at a time when U.S. networks were cutting back on their international coverage. The benefits of this global expansion became apparent in the 1991 Gulf War, when CNN's wall-to-wall coverage produced its highest ratings. Creation of a "CNN factor" was even credited with influencing events by instantaneous coverage. Today, CNN boasts 10 channels, including separate financial and sports networks, along with a radio news network. With 3,000 news staffers in 21 bureaus on six continents, CNN now has access to a potential 500 million viewers.

SOURCE: Don M. Flournoy and Robert K. Stewart, *CNN: Making News in the Global Market*, 1997.

Marc Edge

CANTRIL, ALBERT HADLEY (1940–) is a pollster who gauges the American public's political attitudes and behavior. He obtained his bachelor's and master's degrees from Dartmouth and Massachusetts Institute of Technology, respectively. Following his formal education, he assisted Bill Moyers with the White House's press activities and continued his federal career with the U.S. State Department as an assistant secretary of state for East Asian and Pacific Affairs.

In 1969, he left the government and went to work for the Institute for International Social Research, where he began the research for a book he coauthored with Charles W. Roll, Jr., *Hopes and Fears of the American People*. The book, although brief, received widespread recognition and acceptance for its insights into the thinking of the American public.

In 1975, he became president of the National Council on Public Polls and continued his work on polling as a social science until the present. In 1980, he wrote the book *Polls: Their Use and Misuse in Politics*, a seminal work analyzing the effects polling has had on politics and journalism since its beginnings in the early 1900s. He was especially critical of journalists using polls as proof or the basis for stories, because he felt journalists rarely have the ability to understand the complexities and procedures of social science theory and practices.

SOURCES: *Contemporary Authors*, Vol. 111, 1984; *Who's Who in America*, 1997.

Jacqueline Nash Gifford

CANTRIL, HADLEY (1906–1969) was one of several Princeton University researchers whose work challenged the powerful effects model of media and society and helped in the evolution of modern media theory. His panic research on audience response to the 1938 "War of the Worlds" radio broadcast by CBS and the Mercury Theater provided the first challenge to the idea that media could manipulate all people equally. His work ushered in the selective influence model of mass media effects based on individual differences. His pioneering research pointed out the importance of "critical ability" in determining whether people could be manipulated by the media. Intervening forces such as opinion leaders and psychological variables often were seen to have more influence on people than the media. More important, Cantril refined the survey method and collaborated with George Gallup in adding psychological dimensions to Gallup's polling techniques. Cantril's self-anchoring striving scale illustrated the values underlying the political orientations of the American people. He also influenced the way researchers characterize the relationship between public opinion and government policy. Based on his research, media were viewed as being less politically oppressive and less propagandistic in intent, reinforcing a new view of media as social change agents.

SOURCES: Stanley J. Baran and Dennis K. Davis, *Mass Communication Theory*, 1995; Lloyd Free and Hadley Cantril, *The Political Beliefs of Americans*, 1967; Shearon Lowery and Melvin DeFleur, *Milestones in Mass Communication Research*, 1988.

LeAnne Daniels

CARMICHAEL, STOKELY (Kwame Toure) (1941–) created the term "black power" and applied it to his life and the lives of many African Americans during the Civil Rights movement of the 1960s.

Educated at Howard University, he was very active politically. He joined the Student Nonviolent Coordinating Committee (SNCC) in 1964 and later became its chairman. In that role, he worked throughout the South to register voters and promote political education as it related to African-American causes and issues.

During that time, Stokely developed leadership skills, which he used to instill a militant tone into SNCC, which threatened civil rights supporters, both black and white. Also during this time he coined the phrase "black power" as a way to express the energy that African Americans needed to ensure a future in America.

After leaving the SNCC, he joined the Black Panthers, a national radical group that espoused the same ideas as his. He eventually became the prime minister of that group. Disfranchised with the movement, he left the Black Panthers to study under African leaders in Guinea. He claimed Guinea as his home and in 1978 changed his name to Kwame Toure. In Guinea, he has openly criticized the West, particularly the United States, and has worked with the All African People's Revolutionary Party, which promotes unity of African interests.

SOURCES: Kenneth Estell, ed., *Reference Library of Black America*, 1994; Shirelle Phelps, ed., *Who's Who among African-Americans*, ninth edition, 1996; Jack Salzman, David Lionel Smith, and Cornel West, eds., *Encyclopedia of African-American Culture and History*, 1990.

Jacqueline Nash Gifford

CENSORSHIP is used by government officials to prevent information from reaching the public. The term implies prior restraint of publication, not action after publication. In practice this means that official censors see everything before it is published or aired. The First Amendment prohibits this in the United States, but it is permitted by the military in wartime. In many other countries, censorship is practiced all the time, and everything that is published or aired is with the consent of the government. Censorship should be distinguished from official secrecy, which keeps information from being released and has somewhat the same effect. Secrecy, of course, is practiced by politicians everywhere. However, it is limited by law in the United States and in most free societies.

SOURCE: Ralph L. Holsinger and Jon Paul Dilts, *Media Law*, third edition, 1994.

Guido H. Stempel III

CHAFFEE, STEVEN H. (1935–) obtained his bachelor's degree at the University of Redlands and his master's at the University of California. He obtained his Ph.D. at Stanford University, where he currently is chair of the Department of Communication.

In 1965 he joined the journalism faculty at the University of Wisconsin, where he became director of the Mass Communication Research Center. In 1981, he returned to Stanford University to become director of the Institute for Communications Research, where he is today.

Chaffee has served as a public opinion analyst for political candidates (including polling for the Democratic Party campaign from 1966 to 1984) and as a communication consultant to other groups. He has written many books, including *Political Communications: Issues and Strategies for Research*, which deals with the role of the mass media in the political communications process. Perhaps his major research contribution was the development with Wisconsin colleague Jack McLeod of the theory of co-orientation. (*See also* Co-orientation; Family Communication Patterns.)

SOURCES: *Contemporary Authors*, Vol. 106, 1982; *Who's Who in America*, 1997–1998.

Jacqueline Nash Gifford

CHICAGO TRIBUNE. The *Tribune* has proclaimed itself the world's greatest newspaper (hence the call letters WGN of the radio and television station it owns). It has generally been considered one of the leading newspapers in the United States, but its political heritage has been a handicap. The paper was started in 1847 and came under the control of Joseph Medill in 1855. Medill was one of the leaders in the founding of the Republican Party and was instrumental in getting Abraham Lincoln nominated in 1860. He remained in control of the paper until 1899, except for two years when he was the Republican mayor of Chicago.

In 1910, Robert R. McCormick and Joseph Patterson, cousins, assumed control of the *Tribune*. Patterson went to New York to start the *Daily News* in 1919, and McCormick was in control of the *Tribune* for the next 36 years. Medill had made the *Tribune* Republican and increasingly conservative. McCormick accentuated that and made the *Tribune* isolationist as well. Furthermore, as many studies demonstrated, the Republican bias was all too evident in the news columns of the *Tribune*.

The *Tribune* stayed that way for more than a decade after McCormick's death but changed under the leadership of Clayton Kirkpatrick, who became editor in 1969. Editorializing in news columns was curbed, and the strident editorial voice was restrained. The result has been a newfound respect from both readers and the newspaper industry.

SOURCES: Michael Emery, *America's Leading Daily Newspapers*, 1983; Kenneth Stewart and John Tebbel, *Makers of Modern Journalism*, 1952.

Guido H. Stempel III

CHRISTIAN COALITION was founded in 1989 as a group of private citizens organized to support politicians and political issues that reflect and protect conservative Christian values in America. Although it started as a grassroots organization by religious advocate Marion (Pat) Robertson, it now reportedly has nearly one-half million members throughout the country. It publishes a monthly magazine for its members called *Christian American*. The group is credited with mobilizing conservative Christian interest in the 1992 Republican campaign. It has continued to be active in both presidential and congressional campaigns and is seen as a major segment of the Republican Party.

SOURCE: Allan J. Cigler and Burdett A. Loomis, *Interest Group Politics*, fourth edition, 1995.

Jacqueline Nash Gifford

CHRISTIANITY AND CRISIS was launched in February 1941 by theologian Reinhold Niebuhr and John Bennett as a nondenominational publication. Its purpose was to oppose the isolationist position of another such magazine, *Christian Century*, and, due to the widespread pacifism among Protestant churches after World War I, to provide support for Allied causes in World War II. Niebuhr became known as a theologian in the pages of *Christian Century*, but as an interventionist, he could not tolerate the views of the *Century*'s editor, Charles Clayton Morrison. From the start, *Christianity and Crisis* had trouble locating donors and, in the end, its demise in 1993 was blamed on ''the difficulty involved in maintaining a general-interest religious magazine in a world dominated by television and news briefs.'' A letter to subscribers and supporters from editor Leon Howell and Audrey Miller, president of the Board of Directors, said the board had concluded ''with immense pain and regret, that it cannot responsibly keep the journal going under current circumstances.'' Though circulation had remained steady at 13,000 its last four years, Howell cited ''skyrocketing'' increases in postage, health insurance, and rent as reasons for the budget crisis. Described by some as an ecumenical journal, *Christianity and Crisis* provided a forum ''not only for distinguished U.S. theologians and social commentators but also for a host of new voices, especially those on the margins of public awareness.''

SOURCE: ''Crisis for *Christianity and Crisis*,'' *Christian Century*, March 24, 1993.

Don Ranly

CHRISTIANITY AND POLITICS. Although it can be difficult to separate religion from other factors such as race and socioeconomic status, religious influence is closely related to the ability of religious institutions to make their positions known. Since 1912, when the Seventh-Day Adventist Church created a publicity bureau to counter criticism of its opposition to Sunday blue laws, almost every church has established a communication department in an effort to place its concerns on the public agenda. With recent changes in campaign laws, both lobbying and political fund-raising by churches, ecumenical and parachurch organizations, and religion-related political action committees have become increasingly important.

Like church influence on voting, those efforts to influence political policy are enhanced by the kind of grassroots mobility at which Protestants now excel. Televangelists such as Jerry Falwell and Pat Robertson have capitalized on changes in broadcast regulations and communication technology to speak directly to the public through religious television programs. They create data banks of supporters and mobilize them under the auspices of local congregations working in conjunction with organizations such as the Moral Majority and, more recently, the Christian Coalition. As a result, conservative Protestants can, in close races, affect the outcome of elections. That, in turn, gives them power to affect elected leaders' issue priorities and, in some cases, their issue positions.

Historically, African-American Protestants and white Protestant members of mainline or old-line churches voted Republican. Catholics and more conservative white Protestants voted for Democrats. However, a religiopolitical realignment began with the presidency of Franklin D. Roosevelt, picked up momentum during the 1960s, and became complete in the 1970s, when conservative white Protestants, who had avoided politics, entered the political arena.

As the Democratic Party broadened its concern for the disadvantaged to include protection of civil rights, the Republican Party positioned itself as the party of law and order and traditional values. Because Democratic issue positions were consistent with the concerns that entered mainline Protestantism with the social gospel movement of the late nineteenth century, the Republican Party gradually lost its advantage among mainline Protestants. Conservative white Protestants' concern for personal morality moved them into the Republican camp. Although African-American Protestants hold opinions similar to those of conservative white Protestants and of the Republican Party on personal morality issues such as abortion and family values, as a group they became firmly Democratic because of their overriding interest in civil rights and justice issues. Catholics became the swing voters. Church teachings on abortion and family values now lead many Catholics to vote Republican; however, church emphasis on the common good and a consistent ethic of life as expressed in pastoral letters on peace and on economic and social justice undergird the traditional tendency of Catholics to vote Democratic.

SOURCES: Robert Booth Fowler and Allen D. Hertzke, *Religion and Politics in America: Faith, Culture and Strategic Choices*, 1985; Mark A. Noll, ed., *Religion and American Politics: From the Colonial Period to the 1980s*, 1990.

Judith M. Buddenbaum

CHRISTIANITY TODAY, "A Magazine of Evangelical Conviction," was founded by evangelist Billy Graham and L. Nelson Bell in 1956, with Carl F. H. Henry as editor. In 1975, Harold Myra became president and publisher of the then financially troubled magazine. Today it has a circulation of 185,000 and for the past 16 years has operated in the black. In its 40th anniversary issue, Graham wrote about why he founded the magazine:

Repeatedly in those days I came across men and women in virtually every denomination who were committed to the historic biblical faith, believing it was not only spiritually vital, but socially relevant and intellectually defensible. And yet they had no standard around which they could rally, and no place they could look for spiritual encouragement and intellectual challenge. *Christianity Today* came into being to help fill that vacuum.

Current editor David Neff states that the magazine has engaged "in very little partisan politics." On the other hand, he said, "we do address major social issues, many of which have strong political overtones." Myra, now president of Christianity Today, Inc., which includes eight magazines, says, "Our goal in *Christianity Today* is to apply clear evangelical thinking and perspective to the issues of the day, taking care to be concise, lively, ironic, and thoughtful."

SOURCE: David Neff, "Inside CT—1975: Rescue Operation," *Christianity Today*, June 1995.

Don Ranly

CLEAR AND PRESENT DANGER is a concept introduced by Justice Oliver Wendell Holmes in *Schenck v. U.S.* as a condition for justifying suppression. But as Holmes defined it, it was more nearly perceived danger than clear and present. Nonetheless, it was the standard criterion in such cases until 1957, when the Supreme Court overturned the verdict in *Yates v. U.S.* Yates was prosecuted for being a member of the Communist Party, but the Court said that neither this in itself nor abstract discussion of overthrow of the government constituted clear and present danger. Action was required. That ruling has stood and explains why few dissenters in the Vietnam era were prosecuted.

SOURCES: Kathleen Thompson Hill and Gerald N. Hill, *Real Life Dictionary of American Politics*, 1994; *Yates v. U.S.*, 354 U.S. 298, 1957.

Guido H. Stempel III

CLINTON, HILLARY (1947–) promoted herself in the 1992 presidential campaign with the same "two for the price of one" theme that had described Eleanor Roosevelt in the 1940s, but some Americans didn't appreciate the bargain. They registered dismay with bumper stickers that said "Impeach Hillary" and "I don't trust President Clinton or her husband."

The role of the First Lady has been called the wild card of American politics. The Constitution provides no job description, but most wives of presidents have supervised such semiofficial duties as social hostess and homemaker. In polls, Americans have said they prefer those roles for the First Lady. However, Hillary Clinton, more than most of her predecessors, has politicized the position.

Magazine coverage of her reflected editors' visions of her as both a 1990s woman and a lightning rod. She was a wife, mother, and daughter. Social information described her clothing, hair, and hostess duties. On the other hand, magazine coverage zeroed in on her reputation and on her political activities. This is the negative coverage that made her the lightning rod.

With her appointment as head of her husband's health care reform task force, she attracted more coverage. Such magazines as *Nation, National Review, New Republic, Progressive,* and *The American Spectator,* which had not written at all about Roslyn Carter, Nancy Reagan, or Barbara Bush, commented on her reputation.

Coverage by other media has not been documented, but it undoubtedly has been similar. Her political role indicated that she intended to carry the wife theme in the opposite direction that Nancy Reagan did. While Americans said they thought the Clintons understood the problems of today's family, many did not accept the overtly political role.

SOURCES: Sally Quinn, "Look Out! It's Superwoman," *Newsweek,* February 15, 1993, p. 24; Kenneth T. Walsh, "America's First (Working) Couple," *U.S. News,* May 10, 1993, p. 33.

Liz Watts

COGNITIVE DISSONANCE. *See* Leon Festinger.

COHEN, AKIBA (1944–) has made major contributions to the study of the effects of television news in society, especially in politics. He obtained his bachelor's degree in psychology and sociology from Hebrew University and his master's and Ph.D. in communication from Michigan State University. Cohen started his academic career as a lecturer at the Communications Institute of the Hebrew University of Jerusalem.

His scholarly contributions include three major books: *Almost Midnight: Reforming the Late Night News* (coauthor), *The Television News Interview,* and *Social Conflict and Television News* (coauthor). All of his books explore the impact of television news on social perceptions. *Social Conflict and Television News* uses data collected from a five-nation study and, using content analyses, looks at news practices.

SOURCES: Akiba A. Cohen, *The Television News Interview,* 1992; Akiba A. Cohen, Hanna Adoni, and Charles R. Bantz, *Social Conflict and Television News,* 1996; Susan Herbst, *Contemporary Sociology,* November 1992.

Jacqueline Nash Gifford

COMMUNICATION RESEARCHERS. *See* Jay Blumler; Daniel Boorstin; Albert Hadley Cantril; Hadley Cantril; Steven M. Chaffee; Akiba Cohen; Jack Dennis; George A. Donohue, Clarice N. Olien, and Philip J. Tichenor; Leon Festinger; Johan Galtung; Herbert Gans; George Gerbner; Doris Graber; Kathleen Hall Jamieson; Elihu Katz; Sidney Kraus; Harold Lasswell; Paul F. Lazarsfeld; Maxwell McCombs; Jack M. McLeod; Ralph O. Nafziger; Dan Nimmo; Larry Sabato; Wilbur Schramm; William Stephenson; David M. Weaver; Bruce M. Westley.

COMMUNICATION THEORY. See Agenda Setting; Congruity; Co-Orientation; Cultivation; Diffusion; Family Communication Patterns; Framing;

Gatekeeping; Generation X; Hypodermic Effect; Indexing; Knowledge Gap; Limited-Effects Model; Priming; Reliance versus Use; Selectivity; Spiral of Silence; Third-Person Effect; Voter Need for Orientation.

CONCESSION SPEECH is the speech given by the person who loses a political campaign. The speech's elements often include symbolic statements such as "giving up the good fight" to make way for "a worthy opponent." Speeches also thank those involved in the campaign and its supporters and frequently wish the opponent success in office. They normally are made the evening of the election as soon as the outcome becomes clear.

SOURCES: William Safire, *Safire's New Political Dictionary*, 1993; Jay M. Shafritz, *The HarperCollins Dictionary of American Government and Politics*, 1992.

Jacqueline Nash Gifford

CONGRESSIONAL BLACK CAUCUS is the coalition of African-American congressional members organized to support and advance the causes of blacks. Started in 1969 by Congressman Charles Diggs, Michigan Democrat, it soon generated clout in Washington and throughout the United States. Specifically, the caucus members worked to obtain positions on key committees and flexed their political clout during elections. When caucus members boycotted President Richard Nixon's State of the Union address, Nixon, realizing his blunder in not recognizing the importance of the group, did meet with the caucus.

The group was also successful in establishing the national holiday recognizing Martin Luther King's birthday and recently persuaded President Bill Clinton to adopt his policy on helping Haiti gain independence. The caucus tries to think and act as one on affairs that will affect the African-American community. They are considered one of the most influential groups within the Congress.

SOURCES: Charles D. Lowery and John F. Marszalek, eds., *Encyclopedia of African-American Civil Rights*, 1992; Jack Salzman, David Lionel Smith, and Cornel West, eds., *Encyclopedia of African-American Culture and History*, 1990.

Jacqueline Nash Gifford

CONGRUITY. Individuals tend to have a belief system that is internally consistent, and they strive to keep the system consistent. That means that when one attitude changes, others also change. So, if a person has a strong positive feeling about a politician and a strong positive feeling about cutting taxes, and the politician favors cutting taxes, there is congruity. Now suppose the politician changes his or her mind and comes out in favor of a tax increase. That poses a quandary for the individual. He or she may resolve it by feeling less strongly about both the politician and tax cuts. However, if the person feels strongly about tax cuts, he or she will then probably have a negative feeling about the politician. On the other hand, if the person really is committed to the politician, he or she may view tax cuts much less favorably.

The politician thus must realize that when he or she proposes something, the idea will not be judged solely on its own merits. The public's attitude toward the politician also will come into play. It's often not what was said but who said it that accounts for the public response.

This also affects public attitudes toward the media. When the media expose a politician, the public response often is to "kill the messenger"—that is, to react negatively not to the exposed politician but to the media that exposed him or her.

SOURCE: Charles E. Osgood, George J. Suci, and Percy H. Tannenbaum, *The Measurement of Meaning*, 1957.

Guido H. Stempel III

CO-ORIENTATION is a term for the cognitive transaction between individuals. This approach to communication research was first used by Theodore Newcomb in a 1943 study of political attitudes among college students using his famous A–B–X paradigm. The measurement analyzes the views of two individuals or groups in relation to each other, demonstrating how they view a situation and also how each perceives the view of the other. In the model, X is an external object to which two persons (A and B) co-orient. Newcomb found political attitudes shifted as students became more involved in group memberships at college and became socialized to the views of opinion leaders. Steven Chaffee and Jack McLeod have used the model mostly for public opinion research. They have shown the model to be useful for linking interpersonal and mass communication through the influence of opinion leaders. In co-orientation, the success of communication rests on such criteria as agreement, accuracy, congruency, and understanding. Those people who perceive they agree with one another are most likely to communicate their views to each other. The co-orientation approach has been used to ascertain such things as exposure to political information, voting plans, perceptions of a campaign, and personal orientation to an election. Chaffee and McLeod have suggested that mass media seem to work best for accuracy and understanding in messages but that congruency and agreement are most affected by social interaction. They point out that co-orientation is an important communication system for a pluralistic society. People can agree on content of a message and their understanding of it but still maintain differing opinions. (*See also* Steven H. Chaffee; Jack M. McLeod.)

SOURCES: Steven H. Chaffee and Jack M. McLeod, "Sensitization in Panel Design: A Coorientational Experiment," *Journalism Quarterly*, Winter 1968; Theodore M. Newcomb, "An Approach to the Study of Communicative Arts," *Psychological Review*, No. 6, 1953.

LeAnne Daniels

CORPORATION FOR PUBLIC BROADCASTING (CPB) is a private, nonprofit corporation created by Congress in 1967. The corporation is not a government agency. It is designed to develop public communications service for the American people. About 600 public radio stations exist throughout the nation. There are more than 350 public television stations. CPB is the largest source for funding for public television and radio programming.

Public broadcasting began as an alternative to commercial broadcasting. In 1952 the Educational Radio and Television Center was developed in Chicago. Because of the great growth in public television, the Carnegie Commission on Educational Television called for a well-financed system to serve the needs of the American public. Congress responded by passing the Public Broadcasting Act of 1967, which created the Corporation for Public Broadcasting. The Public Broadcasting Service was initiated in the fall of 1970. It is a private, nonprofit program company owned by America's public television stations. Through the National Program Service, PBS funds the creation and acquisition of programs for its member statons and distributes those programs. National Public Radio began operation in May 1971. It is a private organization that produces and distributes news and cultural programming for member stations throughout America. Lawrence Grossman was named president of PBS in 1976, and he brought popular programs to what had not been a very entertaining programming organization.

SOURCES: Robert J. Blakely, *The People's Instrument*, 1971; Les Brown, "A Bigger Picture for Public Television," *New York Times*, September 12, 1976, pp. 31–32; Donald N. Wood, "The First Fifteen Years of the Fourth Network," *Journal of Broadcasting*, Spring 1969.

Will Norton

COWLES, JOHN AND GARDNER (MIKE), JR., were leaders in a twentieth-century era of newspaper journalism whose hallmarks included family-owned newspapers that dominated regions of the nation, with their publishers also active in national and international public affairs.

For the Cowles family and the two brothers, the flagship newspapers were the *Des Moines Register*, owned by the Cowleses from 1903 until its sale to Gannett in 1985, and the *Minneapolis Star and Tribune*, purchased in the mid-1930s and remaining under Cowles ownership.

John (1898–1983) oversaw the family holdings in Minnesota and the upper Midwest. Mike (1903–1985) had leadership of the *Des Moines Register* and the *Des Moines Tribune* (1946–1982). The brothers also published a national magazine, *Look*, from 1937 to 1971 and shared in a family enterprise that included newspapers in Gainesville, Lakeland, Leesburg, and Palatka, Florida; Rapid City, South Dakota; Great Falls, Montana; Waukesha, Wisconsin; Jackson, Tennessee; and San Juan, Puerto Rico.

The family journalism formula, found in many of John's speeches and articles, was to "give readers a superior product, deliver it better and promote it effectively." The *Des Moines Register*, into the 1980s, was second only to the *New*

York Times in the number of Pulitzer Prizes won by its staff. As early as the 1930s, the Cowles newspapers emphasized photojournalism and graphic design. This was partly because a young pollster in Iowa, George Gallup, found that newspaper readership increased when even small illustrations accompanied news items.

Politically, in the 1940s and 1950s, the Cowles brothers battled on behalf of the liberal or international wing of the Republican Party against the conservative, isolationist influences represented by other publishers, chief among them Colonel Robert R. McCormick of the *Chicago Tribune.*

The Cowles brothers were among the strongest supporters of the 1940 GOP presidential candidacy of Wendell Willkie and were advisers to Republican president Dwight D. Eisenhower.

John Cowles' wife, Elizabeth, who helped found birth control and Planned Parenthood programs in Iowa and Minnesota in the 1930s, influenced her husband's political views. Mike Cowles was married four times. His third wife, Fleur, caused him to support the innovative, avant-garde, and prohibitively expensive *Flair* magazine from February 1950 to February 1951.

SOURCE: The papers of John and Gardner (Mike) Cowles, Jr., on file in the Cowles Library at Drake University in Des Moines.

Herb Strentz

CREEL COMMISSION was the first government organization created to use public relations techniques for the United States. George Creel was a well-noted writer, editor, and muckraker who was appointed by President Woodrow Wilson in 1917 to be the chairman of the Committee on Public Information. The committee, later called the Creel Commission, was charged with implementing a public relations campaign aimed at generating support for the American effort in World War I. The commission also produced printed materials, such as pamphlets and brochures, to offset anti-American information sent out by the Germans. It also issued guidelines for voluntary censorship by the press.

Creel was best known for generating the support of journalists and companies to help with the government's endeavor. Personally, he was under much scrutiny, as many felt he sold out from his early days as a journalist when he was openly suspicious and wrote against big government. Despite the personal controversy, his work with the Creel Commission is considered one of the most successful publicity programs on behalf of the federal government.

SOURCES: Joseph P. McKerns, *Biographical Dictionary of American Journalism*, 1989; Dennis L. Wilcox, Phillip H. Ault, and Warren A. Agee, *Public Relations Strategies and Tactics*, third edition, 1992.

Jacqueline Nash Gifford

CRONKITE, WALTER (1916–). This veteran newsman anchored the CBS Evening News for 30 years, and his effect on television journalism was such that he was once voted "the most trusted man in America." The son of a St. Joseph, Missouri, dentist whose family moved to Houston while he was still in school, Cronkite enrolled in the University of Texas in 1933 to study economics and political science but soon began working for the *Houston Post* and Scripps Howard. In 1936, Cronkite went to work for a Kansas City radio station for a year. He then joined the staff of United Press, for which he would report for more than a decade. When World War II broke out, Cronkite went to Europe as a correspondent. He parachuted into Holland with the 101st Airborne Division and joined the Third Army at the Battle of the Bulge. After the war, he was United Press' chief reporter at the Nuremberg war crimes trials, then moved to Moscow for two years as a bureau chief. Cronkite returned to the United States in 1948 as a radio reporter and joined CBS in 1950. He virtually created the post of "anchorman," sitting at a news desk with his television coverage of the 1952 national political conventions from Chicago. He began hosting CBS Evening News as managing editor in 1962 and became known for his reassuring, unflappable manner. His replacement by CBS as anchor at the 1964 Republican Convention with a team of reporters prompted a reassessment of the nature of television news. After a *Life* magazine article questioned the scramble for ratings behind that move, Cronkite was returned to the anchor desk for election night. In 1968, he went to Vietnam and is credited by some historians with turning majority opinion against the war by reporting during the Tet offensive that America was losing. Since his retirement in 1981, Cronkite has been a special correspondent for CBS.

SOURCES: *Contemporary Authors* (CD-ROM), 1993; John Jakes, *Great War Correspondents*, 1968.

Marc Edge

CROUSE, TIMOTHY (1947–) is the reporter who coined the phrase "pack journalism" to describe the reporters who follow political candidates during an election. Crouse, a Harvard graduate, covered the rock music scene for many East Coast newspapers, including the *Boston Herald*, before joining *Rolling Stone* as a contributing editor in 1971.

There Crouse had an unlikely opportunity—to fill in for the regular political reporters during the 1972 presidential election. At first he refused but resigned himself to the task, deciding to report on only what he saw because he lacked the political background for analysis.

His observations led to the widely accepted book *The Boys on the Bus*, which takes a refreshing look at the workings of political reporters. Among the points Crouse made in his book is that the process of trailing candidates around for months leads to the phenomenon he called "pack journalism." Journalists in a pack were likely to think and behave similarly because all of them are exposed to the same information (created by a press agent on behalf of the political candidate). This common thinking led to the same rehash of facts throughout the press. In addition, the demand upon pack journalists to beat the competition often outweighed their ability to give analysis to the stories they covered daily. In Crouse's view, this phenomenon meant that the articles failed to enlighten the American public about important information during the election process.

SOURCES: Steven d'Arazien, book review, *The Progressive*, February 1974; Frances Carol Locher, ed., *Contemporary Authors*, Vols. 77–80, 1979.

Jacqueline Nash Gifford

C-SPAN was the brainchild of Brian Lamb, Washington bureau chief for *Cablevision* magazine in 1977, when, as a sidelight, he began taping 15-minute interviews with members of Congress for broadcast by 15 capital-area cable systems. In June of that year, House speaker Tip O'Neill had a fixed, black-and-white camera begin broadcasting proceedings on a trial basis via cable to Arlington, Virginia, where many members lived. Lamb raised $400,000 from 22 cable system operators to create C-SPAN, and regulatory approval was quickly gained from the Federal Communications Commission (FCC) for broadcast of gavel-to-gavel coverage of House proceedings to 3 million households. The first transmission was on March 19, 1979, and service was soon expanded to include non-House programming, with student seminars, National Press Club speeches, call-in shows, and federal agency hearings. In 1981 the first congressional hearings were broadcast, and the following year C-SPAN began broadcasting 24 hours a day, seven days a week. During the 1984 election campaign, the network covered the national party conventions. In 1986 C-SPAN II was created to carry Senate proceedings. By the mid-1990s, more than 60 million households had access to C-SPAN. The network was credited with launching the political rise of Newt Gingrich and the television career of talk-show host Larry King, whose Mutual Radio call-in show was first simulcast in 1983.

SOURCE: Stephen Frantzich and John Sullivan, *The C-SPAN Revolution*, 1996.

Marc Edge

CULTIVATION is a theory developed by George Gerbner and his colleagues about the effect of television. Research has shown that heavy viewers of television are more likely than light viewers of television to perceive the world as an unsafe, violent place. Yet, while television affects our perception of the world, it is hardly the only influence. Heavy viewers of television differ from light viewers in such things as age, education, gender, and use of news media.

Given the relation between extent of television viewing and perception of the world as unsafe, which is cause, and which is effect? Does television watching create the impression, or do people who view the world as unsafe have a tendency to become heavy viewers?

More recent studies that have attempted to control other variables related to television viewing find the cultivation effect less pronounced. Still, if there is any effect at all, it raises concerns about what television is injecting into our minds.

Some recent studies also have made the obvious point that a cultivation effect for any individual depends on what television programs that person watches.

The concept is important in political communication to the extent that the cultivation that occurs relates to political issues. The obvious example is crime, which has been an effective political issue for years. Yet, study after study shows that the public overestimates the extent of crime. The media—both print and broadcast—must share some of the blame for this.

SOURCE: Werner J. Severin and James W. Tankard, Jr., *Communication Theories*, fourth edition, 1997.

Guido H. Stempel III

D

DAISY COMMERCIAL was a controversial television advertisement in Lyndon Johnson's 1964 presidential campaign. The advertisement, produced by Tony Schwartz, attacked Republican nominee Barry Goldwater by playing upon the emotions regarding atomic warfare. Goldwater had said he would use nuclear weapons in Vietnam to defoliate the forests, and Johnson had said he would not.

The ad featured a fair-haired young girl smelling the daisies and counting off the flower's petals. As she got closer to removing all the petals, a male voice supersedes her voice and counts backward. The scene then switches to a blast of a nuclear weapon.

Amid the mushroom cloud of the nuclear weapon, Johnson's voice says, "These are the stakes—to make a world in which all God's children can live or to go into the dark. We must either love each other, or we must die."

The ad ran only once, on September 7. Viewers phoned in their protests, and over the next few days the ad was the most talked-about aspect of the campaign.

A formal complaint from Goldwater's staff was filed with the Fair Campaign Practices Committee, but it never made a determination about the ad. The truthfulness of the ad is questionable, but the emotional impact is not. It helped to paint Goldwater as a warmonger who could not be trusted.

SOURCES: Edwin Diamond and Stephen Bats, *The Spot*, 1992; Joanna Morreale, *The Presidential Campaign Film: A Critical History*, 1993; L. Patrick, "An Analysis of Presidential TV Commercials," in Lynda Lee Kaid, Dan Nimmo, and Keith Sanders, eds., *New Perspectives on Political Advertising*, 1986.

Jacqueline Nash Gifford

DAMAGE CONTROL. Communication efforts by political consultants, spin doctors, and public relations practitioners to try to limit the harm done by a statement, action, or event. It is done with the recognition and admission that there is a problem, but with the suggestion that it is minimal or that the statement, action, or event has been misunderstood. The term was once jargon of those in the political arena, but now even the media use it.

SOURCE: Jay M. Shafritz, *The HarperCollins Dictionary of American Government and Politics*, 1992.

Guido H. Stempel III

DAVIS, ELMER (1890–1958), newspaper reporter and radio commentator, born in Aurora, Indiana. A graduate of Franklin College and a Rhodes scholar, Davis worked for the *New York Times* for 10 years beginning in 1914. Davis quit the paper in 1923 to write novels and occasionally contribute political analyses to the *Times* and to magazines. After a troubling visit to Europe in 1936, Davis devoted most of his energies to warning Americans of Germany's threat to world peace. On the eve of World War II, in August 1939, Davis joined the staff of CBS News. He anchored live reports from Europe and presented analysis. Although Davis had a midwestern twang, his concise and informed commentary endeared him to his superiors at CBS and to many listeners. "He was telling you in the fewest possible words what you wanted to know," his biographer Roger Blassingame observed. Davis, Blassingame wrote, possessed "a state of mind that is always ready for split-second interpretation."

After Hitler's invasion of the Low Countries in May 1940, Davis made no effort to cloak his support of U.S. involvement in the European war. Soon after America entered the war, President Franklin D. Roosevelt named Davis to head the new Office of War Information (OWI). OWI assumed all war-related functions. Davis, though admired by many Americans, was a curious choice. He had no administrative experience. Furthermore, the agency operated under severe handicaps. Roosevelt himself had little enthusiasm for creating the OWI and lent Davis, whom he barely knew, little support. The navy and sometimes the army proved uncooperative. Congress, suspicious that the OWI was doing the partisan work of the administration, slashed the agency's budget.

When the OWI ceased operation late in 1945, Davis became a commentator for ABC. He tended to take progressive positions while criticizing the Soviet Union's growing hegemony in Eastern Europe. He was an early and relentless critic of the excesses of domestic, anticommunist crusades led by Senator Joseph R. McCarthy and others, and a tireless champion of civil liberties. He retired in 1955.

SOURCES: Roger Blassingame, *Don't Let Them Scare You: The Life and Times of Elmer Davis*, 1961; Alfred Haworth Jones, "The Making of an Interventionist on the Air: Elmer Davis and CBS News, 1939–1941," *Pacific Historical Review*, February 1973, pp. 74–93; Allan M. Winkler, *The Politics of Propaganda: The Office of War Information, 1942–1945*, 1978.

James L. Baughman

DAY, BENJAMIN (1810–1889) is credited with starting the first successful "penny press" newspaper when he published the initial edition of the *New York Sun* on Tuesday, September 3, 1833. Day, who served as publisher, editor, chief pressman, and mailing clerk, began publishing the *Sun* from one small room. One boy assisted him. The *Sun* was the 12th daily newspaper in New York. All the others cost six cents. A number of other attempts at penny papers had failed. However, while working at the *Journal of Commerce*, Day developed the formula for a successful penny paper: it had to have interesting stories and lots of advertising. Thus, the *Sun* devoted more space to Susan Allen, "who smoked a cigar and danced on the street," than to a visit by Henry Clay. Day tried to show his prosperity by publishing advertisements on his front page. For the first edition, in fact, Day republished advertisements that had been regularly appearing in other papers. Many page 1 ads dealt with shipping, since Day was committed to pleasing ship captains, who, in turn, provided Day with news from outside New York. Day, 23 years old when he began publishing the *Sun*, printed 1,000 copies of his first edition. All of them sold. By December, circulation reached 4,000, and a year later it was 10,000. On August 20, 1836, less than three years after the first *Sun* was published, Day claimed that his newspaper's circulation was more than that of all 11 six-cent newspapers in New York combined.

SOURCE: Francis B. Whitlock, "Two New Yorkers: Editor and Sea Captain 1833," *Newcomen Address*, 1945.

Wayne Wanta

DEBATES are the most common form of political communication used between political candidates to discuss the issues, present their platform, and poke holes in the opposition's arguments. While people tend to think of debates in presidential campaigns and date them from the televised Kennedy–Nixon debates of 1960, debates have been used much more widely. Some are not televised, but many are, even at the local level.

Typically, one political candidate will challenge another to a debate, conducted publicly, or a special interest group or television network will invite speakers to participate. Sometimes they are pure debates following accepted rules of debating, but more often there is a moderator or panel of moderators to ask questions or to take questions from the audience.

For political candidates, it is a chance to speak directly to the public without the mass media's objectivity or spin. It also is an opportunity for a candidate to reach voters of the opposite political party who might otherwise ignore him or her. The debate format makes the voter watch the candidate he or she doesn't favor in order to watch the one he or she does favor.

SOURCE: Jay M. Shafritz, *The HarperCollins Dictionary of American Government and Politics*, 1992.

Jacqueline Nash Gifford

DEMOCRATIC CONVENTION OF 1968 became a flash point for the deep divisions in this country over the United States' involvement in the Vietnam War. Instead of seeing the usual hoopla and party camaraderie leading up to the nomination of the presidential candidate, the American public saw live on television a society at war with itself: police, army, and National Guard troops battling protesters outside the convention hall while a deeply divided Democratic Party clashed on the floor of the convention hall. President Lyndon Johnson may have set the stage for the Chicago confrontation when he announced he would not seek reelection and instead would devote himself to ending the war. Most party faithful threw their support to Vice President Hubert Humphrey, who had backed the president's hawkish stand in Vietnam. But antiwar protesters backed the candidacy of Eugene McCarthy, a senator from Minnesota who ran on a peace platform. Members of the antiwar movement, led by Yippie protesters Abbie Hoffman and Jerry Rubin, decided to use the Democratic Convention as an opportunity to sway public opinion. They and other members of the antiwar movement descended on Chicago, where Mayor Richard Daley was prepared to use force to maintain law and order. Soon the protest turned violent, and riot police reacted by beating protesters and even journalists who were covering the confrontation. Tempers flared inside the convention hall as well. At one point a security guard slugged CBS reporter Dan Rather, prompting network anchor Walter Cronkite to call the guards "thugs." The chaotic and violent images of the Democratic Party Convention may have cost Humphrey the 1968 presidential election. By a narrow margin, Richard Nixon, the Republican candidate, won.

SOURCE: Norman Mailer, *Miami and the Siege of Chicago: An Informal History of the Republican and Democratic Conventions of 1968*, 1968.

Churchill L. Roberts

DEMONSTRATION. Protest by which members picket, carry signs, march, sing, and/or convene to show their support for a candidate, cause, or issue. Demonstrations were a popular form of political protest in the 1960s during the Civil Rights movement and the Vietnam War era. Another form of demonstration is picketing during a labor strike. Still another is the parade. All are recognized as means of communication and, by various Supreme Court decisions, are protected by the First Amendment. Some demonstrations become violent, and such violence is not protected by the First Amendment and is unlawful.

SOURCE: Jay M. Shafritz, *The HarperCollins Dictionary of American Government and Politics*, 1992.

Guido H. Stempel III

DENNIS, JACK, professor of political science at the University of Wisconsin, is a leading authority on political socialization and electoral behavior. He joined the political science faculty at Wisconsin in the early 1960s after earning his Ph.D. in political science at the University of Chicago. Dennis has mentored dozens of graduate students over the years in political communication, political socialization, and public opinion. Particularly important are his contributions to our understanding of mass media as agencies of political socialization among children and preadults.

SOURCES: Jack Dennis, "Political Independence in America," *British Journal of Political Science*, January 1988; Jack Dennis, "Preadult Learning of Political Independence: Media and Family Communication Effects," *Communication Research*, July 1986; Jack Dennis, ed., *Socialization to Politics: A Reader*, 1973.

Lowndes F. Stephens

DEREGULATION OF THE FEDERAL COMMUNICATIONS COMMISSION.

Efforts to deregulate broadcasting and cable television in the United States stem largely from a view that seeks to limit government intervention in a variety of areas and instead advocates reliance on marketplace forces as the optimum means of control. Within the context of the electronic media, as in other areas, this political philosophy took root and blossomed during the Reagan administration, which began in 1981. More recently, particularly when Newt Gingrich became Speaker of the House of Representatives in 1995, calls were heard for the eventual elimination of the Federal Communications Commission (FCC).

Deregulating broadcasting and/or cable television necessarily means limiting the scope and power of the FCC. While the FCC itself chose to abandon several minor regulations in the 1970s, not until 1981 did it begin to remove more substantive rules in earnest. These included regulations dealing with stations ascertaining local community needs, program log keeping, and maximum allowable advertising airtime. Subsequently, a host of other rules and regulations was modified in an effort to reduce FCC involvement. Most recently, the Telecommunications Act of 1996 liberalized licensing, ownership, and programming rules. For example, where prior to 1980 broadcast stations were licensed for three years at a time, the 1996 act extends that to eight years. Where a single company was limited to owning seven AM, seven FM, and seven television stations prior to 1980, national ownership limits have been eliminated in radio. In television, the limit is that the number of people reached by a single owner's stations may not exceed 35 percent of the country's population. Where broadcasters were required to air and treat fairly all sides of controversial issues, in 1987 the FCC eliminated that requirement when it ceased enforcing the Fairness Doctrine.

The future of broadcast and cable deregulation is unclear. While there is a desire to reduce the intrusion of government, even legislation like the Telecommunications Act of 1996 introduced some new regulation and bureaucracy. It did so specifically by a provision that requires new television sets to be equipped with a chip to block certain programming.

SOURCE: Sydney W. Head, Christopher Sterling, and Lemuel B. Schofield, *Broadcasting in America: A Survey of Electronic Media*, seventh edition, 1994.

Joseph A. Russomanno

"DEWEY DEFEATS TRUMAN" is perhaps the most remembered headline in the history of political communication. It was the banner across the top of the front page of the *Chicago Tribune* the morning after the 1948 election. Like most of the press and the pollsters, the *Tribune* got it wrong. In a stunning turnaround, incumbent Harry Truman upset Republican candidate Thomas Dewey. Only three weeks before the election, polls were showing an easy win for the popular governor of New York. *Newsweek* surveyed political writers for its October 11 issue and reported that every single one of them believed that Dewey would win. While Dewey coasted, Truman barnstormed the country in a "give 'em hell, Harry" whistle-stop campaign. His main themes were "the do-nothing eightieth Congress" and the "one-party press." The latter referred to the fact that most major newspapers endorsed Dewey and predicted an electoral sweep. Ten days before the election, *Life* magazine ran a picture of Dewey that identified him simply as "the next president of the United States." On election night, despite Truman's mounting lead in the popular vote, NBC commentator Hans Von Kaltenborn predicted the tide would turn as votes from traditional Republican strongholds were tabulated. When the *Tribune* went to press, Truman was leading in the popular vote, but it was not until 8:30 Wednesday morning that the electoral vote count put Truman over the top. In a postmortem, stunned pollsters, publishers, and political columnists acknowledged they had failed to see the surge of excitement for Truman in the final weeks of the campaign. The last Gallup Poll, released shortly before Election Day, actually was taken several weeks earlier. As a triumphal presidential train traveled through St. Louis on its way back to Washington from Truman's hometown in Independence, Missouri, the president stepped out on the rear platform, where someone handed him a copy of the *Chicago Tribune* with its erroneous headline. Smiling broadly, Truman held it up for what would become one of the most famous photographs in campaign history. (*See also* One-Party Press.)

SOURCE: David McCullough, *Truman*, 1992.

Churchill L. Roberts

DIFFUSION. Information does not usually reach everybody immediately. Studies of diffusion show that there are varied patterns. People tend to find out about major news events first from television and do so within a few hours of the event. Thus, one study found that when the space shuttle Challenger exploded, 58 percent knew about it within 15 minutes, and 85 percent within an hour. Most found out from television.

On the other hand, a study of diffusion of news of a fraternity house fire on a college campus found that most people found out about it from other people and that the newspaper was the most relied-upon source.

It would thus appear that for major events in a political campaign, television will be the first source, but for many events, either the print media or other people will be the main source.

SOURCES: Walter Gantz, Kathy Krendl, and Susan R. Robertson, "Diffusion of a Proximate News Event," *Journalism Quarterly*, Summer 1986; Daniel Riffe and James Glen Stovall, "Diffusion of News of Shuttle Disaster: What Role for Emotional Response," *Journalism Quarterly*, Autumn 1989.

Guido H. Stempel III

DIPLOMACY is used as an instrument of a nation's or group's foreign policy. Diplomacy is how that nation or group interacts with others in a local or global environment. It can be formal or informal but always involves communication or personal interaction such as meetings, negotiations, and public events. Diplomacy is usually conducted by representatives of a nation, such as an ambassador or a group. Generally, the role of a diplomat is to discuss political issues outside the realm of formal politics and to attempt to reach solutions to problems through negotiations.

SOURCE: Jack C. Plano and Ray Olton, *The International Relations Dictionary*, fifth edition, 1995.

Jacqueline Nash Gifford

DISINFORMATION. The deliberate actions of governments or political parties in distributing incorrect or incomplete information or lies meant to cause harm or mislead. It is common during wartime because governments want to mislead the opposing forces and because governments are reluctant to tell their own people the entire truth. It is also common in political campaigns. A candidate may put out false information about his or her opponent to gain political advantage. Disinformation succeeds in part, because it is spread unknowingly by the mass media.

SOURCE: Jay M. Shafritz, *The HarperCollins Dictionary of American Government and Politics*, 1992.

Guido H. Stempel III

DONOHUE, GEORGE A. (1924–), **OLIEN, CLARICE N.** (1933–), **AND TICHENOR, PHILIP J.** (1931–). The collaboration of this trio over a period of more than 30 years is unprecedented in the annals of social science research. So closely are they linked together that the Association for Education in Journalism and Mass Communication presented the Paul J. Deutschmann Award for Excellence in Research to all three in 1994. Never before had collaborators been so honored.

The focus of their research has been knowledge gain from the media, and their major contribution is the concept of the knowledge gap. They have demonstrated that this gap tends to be widened, rather than narrowed, by the media because the media reach the informed more than they reach the uninformed.

Their varied backgrounds have enriched the combined effort. Donohue is a sociologist with a Ph.D. from Washington State. Olien is a rural sociologist with a master's in sociology from Minnesota. Tichenor received his bachelor's and master's in agricultural journalism from Wisconsin and his Ph.D. in mass communication research from Stanford.

They have used the state of Minnesota as their laboratory as they have examined such issues as what news gets published, how news of conflict gets reported, the social consequences of information, and accuracy in news. (*See also* Knowledge Gap.)

SOURCE: William David Sloan, *Makers of the Media Mind*, 1990.

Guido H. Stempel III

DOUGLAS, WILLIAM O. (1898–1980) was a U.S. Supreme Court justice. He was appointed by President Franklin Roosevelt in 1939, replacing Louis Brandeis. He was born in Yakima, Washington, and had a bout of polio that left him with the challenge of strengthening his legs. After putting himself through Columbia Law School, he worked on Wall Street and taught at prestigious East Coast law schools, including Yale. However, an early clerkship with Associate Justice Harlan Fiske Stone sparked his interest in the judicial system.

Douglas was considered a liberal and an absolutist when it came to the First Amendment. He believed that individual rights, such as freedom of speech and freedom of the press, were protected in all circumstances under the amendment. However, he also did not believe in heavy government involvement. He held that liberty was achievable only if there were no restrictions on speech—even speech that proposes unpopular beliefs. This was important during the 1960s, when he supported the rights of civil rights and Vietnam protesters.

Douglas also is credited for shaping opinions regarding free press and fair trial cases. He believed that trials, as public events, were open to be covered by the press and that the government could not interfere with the reporting of the information.

SOURCES: Leonard W. Levy, *Encyclopedia of the American Constitution*, 1986; Melvin Urofsky, *The Supreme Court Justices: A Biographical Dictionary*, 1994.

Jacqueline Nash Gifford

DOUGLASS, FREDERICK (1817–1895). Born the son of a black slave woman and a white man, Frederick Douglass educated himself, escaped slavery in 1838, and became an outstanding spokesman for his race, giving notable service to the cause of freedom throughout his life. His first speech at an antislavery convention in Nantucket, Massachusetts, in 1841 made him famous. William Lloyd Garrison gave this account of the speech:

I shall never forget his first speech at the convention—the extraordinary emotion it excited in my own mind—the powerful impression it created upon a crowded auditory—the applause which followed from the beginning to the end of his felicitous remarks. I think I never hated slavery so intensely as at that moment.

After speaking there, Douglass was employed by several societies as a lecturer and became known as one of the best orators in the United States and in England. In 1845, he published his first autobiography, *Narrative of the Life of Frederick Douglass*, a powerful account of the cruelty and oppression of the Maryland plantation culture into which he was born. Two years later he became associate editor of the *Ram's Horn*, a strong antislavery paper. Later in the same year, Douglass announced the publication of his own paper, the *North Star*, in the *Ram's Horn*: "The object of the *North Star* will be to Attack Slavery in all its forms and aspects: advocate Universal Emancipation; exalt the standard of Public Morality; promote the Moral and Intellectual Improvement of the Colored People; and hasten the day of Freedom to the Three Millions of our Enslaved Fellow Countrymen."

Douglass saw early that the Negro's cause and the women's cause were intertwined. Therefore, the *North Star* carried in its masthead: "Right is of no sex—Truth is of no Color—God is the Father of us all, and we are all Brethren." In 1851, the name of the paper was changed to *Frederick Douglass' Paper*. It lasted 16 years.

In his second autobiography, *My Bondage and My Freedom*, published in 1855, Douglass expanded the account of his slave years. It included his views and lectures on antislavery. For example, in a speech in Rochester on July 5, 1852, on "What to the Slave Is the Fourth of July?" he said that it revealed to him "the gross injustice and cruelty to which he is the constant victim." After the Civil War, Douglass started another paper in 1870, the *New National Era*, the motto of which was "free men, free soil, free speech, a free press, everywhere in the land. The ballot for all, fair wages for all."

His last autobiography, *Life and Times of Frederick Douglass*, published in 1881, records his efforts to keep alive the struggle for racial equality in the years following the Civil War. In the conclusion of his book, he wrote, "Forty years of my life have been given to the cause of my people, and if I had forty more they should all be sacredly given to the same great cause. If I have done something for that cause, I am, after all, more a debtor to it, than it is a debtor to me."

SOURCES: Douglass' autobiographies published by the Library of America, 1994; Philip S. Froner, ed., *Frederick Douglass on Women's Rights*, 1976; Nathan Irvin Huggins, *Slave and Citizen: The Life of Frederick Douglass*, 1980.

Anju G. Chaudhary

E

EARLY, STEPHEN TYREE (1889–1951), the first effective presidential secretary, served Franklin D. Roosevelt throughout his White House years from 1933 to 1945. Early's experience in mass communications made him well prepared to carry out his duties. Beginning as a wire-service reporter, first for the United Press and then for the Associated Press, he worked as director of publicity for the U.S. Chamber of Commerce before acting as an advance man for Roosevelt's unsuccessful campaign for the vice presidency in 1920. After the defeat, Early returned to the Associated Press, but he left the wire service in 1927 to become Washington editor of Paramount News, a newsreel company. He also familiarized himself with the new field of radio. Appointed assistant secretary in charge of press relations in 1933, he was promoted to presidential secretary in 1937 along with Marvin McIntyre, but McIntyre became ill, and Early took charge. Under Early's guidance, Roosevelt used both newsreels and radio to great advantage to communicate directly to the public. Early made sure that photographs of Roosevelt did not show his physical handicap. Since many newspaper publishers disliked the New Deal, Early orchestrated contacts between Roosevelt and individual reporters, including frequent press conferences, that countered this hostility. Understanding reporters' needs, Early held briefings and identified news angles. In spite of showing anger toward reporters he thought were biased, Early gained a reputation for fair dealings. Although Roosevelt became somewhat bitter toward the press by 1940, Early facilitated good working relationships between the president and the press.

SOURCE: Betty Winfield, *FDR and the News Media*, 1990.

Maurine H. Beasley

EICHMAN CASE (*United States v. Eichman*) is the most recent U.S. Supreme Court case that challenged the constitutionality of laws to protect American flags from desecration as political symbols. In the 1980s a group of protesters in Texas burned a flag to protest the Reagan administration's close ties with big American businesses. In that case, *Texas v. Johnson*, the U.S. Supreme court ruled, in a 5–4 decision, that a Texas appellate court's conviction of Gregory Lee Johnson's act of "desecrating a venerated object" was unconstitutional. In the U.S. Supreme Court's majority opinion, the state's objection was to the message that the flag burning sent and not so much to the flag burning itself. This distinction, in their view, was critical because the First Amendment protects political speech, even that which is controversial or criticizes American government.

Following the Supreme Court's decision, President George Bush picked up flag burning as a political issue and sought an amendment to the Bill of Rights that would overturn the Court's opinion. In 1989, Congress passed a law making it a federal crime to destroy or mark a U.S. flag but could never reach consensus on adding it to the Bill of Rights. In *United States v. Eichman*, protesters of the federal law burned flags to show their disapproval. Again, the U.S. Supreme Court stuck to its 5–4 vote that it was unconstitutional to ban flag burning as a form of political protest, thus killing interest in making the issue an amendment.

SOURCES: *Texas v. Johnson*, 491 U.S. 397, 1989; *United States v. Eichman*, 496 U.S. 310, 1990.

Jacqueline Nash Gifford

ENDORSEMENTS. Newspapers have endorsed presidential candidates in editorials since the middle of the nineteenth century. However, there was no comprehensive record of those endorsements until 1940, when *Editor & Publisher*, trade magazine of the newspaper industry, began polling daily newspapers about their endorsements. Republican candidates have had more endorsements than

Percentage of U.S. Daily Newspapers Endorsing Presidential Candidates, 1940–1996

Year	Republican	Democratic	Uncommitted
1940	63.9	22.7	13.4
1944	60.1	22.0	17.9
1948	65.1	15.3	15.6
1952	67.3	14.5	18.2
1956	62.3	15.1	22.6
1960	57.7	16.4	25.9
1964	35.1	42.3	22.6
1968	60.8	14.0	24.0
1972	71.4	5.3	23.2
1976	62.3	12.1	25.6

Year	Republican	Democratic	Uncommitted
1980	42.5	12.9	40.7
1984	57.7	9.4	32.7
1988	29.5	7.7	62.8
1992	14.9	18.3	66.7
1996	18.7	10.9	60.9

Note: Small number of endorsements for Henry Wallace and Strom Thurmond in 1948, George Wallace in 1968, John Anderson in 1980, and Ross Perot in 1992 not included.

Democratic candidates in every year except 1964 and 1992. In the last three presidential elections, a majority of the newspapers responding did not endorse a candidate. Why not? First, it's obvious that the endorsements are not particularly influential. Democratic candidates won in 1940, 1944, 1948, 1960, and 1976 despite a wide margin of endorsements for the Republican candidates. Some newspaper people also question the appropriateness of endorsements. Also, endorsements generate sharp letters from readers who criticize newspapers for the fact that it is nearly always the Republican candidate who gets endorsed.

SOURCE: *Editor & Publisher*, last issue before the election in each of the years mentioned.

Guido H. Stempel III

EQUAL TIME RULE. Enshrined in the 1927 Radio Act and continued in the Communications Act of 1934, the Equal Time Rule has been amended several times since. The original provision was a compromise between forces in Congress that sought to mold the new medium of radio into a common carrier along the British model and those who favored commercial development. Concerns over political abuse of monopoly ownership of radio resulted in a requirement that "if any licensee shall permit any . . . candidate . . . to use a broadcasting station, he [*sic*] shall afford equal opportunities to all other such candidates for that office." This prevented broadcasters from discriminating against candidates but allowed them limited discretion as to whether to air political debate at all. Congress created the Federal Radio Commission to regulate the act. The Federal Communications Commission (FCC) was created in 1934 to regulate broadcasting, and it took over responsibility for the equal time provision. When television came into being, the rule applied to it as well. Following an FCC ruling in 1959 that required broadcasters to provide equal time for candidates in newscasts, Congress quickly amended the law to exempt news, interviews, and documentaries from the Equal Time Rule. This paved the way for staged "media events" designed to obtain free airtime for candidates. The FCC extended the exemption to talk shows in 1984.

Under a major rewrite in 1991, broadcasters were left legally compelled only to provide equal access to political advertising. Any candidate must be allowed to purchase airtime at the same price as a competing candidate or for free if no price was charged. The courts have also upheld an FCC ruling that if broadcasters themselves seek political office, equal airtime must be given to their opponents for free. This has usually resulted in broadcaster candidates going off the air during an election campaign.

SOURCES: Hugh Cater Donahue, *The Battle to Control Broadcast News*, 1989; Wayne Overbeck, *Major Principles of Media Law*, 1997–1998.

Marc Edge

F

FAIRNESS DOCTRINE. This most controversial policy of the Federal Communications Commission (FCC) arose in 1949 out of a series of rulings on broadcast editorializing. It died a political death in 1987 during the administration of President Ronald Reagan. The FCC had first banned broadcasters from editorializing at all. When that proved unrealistic, the FCC established guidelines in 1949 for stations it licensed. A twofold duty both to cover public affairs and to seek opposing views was placed on licensees, requiring them to seek out and provide free airtime for other opinions. Congress amended the Communications Act in 1959 to specifically exempt news programs from the Fairness Doctrine.

The issue reached the Supreme Court in 1969 in *Red Lion Broadcasting v. FCC*, and the Court ruled unanimously that the First Amendment rights of the public as expressed in the Fairness Doctrine outweighed the First Amendment rights of broadcasters. However, in 1974, the Court ruled in *Tornillo v. Miami Herald* that print media had no such duty to carry opposing viewpoints. Broadcasters then began to lobby for the same freedom to editorialize, arguing that the Fairness Doctrine had a chilling effect on electronic journalists. In 1987, a lower court ruling said that the Fairness Doctrine was not, in fact, law but rather an administrative rule of the FCC. The FCC then took an action that has been widely misreported. The FCC did not abolish or repeal the Fairness Doctrine. It merely indicated it would no longer enforce it. It is still on the books and could be enforced at any time the FCC wishes to do so. The Democratic Congress did pass a bill making the Fairness Doctrine law, but Reagan vetoed the bill.

SOURCES: Donald J. Jung, *The Federal Communications Commission, the Broadcast Industry, and the Fairness Doctrine, 1981–1987*, 1996; Wayne Overbeck, *Major Principles of Media Law*, 1997–1998, 1997 edition; *Red Lion Broadcasting v. FCC*, 395 U.S. 367, 1969.

Marc Edge

FALWELL, JERRY (1933–). Soon after graduating from Baptist College in 1956, Falwell established his own church in an abandoned pop-bottling plant in his hometown of Lynchburg, Virginia. Within a week, he was broadcasting his sermons on radio, and within 18 months he had his own television specials. By 1967 his *Old-Time Gospel Hour* aired weekly on local television. By the 1970s, his congregation numbered 18,000, and his audience on television and radio exceeded 25 million. His radio show, carried by almost 400 stations, at one point had a bank of 62 telephone operators standing by to take pledges. Falwell's influence even extends to academe because he founded Liberty University. In 1979, a group of secular "New Right" leaders became disaffected from the Republican Party due to their inability to move the party from the middle politically. They approached a number of popular evangelists to lure them into politics. Falwell at first refused, but when asked a second time, he agreed to front the Moral Majority. He has since served both as president and as chairman of the Moral Majority, which operates a $100 million annual budget. An outspoken opponent of pornography, this group successfully orchestrated a boycott against 7–11 stores that forced them to stop selling adult magazines.

SOURCES: Sharon Linzey Georgiannam, *The Moral Majority and Fundamentalism*, 1989; David Snowball, *Continuity and Change in the Rhetoric of the Moral Majority*, 1991.

Marc Edge

FAMILY COMMUNICATION PATTERNS. The family has long been considered a key agency in the political socialization of children—or the process by which they acquire their orientation to the political world. Yet the evidence indicates that few political orientations, with the limited exception of partisanship, are transmitted directly from parent to child. Instead, the family environment, as characterized by the patterns of parent–child communication, appears to be more influential in developing the political character of children.

Research by Jack McLeod and Steven Chaffee at the University of Wisconsin-Madison in the 1960s demonstrated two politically relevant dimensions of parent–child communication in the family. In socio-oriented families, children are consistently told to maintain good relationships with their parents and other authority figures, often being advised to repress their anger, to avoid expressing their own points of view, and to stay away from trouble in general. In the concept-oriented family, children are encouraged to express their own ideas and to challenge those of other people, resulting in frequent participation in controversial discussions at home, where they are exposed to differing points of view.

Although these were originally assumed to be polar opposites, research has indicated that some families actually have a mix of both socio- and concept-oriented communication, while others exhibit no clear patterns of parent–child interaction along either dimension. However, children from homes with higher levels of concept-oriented communication tend to be heavier users of the public affairs media; to be more knowledgeable about politics; to have more interest in, and participate more in, election campaigns; to express greater trust in the government; and to have greater admiration for political leaders.

SOURCES: Steven H. Chaffee, Jack M. McLeod, and Daniel Wackman, "Family Communication Patterns and Adolescent Political Participation," in Jack Dennis, ed., *Socialization and Politics: A Reader*, 1973; Jane Meadowcraft, "Family Communication Patterns and Political Development: The Child's Role," *Communication Research*, August 1990.

Kim A. Smith and Milena Karagyazova

FAMOUS EPISODES. *See* Spiro T. Agnew; Bush-Rather Interview; Daisy Commercial; Democratic Convention of 1968; "Dewey Defeats Truman"; Grenada Invasion; Gary Hart; Huey Long; Joseph McCarthy; Panama Invasion; Persian Gulf War; Scopes Monkey Trial; Clarence Thomas; Truman Firing of MacArthur; Watergate.

FDR AND RADIO. Franklin Delano Roosevelt used radio to manage national and international news and provide peace of mind for millions of Americans during his presidency from 1933 to 1945. Using what the press called "fireside chats," Roosevelt managed to discuss news with his listeners on a personal level. He used folksy language and an informal style to talk to the American public about the important issues of the day. Historians' estimates of the number of fireside chats range from 27 to 31 in the slightly more than 12 years he was in office. The words "fireside chat" originated in a CBS press release written by Harry Butcher prior to Roosevelt's second broadcast. The term captured the imagination of the press and the public.

The broadcasts were normally delivered in the evening, and more than a third were on Sundays, allowing for a "one-two rhetorical punch." His chats would be heard that night and covered by the newspapers the next day. Roosevelt's radio success was, in large part, because of his voice quality. His voice was described as "golden," "rich," and "melodious." Roosevelt was said to inspire confidence through his voice alone. He achieved a feeling of genuine concern and intimacy among his listeners, calling them "my friends" or "my fellow Americans." He spoke using at least 75 percent of the thousand most commonly used words and slowed his speech to about nine-tenths the speed of most exceptional speakers. FDR used radio to relay good news to the nation, to provoke thought among his listeners, and to boost morale in times of national crisis.

SOURCES: Russell D. Buhite and David W. Levy, eds., *FDR's Fireside Chats*, 1992; Betty Houchin Winfield, *FDR and the News Media*, 1990.

J. Sean McCleneghan and Churchill L. Roberts

FESTINGER, LEON (1919–) was a psychology professor at Stanford when he developed the theory of cognitive dissonance. Cognitive dissonance theory explains the thinking process when a person chooses one option versus another. After the decision is made, the person will have some degree of doubt or uncertainty about the choice. The degree or intensity of that doubt relates to the degree or intensity of the similarities of outcomes between the two choices in the person's mind. The cognitive dissonance concept is important to political communications because it may explain why people are not persuaded by information they receive from candidates or the media. What Festinger demonstrated was that people experiencing dissonance seek consonant information— that is, information supporting their decision or choice—and avoid information that will add to their dissonance. Festinger also taught at Massachusetts Institute of Technology, the University of Michigan, and the University of Minnesota. His book, *Theory of Cognitive Dissonance*, was published in 1957.

SOURCES: David Cohen, *Psychologists on Psychology*, second edition, 1995; Vernon J. Nordby and Calvin S. Hall, *A Guide to Psychologists and Their Concepts*, 1974.

Guido H. Stempel III

FIRST AMENDMENT. *See Abrams v. United States*; Clear and Present Danger; Eichman Case; *Hustler v. Falwell; Miami Herald v. Tornillo; Near v. Minnesota; New York Times v. Sullivan;* Pentagon Papers; *Progressive* Case; *Richmond Newspapers v. Virginia*; *Schenck*; Seditious Libel; Symbolic Speech; John Peter Zenger.

FRAMING is agenda setting by the media to create a particular context around an issue or a candidate. This is done by selecting certain aspects and emphasizing them continuously while ignoring other equally important aspects.

Media are being criticized for creating a negative frame for political candidates. Any presidential candidate becomes subject to negative coverage by the media, and many feel that such coverage is out of proportion. However trivial the negatives, they outweigh the positives, no matter how significant.

Some critics are suggesting that this is one reason voter participation is declining in this country. Others have suggested that such coverage discourages people from running for office.

Framing is not restricted to coverage of political candidates. In particular, it applies to political issues. For example, welfare has been cast largely in the frame of the lazy poor and welfare fraud. Likewise, health care reform has been cast in the frame of socialized medicine. Like stereotypes, frames restrict the dialogue on issues.

SOURCE: Michael B. Salwen and Don W. Stacks, *An Integrated Approach to Communication Theory and Research*, 1996.

Guido H. Stempel III

FRANKLIN, BENJAMIN (1706–1790) is often best known for his impressive achievements as colonial printer, editor, entrepreneur, and author of a widely read (and still popular) book of sayings and witticisms, *Poor Richard's Almanac*, which went through numerous editions. However, he more properly should be known for his achievements in the field of politics.

His skill as an organizer and communicator were put to use early in Philadelphia, where he helped to found such institutions as a library, a fire department, an insurance company, and a hospital. He was elected to the Pennsylvania Assembly, thus beginning 40 years of political life. In 1753, along with William Hunter, he was appointed deputy postmaster general of the colonies and within a short time had turned a losing proposition into one that showed a profit. By that year his wit, wisdom, and political insights had brought him honorary degrees from Yale and a Copley medal from the Royal Society. The Pennsylvania legislature sent him to London in 1757 for the first of three extensive periods abroad when he represented his state or the new nation (1757–1762 and 1764–1775 in England and 1776–1785 in France). During the latter period he played a key role in negotiating, under a charge from Congress, a pact of ''amity and commerce.'' In doing so, he immeasurably aided the American war effort by raising money, securing ships for the American navy, and recruiting forces to serve in America. This success was accomplished by persistent courting of the right French officials. After the 1781 surrender at Yorktown, he began drafting a peace treaty—signed in 1783—that was close in terms and language to the final document. He returned to this country in 1785 to universal accolades for his service. He became president of the Supreme Executive Council of Pennsylvania and president of the Pennsylvania Society for Promoting the Abolition of Slavery. His final service was as delegate to the Constitutional Convention. Though in failing health, he provided a persistent, often humorous, compromising force that helped the authors of the convention stick to their difficult task.

SOURCE: Leonard Lebaree, ed., *The Autobiography of Benjamin Franklin*, 1964.

Wallace B. Eberhard

THE FREEDOM FORUM is a nonpartisan, international foundation with a focus on free press, free speech, and free spirit. Previously known as the Gannett Foundation, it is supported by an endowment established by Frank E. Gannett, founder of what is now known as Gannett Co., Inc. The initial investment of $100,000 in Gannett stock has increased to an endowment of more than $900 million. Allen H. Neuharth became chief executive officer (CEO) of Gannett in 1973 and led the company through more than a decade of rapid growth. During that time, the foundation and Gannett were closely tied. Neuharth became chairman of the Gannett Foundation in 1986. He retired from Gannett in 1989, and the foundation was renamed the Freedom Forum in July 1991. Through a series of negotiations, the Gannett Co., Inc. purchased back Gannett stock owned by the foundation, and the Freedom Forum diversified its assets. The foundation does not solicit or accept financial contributions. It funds only its own programs and related partnerships and sponsors conferences, educational activities, publishing, broadcasting, training, research, and on-line services. Operating programs are the Media Studies Center in New York City, the First Amendment Center at Vanderbilt University, the Newseum in Arlington, Virginia, and the Freedom Forum Pacific Coast Center in San Francisco. Charles Overby is chairman and CEO of the foundation, and Peter Pritchard is its president.

SOURCE: *The Freedom Forum 1995 Annual Report.*

Will Norton

FREEDOM OF INFORMATION ACT (FOIA) is an act passed by Congress in 1966 that created an ''open policy'' for obtaining federal government documents. The FOIA makes government documents available to average citizens. The requester does not have to specify why he or she wishes to obtain the information or how the information will be used. Requests must be made in writing, and government agencies are expected to respond within 10 days, although rarely does this occur. A government agency does have the right to deny a request. However, if the request goes to court—and 18 have to date—the agency must prove in a court of law why the information should not be released. The access provided is limited, however, because there are nine exceptions that a government agency can claim as reasons for denying permission. These are national security, internal agency rules, information exempted by federal statute, trade secrets, internal memoranda, personal privacy, investigatory records, financial institutional records, and oil well information. FOIA applies to federal government agency records only, and state and local government agencies are free to enact their own disclosure policies.

SOURCES: ''How to File an FOIA Request,'' *Quill*, October 1994; John W. Smith and John S. Klemanski, *The Urban Political Dictionary*, 1994.

Jacqueline Nash Gifford

FREEDOM OF SPEECH describes the provisions of acceptable and permissible speech as outlined in the First Amendment. The First Amendment says that ''Congress shall make no law respecting an establishment of religion, or prohibiting the free exercise thereof; or abridging the freedom of speech, or of the press; or the right of the people peaceably to assemble, and to petition the government for a redress of grievances.''

Despite the ''absolute'' tone of the provisions of freedom of speech, the U.S. Supreme Court, over the years, has ruled that certain types of speech are not protected by the Constitution. Among those types of speech are fighting words and obscenity. In the Court's opinion, free speech, including the right to peacefully protest, is critical to the well-being of a healthy democratic state. Specifically, there must be an environment that permits public debate and allows for the expression of unpopular ideas. In essence, freedom of speech is the cornerstone of political communication because it encourages the open exchange of political ideas—even radical ideas—which ultimately serves the best interest of the nation's citizens.

SOURCE: Leonard W. Levy, ed., *Encyclopedia of the American Constitution, Supplement One*, 1992.

Jacqueline Nash Gifford

FREEDOM OF THE PRESS refers to the rights of the media as protected by the First Amendment of the U.S. Constitution. Freedom of the press is essential to a democracy. Thomas Jefferson wrote in the Declaration of Independence that governments exist to protect our God-given rights and that governments derive "their just powers from the consent of the governed." This implies an informed electorate, but if the government controls the press, the electorate cannot be fully informed.

Under the First Amendment, the press is permitted to write about governmental abuses and to analyze governmental policies and actions. The public can make intelligent choices for political candidates and issues based on the information provided by the press.

The U.S. Supreme Court has given the press great latitude to do its job without censorship. Over the Court's history, it made rulings limiting government action in such areas as libel, prior restraint of printing or airing information, access to government events and files, and discriminatory taxation.

SOURCES: Kermit L. Hall, ed., *The Oxford Companion to the Supreme Court of the United States*, 1992; Leonard W. Levy, ed., *Encyclopedia of the American Constitution, Supplement One*, 1992.

Jacqueline Nash Gifford

FRIENDLY, FRED (1915–1998) created the standards for today's broadcast news journalists and helped create the Corporation for Public Broadcasting. Born in New York City, Friendly had a comfortable life as an only child. He attended the Nicols Junior College in Massachusetts, where he majored in business administration and was the yearbook editor.

In 1937, he landed his first radio announcing and news job at WEAN in Providence, Rhode Island. There he started his famous *Footprints in the Sand* series, a collection of on-air biographical sketches and stories of famous historical figures. The series was so popular it was eventually made into a record.

Friendly is best known for his work with Edward R. Murrow, considered one of America's best news broadcasters. Together, Friendly and Murrow produced a series of albums, again based on history, called *I Can Hear It Now*. Their recordings won many awards, and in 1951, the concept was changed to a television program called *See It Now*. Those watching *See It Now* could see documentaries and news from around the world. The most famous of those programs was the exposé of Senator Joseph McCarthy during the "Red Scare." That program is generally considered a major factor in the downfall of McCar-

thy. *See It Now* was on the air until 1958. It won more than 30 awards, including the George Peabody Award. The end of the program did not signal an end to their relationship; the pair then coproduced a program called *Small World*, which used new technology to connect people from different parts of the world to discuss various topics.

Eventually, Friendly was asked by CBS to produce another documentary program called *CBS Reports*, a program that produced quality, informative documentaries. In 1964, Friendly was appointed president of CBS News. It was a heady time for journalists as the 1960s continued to see the country in turmoil, and Friendly made sure that CBS News did more than just cover the facts by also providing news analysis.

But gradually he became disenchanted with management at CBS. When they insisted on running *I Love Lucy* instead of congressional hearings on the Vietnam War in 1966, he resigned. He was asked to be president of the Ford Foundation, a group dedicated to producing quality educational television programs. He did so and over the next few years helped set the groundwork for what was to become today's Corporation for Public Broadcasting (CPB). He continued to lend his expertise to producing documentaries on CPB. Friendly also became very active in teaching broadcast journalism at Columbia University. (*See also* Joseph McCarthy.)

SOURCES: *Contemporary Authors*, Vol. 14, 1985; *Who's Who in America*, 1997–1998.

Jacqueline Nash Gifford

G

GALLUP POLL. The term Gallup Poll is used in a variety of ways. It is applied to a series of surveys about public opinion, such as the CNN/USA Today Gallup Poll, conducted by the Gallup Organization. The term is also used more generally to refer to any survey project conducted by the Gallup Organization. However, its original use refers to a newspaper poll about American public opinion that was started by George Gallup. In 1972, the results of the various Gallup Polls since 1935 were combined into a book called *The Gallup Poll.* Each year, the Gallup Organization's collected research continues to be published under the same title.

George Gallup was a pioneer in the field of survey and public opinion research. Gallup began conducting survey research while teaching journalism at the University of Iowa, Drake University, and Northwestern University. He left academe to become a full-time researcher for Young & Rubicam, a Manhattan advertising agency. In 1935, Gallup joined with Harold A. Anderson to start the American Institute for Public Opinion (AIPO). The AIPO started the syndicated newspaper column based on public opinion research and conducted research for various business and political organizations. In 1940, the column was renamed "The Gallup Poll."

In 1938, Gallup founded Audience Research Incorporated (ARI) to conduct research for media companies. In 1950, ARI became the Gallup Organization, and by 1958, all of George Gallup's many research enterprises were consolidated under that name. George Gallup died in 1984, but the Gallup Organization continues as one of the world's most respected research and public opinion polling organizations. Gallup was one of the most influential people in promoting the use of survey research methods for political and business purposes.

SOURCES: George Gallup, ed., *The Gallup Poll: Public Opinion 1935–1971*, 1972; Richard D. Smith, "Letting America Speak," *Audacity*, Winter 1997.

Stephen Lacy

GALTUNG, JOHAN (1930–) is the founding father of peace studies as an academic discipline. His formal education is in mathematics and sociology. In 1959, he founded and directed the International Peace Research Institute. In 1969, he left the institute formally and became a professor at the University of Oslo. This academic career spans major international universities, including the University of Hawaii and the University Witten-Herdecke, Germany.

For his prestigious work, he received an alternative Nobel Peace Prize for an essay. He returned to social sciences in 1974 as director-general of the Inter-University Centre and president of the World Future Studies. He also was project coordinator for the United Nations.

His most recent book, *Global Glasnost: Toward a New World Information and Communication Order*, examines how economics and information management affect the Third World, particularly through international governmental agencies such as the United Nations Educational, Scientific, and Cultural Organization (UNESCO). He also analyzes journalism's contribution to cover war and peace stories as part of the international political dialogue.

SOURCE: *The International Who's Who*, 1995–1996.

Jacqueline Nash Gifford

GANS, HERBERT (1927–) is a sociologist with a strong interest in analyzing and describing gatekeeping. Gans was born in Germany and came to the United States in 1940. He has advanced degrees from the University of Chicago and the University of Pennsylvania. During his career, he has worked in many research capacities, including urban and city planning research, and as a professor at Massachusetts Institute of Technology and Columbia University. He also has been a consultant for many governmental agencies and private philanthropy organizations.

Gans is the author of *The Uses of Television and Their Educational Implications* and *Deciding What's News*. Perhaps his most important contribution is his analysis on the press' cultural bias, which influences news decision making. Specifically, Gans identified several perspectives, which he called "enduring values." Two of those values were ethnocentrism and individualism. He argues that themes such as these constantly appear in the news for two reasons— because journalists respect them as part of their professional values and because journalists share those values with their audience's cultures. Gans' work gives a credible nod to recognizing the power of the press to persuade society, even when attempting to be objective.

SOURCES: Ann Evory, ed., *Contemporary Authors*, Vol. 6, 1982; Werner J. Severin and James W. Tankard, Jr., *Communication Theories: Origins, Methods and Uses in the Mass Media*, fourth edition, 1997; *Who's Who in America*, 1992–1993.

Jacqueline Nash Gifford

GARRISON, WILLIAM LLOYD (1805–1879), a prominent abolitionist, put forward the law of "nonresistance" to combat slavery. He believed that the slavery of the Negroes was only a particular instance of universal coercion and advanced the principle that under no pretext has any man the right to dominate or use coercion over his fellows. Leo Tolstoy credits Garrison with being "the first to proclaim this principle as a rule for the organization of the life of men" and proclaimed him as "one of the greatest reformers and promoters of true human progress."

Garrison used the power of the press to spread his creed far and wide. In January 1831, the first issue of his paper, the *Liberator*, appeared with a motto: "Our country is the world—our countrymen are mankind." Although its primary objective was the abolition of slavery, it did not overlook other moral and social evils. Garrison was also an activist in other movements such as women's and civil rights and religious reform. He spoke strongly in favor of the enfranchisement of women at the Women's Rights Convention in Worcester, Massachusetts, in 1850. Garrison's views on women's issues are expressed in these words: "I have been derisively called a 'Women's Rights Man.' I know no such distinction. I claim to be a Human Rights Man, and wherever there is a human being, I see God-given rights inherent in that being, whatever may be the sex or complexion."

On the same principle of human fraternity and true to his motto, he espoused the cause of the Chinese by denouncing the national policy of excluding them from the country on the grounds of race.

In addition to being a newspaperman, Garrison was active as a lecturer in the antislavery cause. Frederick Douglass, awed by his marvelous power as a speaker, narrated the following account of an address by Garrison in Nantucket in 1841:

Those who heard him oftenest and known him longest, were astonished at his masterly effort. . . . The orator swayed a thousand heads and hearts at once, and by the simple majesty of his all-controlling thought, converting his hearers into the express image of his own soul. That night there were a thousand Garrisons in Nantucket.

SOURCES: V. G. Chertkoff and Florence Holah, *A Short Biography of William Lloyd Garrison with an Introductory Appreciation of His Life and Work by Leo Tolstoy*, 1904; Archibald Henry Grimke, *William Lloyd Garrison: The Abolitionist*, 1891; Oliver Johnson, *W. L. Garrison and Times*, 1881; *Selections from the Writings and Speeches of William Lloyd Garrison*, 1852.

Anju G. Chaudhary

GATEKEEPING. Even in the simplest of communication, a sender and a receiver serve as gatekeepers, allowing some information to be transmitted and received, while slamming the gates on other information that could have been shared. The term "gatekeeper," however, often is reserved for those in relatively large and complex communication organizations, especially the news media, whose job it is to select information to transmit. Because space and time for their products are limited, and because they must deliver these products quickly, news media have developed highly structured routines for the fast-paced, zero-sum game that is gatekeeping. Consequently, there has been much interest in how the mass media, especially the news media, decide what information to convey and what information to ignore. Social psychologist Kurt Lewin has been credited with coining the term in a 1947 study of decision rules within families. The seminal gatekeeping study was conducted by David Manning White in 1950; he observed a newspaper wire editor for a week as he selected news. Since then many other studies have been conducted to examine the criteria reporters and editors use in making gatekeeping decisions as well as the effects of these rules and routines.

SOURCES: David Manning White, "The 'Gatekeeper': A Case Study in the Selection of News," *Journalism Quarterly*, Fall 1950; Pamela J. Shoemaker and Stephen D. Reese, *Mediating the Message: Theories of Influences on Mass Media Content*, second edition, 1996.

Dominic L. Lasorsa

GENERATION X. A term coined by modern media to describe young adults between the ages of 18 and 29. This group is often characterized by the media as being politically unmotivated compared to their parents, who are generally baby boomers. Media magazine articles in the 1980s describe Generation Xers (the X implies that they are an anonymous breed with no legacy) as disenchanted with societal norms and exceptions. They often choose untraditional career paths and life choices, including marriage, families, and religion. Reaching this generation is seen as a major challenge for political communicators.

SOURCE: Kathleen Thompson Hill and Gerald N. Hill, *Real Life Dictionary of American Politics*, 1994.

Jacqueline Nash Gifford

GERBNER, GEORGE (1919–). Research into television violence by this Hungarian-born scholar has led to increased awareness of the powerful effects of the medium. Gerbner enrolled in journalism at Berkeley after fleeing his homeland before World War II. He worked as a reporter for the *San Francisco Chronicle* before joining the Office of Strategic Services (OSS) after the United States entered the war.

Gerbner took his master's and Ph.D. degrees at Southern California, where he developed his "General Theory of Communication" as his dissertation. After teaching at the University of Illinois for eight years, he became dean of the Annenberg School of Communication at the University of Pennsylvania in 1964.

In the late 1960s, he conducted a series of content analyses of television violence as part of two federal government projects. He hypothesized that rather than imitating acts of violence, viewers would tend to identify with the victims.

This led him to develop the "cultivation theory," which states that heavy viewers of television tend to see the world as it is portrayed on the small screen. By cultivating fear, television was seen as a vehicle for the possible acceptance of repression. This contradicted the hitherto accepted theory of limited effects of media. As editor of the *Journal of Communication*, Gerbner published much of his own work on cultivation theory as well as some of the reaction to it. (*See also* Cultivation.)

SOURCES: John A. Lent, ed., *A Different Road Taken; Profiles in Critical Communication*, 1995; Shearon A. Lowery and Melvin L. DeFleur, *Milestones in Mass Communication Research: Media Effects*, third edition, 1995.

Marc Edge

GODKIN, EDWIN LAWRENCE (1831–1902) founded the *Nation* in 1865 in a joint-stock arrangement with Carl Schurz and Henry Villard. Godkin was editor of the *Nation* from 1865 to 1899 and associate editor of the *New York Evening Post* from 1881 to 1899. The *Evening Post* was also owned by Godkin, Schurtz and Villard. Neither publication had a very large circulation, but both were noted for readership among leaders in business, politics, and intellectual life and for well-written, thoughtful editorials. Godkin's political views were generally liberal. He supported limited government and construed individual rights very broadly. The influential *Nation* was reportedly the target of a Joseph Pulitzer quip that he was interested in talking "to a nation, not a select committee." Godkin was a harsh critic of contemporary journalism, and his high standards for journalism put him at odds with *New York Tribune* editor Horace Greeley, whom Godkin saw as a symbol of both personal and professional lowliness. He called Greeley "ambitious and scheming" and said that as long as the American press remained a "moral and intellectual dunghill," it would produce such people as Greeley. He believed journalists and newspapers should promote public life and cultivate society. His acidic style of journalism was characterized by one of his attorneys (he was sued several times for libel) in describing the *Post* as a "pessimistic, malignant, and malevolent sheet, which no good citizen ever goes to bed without reading."

SOURCES: William A. Armstrong, *E. L. Godkin: A Biography*, 1978; Alan P. Grimes, *The Political Liberalism of the New York "Nation,"* 1953.

Charles Caudill

GRABER, DORIS (1923–) is a leading researcher in political communication. Her work has addressed fundamental questions about the role of the media in the political process. A native of St. Louis, Graber passed the entrance exam at local Washington University as a high school freshman. She had her M.A. in political science at age 18, having worked her way through school as a newspaper reporter. She took her Ph.D. in international law and relations at Columbia and began teaching at several Chicago-area schools, settling at the University of Illinois at Chicago in 1963.

Her best-known research has been on information processing—how people choose, interpret, and retain information from the news media. Graber draws heavily on "schema" theory in her work, arguing that people evaluate new information according to their preexisting belief structures. Her 1984 book on this subject, *Processing the News: How People Tame the Information Tide*, was released in a third edition in 1994. Graber also contributed to a major study of the agenda-setting function of the media, which was published in the 1993 book *Media Agenda Setting in a Presidential Campaign*. Her 1980 book, *Mass Media and American Politics*, released in a fifth edition in 1997, is a compendium of current knowledge on the subject. In 1984, she edited a companion volume, *Media Power in Politics*, which was released in a third edition in 1994.

When the American Political Science Association and the International Communication Association began joint publication of the scholarly journal *Political Communication* in 1992, Graber was chosen as its first editor.

SOURCES: *Contemporary Authors* (CD-ROM); Douglas M. McLeod, *Women in Communication*, 1994.

Marc Edge

GREELEY, HORACE (1811–1872) was truly a legend in his own time. Born to a large, poor family in New Hampshire, he was self-educated. Yet, with assets of $3,000 he started what would become the best-known newspaper of his time and became a major figure in national politics. He went to New York City in 1830 to be a reporter, and three years later he and a friend started the *Morning Post*. It lasted three weeks, but a year later he started a weekly, the *New Yorker*. Then in 1841, at the age of 30, he started the *New York Tribune*. It was a success from the start, and from it sprang the *Weekly Tribune*, which circulated nationally and achieved a circulation of 200,000.

He was an idealist and a reformer. He was a proponent of Fourierism, a type of collectivism. He was for labor unions and against capital punishment and had some success on both issues. He also favored high tariffs and free homesteads. He was a strong abolitionist. His newspaper was a strong advocate on all these issues and thus different from most of its contemporaries.

He was a supporter of the Whig Party and became one of the founders of the Republican Party. Yet in 1872, disillusioned with the Republicans and President Grant, he ran for president on the Democratic ticket. Grant won easily, and Greeley, crushed by that and the death of his wife just before the election, died later that month.

SOURCES: Joseph McKerns, *Biographical Dictionary of American Journalism*, 1989; Kenneth Stewart and John Tebbel, *Makers of Modern Journalism*, 1952.

Guido H. Stempel III

GRENADA INVASION. The October 1983 storming of this Caribbean island by U.S. troops created some of the deepest-ever tensions between press and government. A Marxist coup and the subsequent execution of Prime Minister Maurice Bishop prompted President Ronald Reagan to divert to Grenada a 10-ship navy task force bound for Lebanon. The reason for the "intervention"— dubbed "Operation Urgent Fury"—was ostensibly to protect U.S. students at a medical school on the island. But in an unprecedented move, reporters were barred from accompanying the invasion forces. Those who chartered private boats were either forced back by the U.S. military, sometimes under fire, or detained by troops if they did land. On the third and final day of hostilities, a contingent of 15 television and wire-service reporters was taken in by military transport plane but brought out the same day. Massed in nearby Barbados was a force of 300 journalists trying to get into Grenada. The extraordinary measures were felt to be a result of resentment by military commanders, many of whom served in Vietnam and blamed press coverage for losing the war. Outrage at the restrictions, however, led to the establishment of a media pool cleared and ready to join military maneuvers on short notice. This system was implemented in the invasion of Panama six years later.

SOURCES: Peter M. Dunn and Bruce W. Watson, eds. *American Intervention in Grenada: The Implication of Operation "Urgent Fury,"* 1985; Gordon K. Lewis, *Grenada, the Jewel Despoiled*, 1987.

Marc Edge

H

HAGERTY, JAMES CAMPBELL (1909–1981), press secretary to President Dwight D. Eisenhower, set a precedent for frank discussion of a president's illness when he disclosed the complete details of Eisenhower's heart attack in 1955. Instead of following the tradition of attempting to conceal a health crisis, Hagerty made a point of giving timely and accurate information to the public. In doing so, he established a policy followed by subsequent administrations, except in the case of President John F. Kennedy, whose back ailment and general physical condition were not publicized.

Serving as press secretary during Eisenhower's two terms from 1953 to 1961, Hagerty established a reputation for innovative and successful news management based on extensive experience. Before taking the White House position, he had been a political reporter and political aide, first covering the New York legislature for the *New York Times* and then working as an assistant for Governor Thomas E. Dewey, who twice ran unsuccessfully for president on the Republican ticket.

A graduate of Columbia, Hagerty was the son of James A. Hagerty, chief political reporter of the *New York Times*. Enjoying a close relationship with Eisenhower, Hagerty allowed the president to be quoted directly at his press conference, a break with past policies. He also opened the conferences to television cameras for the first time. A champion of small newspapers and broadcast stations, Hagerty sent tapes of press conferences to small-town stations and called correspondents with breaking stories. He prided himself on candid dealings with the press.

SOURCES: Robert H. Ferrell, ed., *The Diary of James C. Hagerty*, 1983; Andrea B. Wagner, "A Study of Political News Management during a Presidential Health Crisis," M.A. thesis, University of Maryland, 1988.

Maurine H. Beasley

HART, GARY (1936–   ), U.S. senator from Colorado from 1975 to 1987, was twice a serious contender for the Democratic nomination for president. He won the New Hampshire primary in 1984 but eventually lost out to Walter Mondale. He was the presumed front-runner for the nomination in 1988. However, on May 3, 1987, the *Miami Herald* reported that a woman who was not his wife had spent the night in Hart's Washington, D.C., town house. There ensued a torrent of media attention to Hart's sex life outside his marriage, much of it based on rumor and innuendo.

Hart had been asked before about these rumors and had challenged reporters to "put a tail on me." The *Miami Herald* did just that. The appropriateness and accuracy of the *Herald*'s reporting were the subject of much scrutiny and heated debate in political and journalistic circles. The effects, however, transcended this one incident and this one candidate.

Aside from the devastating effect this had on his campaign (he shortly withdrew, reentered later, but was no longer a serious contender), the frenzy of media interest in his personal life definitively broke down the barriers that had long existed between a politician's public and private lives. While such interest might have been the stuff of tabloids in the past, the elite newspapers were the major players in this story, with *Washington Post* reporter Paul Taylor asking Hart in a press conference, "Have you committed adultery?" In effect, from this point on, no aspect of a candidate's or elected official's life was off-limits to the press.

SOURCES: John B. Judis, "The Hart Affair," *Columbia Journalism Review*, July/August 1987; "The Sudden Fall of Gary Hart," *Newsweek*, May 18, 1987.

David Kennamer

HEARST, WILLIAM RANDOLPH (1863–1951). This media tycoon was also a significant participant in politics. His father, George Hearst, was a miner who made a fortune mining silver. Later he became a U.S. senator and for political reasons bought the *San Francisco Examiner*. Young Hearst, eager to imitate Pulitzer's style of journalism, convinced his father he could revive the faltering *Examiner*. He took over the paper in 1887 and made good on his promise. His success there led him to move into the New York market and compete directly with Pulitzer by purchasing the *New York Journal* in 1895.

That set the stage for yellow journalism, with its intense competition and sensationalism. It climaxed with the Spanish-American War. Legend has it that Hearst sent the famous artist Frederic Remington to Cuba to make pictures of the war. Remington let Hearst know there was no war, but Hearst wired back, "You furnish the pictures, and I'll furnish the war." When the battleship *Maine* was sunk, both Hearst's *Journal* and Pulitzer's *World* had artists' drawings of the explosion covering more than half the front page. Yet historians now doubt that Hearst was much of a factor in leading the country to war.

Hearst was elected to Congress as a Democrat in 1902 and unsuccessfully sought the Democratic nomination for president in 1904. He ran against Charles

Evan Hughes for governor of New York in 1906 and lost, and after two more unsuccessful attempts to gain office, he renounced his political ambitions. However, he was a major factor in the nomination of Franklin D. Roosevelt for president in 1932. Yet, within a year he turned on Roosevelt and became increasingly more conservative the rest of his life. He was not, however, again to be the political force he had been in earlier years. (*See also* Joseph Pulitzer; Yellow Journalism.)

SOURCE: Kenneth Stewart and John Tebbel, *Makers of Modern Journalism*, 1952.

Guido H. Stempel III

HOAXES are journalists' practical jokes that make it on the pages or airwaves of the American media. They have a history that spans back to the 1800s in England, but they soon found their way into American newspapers and even the folklore of famous American historical events. Newspapers in the 1800s printed outrageous stories—and even hoaxes—to attract readers.

Fred Fedler, author of *Media Hoaxes*, writes that hoaxes were often successful because: (1) the stories were believable and credible, (2) topics were recently in the news, and (3) they used credible sources.

Some of the more famous American media hoaxes were:

1. The moon hoax by the *New York Sun* in 1835, which reported that there really was life on the moon.

2. The widely used story that Mrs. O'Leary's cow turned over a lantern and started the great Chicago fire of 1871.

3. Orson Welles' radio dramatization of H. G. Wells' *War of the Worlds*. The program, broadcast on Halloween in 1938, in the form of news bulletins about an invasion of New Jersey by Martians caused millions to panic.

SOURCE: Fred Fedler, *Media Hoaxes*, 1989.

Jacqueline Nash Gifford

HOWARD, ROY WILSON (1883–1964) was a newspaper journalist and executive. Born in Gano, Ohio, in a turnpike tollhouse, he grew up in Indianapolis. In 1912, at the age of 29, Howard became the United Press' first president and general manager in charge of both editorial and business operations. He broke the story announcing the armistice ending World War I four days before it was officially announced. Admiral Henry Braid Wilson, commander of American naval forces in France, later confirmed that he had given permission to Howard to use this story on November 7, 1918. In 1920, Howard left United Press to become associated with Robert P. Scripps in the management of Scripps newspapers. In 1922, E. W. Scripps changed the company's name to Scripps-Howard Newspapers, and Howard was named chairman of the board. In 1931, Howard bought the *New York World* and the *Evening World* for $5 million and consolidated them with the *New York Telegram*, which he acquired in 1927. The *New*

York World-Telegram won the Pulitzer Prize for public service in 1933. Howard directed the newspaper's attack on Tammany Hall and supported Fiorello H. LaGuardia, the reform candidate for mayor. Throughout his career, Roy Howard maintained a keen interest in reporting. He obtained exclusive interviews with a number of world leaders, including Britain's minister for war David Lloyd George, Japanese emperor Hirohito, and Soviet premier Joseph Stalin. The *New York Times* credited Howard with being a major influence in the election of Franklin D. Roosevelt in 1932. Howard retired officially in 1953 but continued to serve as chairman of the executive committee of Scripps-Howard Newspapers until his death of a heart attack in his New York office at age 81.

SOURCE: Kenneth Stewart and John Tebbel, *Makers of Modern Journalism*, 1952.

David H. Weaver

HOWE, LOUIS HENRY (1871–1936), a political operative who personified the "man behind the scenes," was instrumental in the political development of both Franklin D. Roosevelt and Eleanor Roosevelt. After a somewhat unsuccessful career as a newspaper reporter and political aide in Albany, New York, Howe attached himself to Franklin D. Roosevelt when he led an effort to reform Democratic politics and New York as a new state senator in 1911. When Roosevelt became ill during his reelection bid the following year, his wife, Eleanor, who initially disliked Howe for his heavy smoking and other personal characteristics, was forced to ask him to run the campaign. During the next eight years, Howe wrote speeches for Roosevelt, developed a national network of supporters, and managed his unsuccessful campaign for vice president on the Democratic ticket in 1920. Refusing to give up his belief in Roosevelt's political future when Roosevelt contracted infantile paralysis the following year, Howe kept Roosevelt's name before the public by extensive correspondence and personal contacts with political leaders. He also groomed Eleanor Roosevelt to become politically active. Howe helped bring about political alliances that led to Franklin Roosevelt's election as governor of New York in 1928. Instead of accompanying Roosevelt to Albany, he remained in New York, working on national political strategies that culminated in Roosevelt's election as president of the United States in 1932. By that time, Howe was in failing health. He was given the title of secretary to the president and was an indispensable adviser. He died in 1936 before Roosevelt ran for a second term.

SOURCE: Alfred B. Rollins, Jr., *Roosevelt and Howe*, 1962.

Maurine H. Beasley

HUSTLER V. FALWELL. One of Moral Majority leader Jerry Falwell's several court battles against sexually explicit magazines turned into a landmark Supreme Court case. *Hustler* magazine publisher Larry Flynt lampooned Falwell in print in a liquor ad parody that suggested Falwell's first sexual experience was with his mother in an outhouse. Falwell sued for libel and lost because as a public figure he was required to prove malice. He did, however, win $200,000 for "intentional infliction of emotional distress" because the trial court ruled it was not necessary to prove malice to collect damages for that. But in a unanimous 1988 ruling, the U.S. Supreme Court overturned the damage award and ruled that malice would thereafter be a necessary condition for a damage award for emotional distress.

SOURCES: Wayne Overbeck, *Major Principles of Media Law*, 1997; *Hustler Magazine v. Falwell*, 485 U.S. 46, 1988.

Marc Edge

HUTCHINS COMMISSION. Robert Maynard Hutchins, chancellor of the University of Chicago, chaired the Commission on Freedom of the Press (1942 – 1947). Conceived by Henry Luce and funded by *Time* and *Encyclopaedia Britannica*, the commission was formed in reaction to several challenges to press barons. These included threats posed by media critics to enforce press responsibility through more liberal libel laws and even direct government control or regulation. Another challenge was the increasing tendency of courts to define freedom of the press as the right of individual citizens to accurate and comprehensive information, rather than freedom from government control for the news industry.

The commission's report called for self-regulation. Also, "free press" should provide the public with:

1. A truthful account of the day's events in a context that gives them meaning.
2. A forum for the exchange of comment and criticism.
3. A representative picture of constituent groups in society.
4. The presentation and clarification of the goals and values of society.
5. Full access to the day's intelligence.

Reaction by publishers and editors was negative due to the closed proceedings of the commission, its attacks on the triviality and sensationalism of news coverage, and the lack of direct participation by journalists. Nevertheless, many of the recommendations of the commission have been adopted.

While the main report of the commission was in a brief book entitled *A Free and Responsible Press*, six other books on various aspects and issues of the media were produced by members of the commission.

SOURCES: Stephen Bates, *Realigning Journalism with Democracy: The Hutchins Commission, Its Times, and Ours*, 1995; Margaret Blanchard, "The Hutchins Commission, the Press and the Responsibility Concept," *Journalism Monographs*, No. 49, 1977; Commission on Freedom of the Press, *A Free and Responsible Press*, 1947; Frank Hughes, *Prejudice and the Press*, 1950.

David C. Perlmutter

HYPODERMIC EFFECT, also know as the magic bullet theory, was the name coined to describe the powerful, direct, and uniform effects of the media on a society hypothesized by communication researchers in the early twentieth century. The needle theory was based on incorrect views of modern society. It predicted that an appropriate stimulus message would produce a consistent response from the receiver in line with the intent of the message sender. This led to concerns about government's ability to use media to spread propaganda and influence people in their voting behaviors and their participation in war. Because individuals were viewed as isolated from their institutions and other citizens, media were thought to be able to shape public opinion in oppressive ways. This was the dominant theory of media and society prior to the beginnings of the scientific research ushered in by the Payne Fund studies in the 1920s. This somewhat crude stimulus-response model eventually was replaced by theory that stressed the social and cultural factors that limit the media's power to influence people.

SOURCE: Melvin DeFleur and Sandra Ball-Rokeach, *Theories of Mass Communication,* 1989.

LeAnne Daniels

I

INDEXING refers to creating a scale or index of attitudes. This is done by getting responses to a number of items chosen so that they form a continuum. We can then place individuals at a specific point on that continuum. A simple example is asking the individual whether he or she is very liberal, somewhat liberal, neither liberal nor conservative, somewhat conservative, or very conservative.

More important is the application of this concept to a series of attitude items. Thus, we might have statements about such issues as abortion, gun control, welfare, military spending, and school prayer. We would phrase them so that agreement would mean acceptance of the conservative position. Then the number of items the respondent agrees with is his or her score, and the score reflects the extent of conservative belief.

Such indexing assumes that we have a true continuum and that the continuum is unidimensional. That isn't always tested, and as a result some indexes are not very valid.

SOURCE: Michael W. Singletary and Gerald Stone, *Communication Theory and Research Applications*, 1988.

Guido H. Stempel III

J

JAMIESON, KATHLEEN HALL (1946–) is dean of the Annenberg School of Communication at the University of Pennsylvania and one of the most widely quoted political communication scholars of the 1990s. This is largely because she is clearly the country's expert on political advertising.

Jamieson is attempting to make communications the optimistic social science. Her analysis of how political and media forces manipulate public discourse is not a checklisting of oppression and duplicity but a program of problem solving. In her book *Dirty Politics*, she outlines concrete strategies through which news professionals can verify and critique political ads.

In her book *Eloquence in an Electronic Age*, she explained the decline of Old World oratory under the glaring lights and compressed editing of television. In *Beyond the Double Bind*, she shows that the rhetorically imposed contradiction of femininity versus career success has been and can be transcended. She writes, ''Examined as rhetorical frames, double binds can be understood, manipulated, dismantled.'' No more accurate summary of her method, goals, and attitude toward political communication form and content could be stated.

SOURCES: Kathleen Hall Jamieson, *Eloquence in an Electronic Age*, 1988; Kathleen Hall Jamieson, *Dirty Politics: Deception, Distraction and Democracy*, 1992; Kathleen Hall Jamieson, *Beyond the Double Bind: Women and Leadership*, 1995.

David C. Perlmutter

JEFFERSON, THOMAS (1743–1826). Any study of political communication in the United States must begin with Thomas Jefferson. He provided the basis for political communication when he wrote in the Declaration of Independence:

We hold these Truths to be self evident, that all Men are created equal, that they are endowed by their Creator with certain inalienable Rights, that among these rights are

Life, Liberty, and the Pursuit of Happiness—that to secure these Rights, Governments are instituted among Men, deriving their just Powers from the Consent of the Governed.

If the consent of the governed is required, then the governed must be informed, and that can happen only if there is political communication.

Another significant factor in the evolution of political communication in this country was the election of 1800, in which Jefferson defeated incumbent president John Adams. The main issue was the Alien and Sedition Act of 1798, and Jefferson's victory meant that the oppressive act would not be renewed.

Jefferson is also remembered for saying, "Were it left to me to decide whether we should have a government without newspapers or newspapers without a government, I should not hesitate a moment to prefer the latter." Yet after he became president, Jefferson was often critical of the press, and those comments are often noted. What is overlooked is that in his later years after he had left the presidency, he was supportive of the press. It also needs to be recognized that while he was president, Jefferson endured a great deal of abuse from the partisan press of that era. It was a press committed to political ends much more than to truth.

SOURCE: Leonard Levy, ed., *Freedom of the Press from Zenger to Jefferson*, 1967.

Guido H. Stempel III

JFK AND TELEVISION. In 1950, only 4.4 million American families owned a television set. By 1960, 40 million American families owned one. In a single decade the medium of television had exploded into a dimension shaping the American mind that rivaled America's schools and churches. John F. Kennedy became the first American president to take advantage of, and benefit from, almost every aspect television had to offer. The indisputable power of the medium was realized on September 26, 1960, when Kennedy and Richard Nixon engaged in what became the event of the campaign—the first presidential debate. It left no doubt about television's ability to create a political star's image overnight. Kennedy appeared fresh and relaxed. Nixon was made up poorly for the cameras. Reaction shots showed him sweating, biting his lip, wiping his forehead. Seventy-five million Americans watched the debate, and others listened on radio. The Gallup Poll found that 43 percent thought Kennedy had done a better job, while 23 percent thought Nixon had done a better job. Kennedy, who had trailed Nixon in a Gallup Poll two weeks earlier, moved ahead of Nixon in the poll done right after the first debate. Yet, one study showed that people who heard the debate on the radio thought Nixon had won. Televising the debate thus did no service to the substance of the debate, but it did affect images.

Kennedy continued to use television effectively throughout his presidency. He was the first president to have live televised press conferences, and no president who followed him used them as effectively. At the time of the Bay of Pigs invasion in 1961 and the Cuban missile crisis in 1962, he used television to speak directly and forcefully to the American people. From televised speeches to tours of the White House, Kennedy and television were friends because they complemented each other. The first president to fully utilize television ironically died on television. Four days of uninterrupted coverage informing, consoling the public, and reflecting, honored him.

SOURCES: Michael Tracey, "Non-Fiction Television," in Anthony Smith, ed., *Television: An International History*, 1995; Ann Watson, *The Expanding Vista: American Television in the Kennedy Years*, 1990; Theodore H. White, *The Making of the President, 1960*, 1961.

J. Sean McCleneghan

JOHN BIRCH SOCIETY is an organization that works to stamp out communist activities that threaten American democracy. The organization, founded in 1958 by confectioner Robert W. Welch, Jr., was named after Captain John Birch, a missionary who was killed by the communist Chinese.

The group is categorized as ultraconservative. The group has sought to remove the United States from the United Nations and was highly critical of Presidents Eisenhower and Kennedy and Supreme Court chief justice Earl Warren.

The group, which boasts a membership of approximately 100,000, publishes various magazines and books, including *American Opinion* and *The JB Bulletin*.

SOURCES: John B. Harer, *Intellectual Freedom, a Reference Handbook*, 1992; Ciaran O. Maolain, *The Radical Right: A World Directory*, 1987.

Jacqueline Nash Gifford

JOINT OPERATING AGREEMENTS. The Newspaper Preservation Act is either an effective means to preserve multiple voices in the daily newspaper field during a period of consolidation and death of dailies, or it is a mechanism for already profitable newspapers to preserve their profitability and fend off competition. Joint operating agreements (JOAs) were not new when the act protecting them was passed in 1970. Twenty-two were in effect, the first dating from 1933 in Albuquerque, New Mexico. The agreements were forged by competing newspapers to permit the weaker of the two to escape the trend of daily newspaper failures in the 1920s. The agreements consolidated one or more of the following—mechanical departments, advertising departments, and circulation departments. News and editorial departments were kept separate, and each paper retained its own name and identity. Thus, competition in news gathering and divergence in editorial opinion were kept alive. Because some of the agreements included price fixing, market control, or profit sharing, the U.S. Department of Justice challenged the JOAs as being a violation of antitrust law. The New Mexico agreement was the test case, and that joint operating agreement was held illegal by the U.S. Supreme Court in *Citizen Publishing Co. v. United States*.

Within a year the newspaper industry successfully lobbied Congress for legislation legalizing existing JOAs and setting rules for new ones. That law, the

Newspaper Preservation Act of 1970, requires a court hearing to determine the need for a joint operating agreement. Many journalists say the law works to protect multiple voices, but critics maintain that the law is a sham, permitting JOAs where they are not needed. Perhaps more noteworthy is the fact that while there were 22 JOAs a quarter century ago, there are only 17 now.

SOURCES: John C. Busterna, *Joint Operating Agreements: The Newspaper Preservation Act and Its Application*, 1993; National Newspaper Association, *Facts about Newspapers*, 1997.

Wallace B. Eberhard

K

KATZ, ELIHU (1926–) was a professor of communication and director of the Annenberg Scholars Program at the University of Pennsylvania. He also was the founder of the communication program at Hebrew University in Jerusalem and was instrumental in bringing Israel into the television age in 1968. His research has dealt with the effects of mass media in different social systems, as well as the dynamics of public opinion. Two areas of his research are especially noteworthy.

First, Katz and Paul Lazarsfeld, in *Personal Influence: The Part Played by People in the Flow of Communication* (1955) developed the notion of the two-step flow of communication. They noted that more people engaged in informal interpersonal discussions with other people than were exposed to campaign information directly from the news media. Thus, media influence seemed to pass to the masses through opinion leaders.

Katz was also a pioneer in research dealing with uses and gratifications. According to Katz, Blumler, and Gurevitch in their book *The Uses of Mass Communication: Current Perspectives on Gratifications Research* (1974), uses and gratifications research focuses on the social and psychological origins of need that generate expectations of media that lead to differential patterns of media exposure that result in need gratifications.

Uses and gratifications research thus highlighted the likelihood of audience initiative and activity. Individuals actively select and consume messages from the media in response to their expectations. Individuals thus are viewed as making subjective choices about media and initiating behavior based on their needs and expectations of fulfilling those needs.

SOURCES: Elihu Katz, Jay G. Blumler, and Michael Gurevitch, "Utilization of Mass Communication by the Individual," in Jay G. Blumler and Elihu Katz, eds., *The Uses of Mass Communication: Current Perspectives on Gratifications Research*, 1974; Melvin L. DeFleur and Sandra Ball-Rokeach, *Theories of Mass Communication*, fifth edition, 1989.

Wayne Wanta

KENNEDY, JOHN. *See* JFK and Television; Kennedy-Nixon Debates.

KENNEDY-NIXON DEBATES. The first televised presidential debates were in 1960 between John F. Kennedy and Richard M. Nixon. They were made possible by an act of Congress that exempted presidential debates from the Federal Communication Commission's (FCC) Equal Time Provision for the 1960 campaign only. There were four debates, and it is widely believed that they were a major factor in Kennedy's victory in the election. It was really the first debate that was crucial. Most observers thought that Nixon, with his two terms as vice president, would have the best of it against his less experienced rival. It turned out the opposite. Kennedy was much more adept at spontaneous responses than Nixon. Furthermore, Nixon was the victim of a terrible makeup job that made him look pale. It was so bad that the *Chicago Daily News*, two days after the debate, speculated in a front-page story that it might have been sabotage.

The polls showed a clear Kennedy gain after the first debate. The other three debates were much more even, but the damage had been done to the Nixon campaign. Although the debates were widely acclaimed, there would not be debates between presidential candidates again until 1976. A change in FCC regulations made it possible to have the debates under outside sponsorship, and the League of Women voters agreed to take that responsibility in 1976 and 1980.

SOURCE: Sidney Kraus, *The Great Debates*, 1962.

Guido H. Stempel III

KERNER COMMISSION. In the summer of 1967, nearly 150 cities in the United States reported disorders in black neighborhoods. These involved widespread looting, burning, and destruction of property. The worst came during a two-week period in July, when large-scale disorders erupted first in Newark New Jersey, and then in Detroit, each setting off a chain reaction in neighboring communities. About 80 people died, and 1,900 were injured. Property damage was estimated at more than $100 million.

On July 28, 1967, President Lyndon Johnson appointed the National Commission on Civil Disorders (called the Kerner Commission after its chairman), calling upon it "to guide the country through a thicket of tension, conflicting evidence, and extreme opinions." The president sought the answers to three basic questions about these riots: What happened? Why did it happen? What can be done to prevent it from happening again and again?

The commission made its report on March 1, 1968. The commission found the riots of 1967 were not caused by, or the consequence of, any organized plan or conspiracy. The disorders were the result of racism and poverty. The commission reported that segregation and poverty had created in the racial ghettos a destructive environment totally unknown to most white Americans. In responding to the question "What can be done to prevent it from happening again and again?" the commission found that there was widespread dissatisfaction among blacks, with the unwillingness or inability of local governments to respond. The commission recommended that great sustained national efforts were required to combat racism, unemployment, and poverty.

The commission's recommendations embraced three basic principles: to mount programs on a scale equal to the dimension of the problems, to aim these programs for high impact on the immediate future in order to close the gap between promise and performances, and to understand new initiatives and experiments that can change the system of failure and frustration dominating the ghetto and weakening the society.

SOURCE: *Report of the National Advisory Commission on Civil Disorders*, 1968.

Anju G. Chaudhary

KNOWLEDGE GAP. The knowledge gap hypothesis was introduced by Tichenor, Donohue, and Olien in 1970. They maintained that those in higher socioeconomic conditions would acquire information from the mass media more readily than those in lower social strata. Mass communication would therefore have the general effect of widening differences in information-holding between those in the higher and those in the lower social classes. Thus, the hypothesis holds, those hoping that mass media can be used to level the information playing field between wealthier and poorer members of a community must face the possibility of the very opposite effect. The researchers attributed the differential growth of information to differences between social classes in personal experiences, communication skills, education levels, social circles, economic power, and interests. Because the mass media are generally expected to deliver audiences with high purchasing power to advertisers willing to pay for that service, the mass media target information to those in higher socioeconomic groups. Coupled with the particular characteristics of audiences in different social classes just noted, a knowledge gap is created.

SOURCE: P. J. Tichenor, G. A. Donohue, and C. N. Olien, "Mass Media Flow and Differential Growth in Knowledge," *Public Opinion Quarterly*, Summer 1970.

Dominic L. Lasorsa

KOPPEL, TED (1940–). This unflappable anchor and interviewer has become one of the most respected political commentators in America with the success of the late-night, live-interview television show he has hosted since 1980, ABC News' *Nightline*. Born of German parents who fled to England before World

War II, Koppel attended boarding school there before his parents emigrated again in 1954, this time to the United States. Koppel got his first broadcasting experience working for the campus radio station as a student at Syracuse University. After graduating with a B.A. in speech in 1960, he went to Stanford for his master's in journalism. Failing the Associated Press broadcasters' test, Koppel started work at New York City radio station WMCA as a copy boy. In 1963, he moved to WABC, where he soon began doing news and is said to have been the youngest-ever network correspondent.

Koppel's smooth style became apparent when he had to ad-lib for 90 minutes during a live report when the arrival of newly installed President Lyndon Johnson was delayed. In 1964 he reported on his first presidential nominating convention and the following year became anchor of the nightly ABC newscast in New York. In 1967, Koppel began his television career as an ABC correspondent in Vietnam, then went to Miami and Hong Kong as bureau chief. In 1971, he was named chief diplomatic correspondent for ABC News, covering the Department of State for the next eight years. Meanwhile, Koppel took on the added post of anchor of the ABC Saturday Night News in 1975. When the Iran hostage crisis began in 1979, new head of ABC Roone Arledge created a late-night news program devoted to covering it. That soon gave way to *Nightline*, first hosted by Frank Reynolds, and a new concept in television news was launched. Koppel increasingly began to fill in for Reynolds and in 1980 took over the job permanently.

SOURCES: *Current Biography Yearbook*, 1984; Dan Nimmo and Chevelle Newsome, *Political Commentators in the United States and in the 20th Century*, 1997.

Marc Edge

KRAUS, SIDNEY (1927–) is best known for his studies of political debates. He edited *The Great Debates*, a major compilation of research about the 1960 Kennedy-Nixon debates.

He received B.F.A. and M.F.A. degrees from the Art Institute of Chicago and his Ph.D. from the University of Iowa. He has taught at DePaul University, Indiana University, Roosevelt University, Cleveland State University, and the University of Massachusetts.

Other books he authored, coauthored, or edited include *The Effects of Mass Communication upon Political Behavior* and *Handbook of Political Communication*.

SOURCE: *Contemporary Authors*, New Revision Series, Vol. 10, 1983.

Jacqueline Nash Gifford

KROCK, ARTHUR (1886–1974) shaped both the journalism and the politics of twentieth-century America in a 60-year career, most of which he spent as the most influential reporter and columnist on the nation's most influential newspaper, the *New York Times*. From 1932 until his retirement in 1966, AK or Mr.

Krock, as he was known to colleagues, served as the *New York Times* Washington Bureau chief, the paper's Washington correspondent, and columnist, handling all three assignments at the same time for 20 years.

In the course of that career, he won three Pulitzer Prizes and suggested that another not be awarded to him—even though a majority of the Pulitzer Board had decided to do so—for fear it would show favoritism. That award would have been for his 1950 exclusive interview with President Harry Truman. Like the exclusive, Pulitzer Prize-winning interview Krock had with President Roosevelt in 1937, the Truman interview nettled other journalists, perhaps more upset with the president than with their competitor.

Arthur Krock, Walter Lippmann, and David Lawrence were considered pioneers of the newspaper column and links between the nation's isolationist past and its emergence as a world power. Through those years, Krock was a confidant and consultant to all the presidents he reported on and to congressional leaders as well. Nevertheless, his colleagues and competitors marveled at how he maintained his objectivity when it came to reporting events about those he knew well.

Born in Glasgow, Kentucky, Krock attended Princeton for a semester before having to leave for financial reasons. He did earn a two-year degree in 1906 from the Lewis Institute in Chicago and then returned to Kentucky, where his early journalism career consisted of Louisville newspapers. He first tenure in Washington, D.C., began in 1910, covering the presidency of William Howard Taft. Krock later became editorial manager of the *Louisville Courier-Journal* and the *Louisville Times* and then editor of the *Times*. He worked, too, for the Pulitzer family's *New York World* before joining the *New York Times* in 1927.

SOURCE: Arthur Krock, *Memoirs: Sixty Years on the Firing Line*, 1972.

Herb Strentz

KU KLUX KLAN (KKK) is a group of loosely related organizations that support white supremacy and the Protestant religion. The groups are primarily based in the South and claim to be descendants of the original KKK founded in Tennessee in the late 1800s.

In addition to the advocacy of a separatist movement by race and religion, Klan members are also very conservative. Nationwide, the Klan reportedly has tens of thousands of members.

While the Klan heritage is one of violence, it has in recent years operated, to some extent, in the political arena, supporting candidates and promoting its views in the media. It also tries to engage in nonviolent protest, but its heritage tends to draw groups to counter them, and violence often ensues. The Klan movement has offshoot groups for women and youth interested in following the Klan's beliefs.

SOURCES: John B. Harer, *Intellectual Freedom: A Reference Handbook*, 1992; Ciaran O. Maolain, *The Radical Right: A World Directory*, 1987.

Jacqueline Nash Gifford

L

LASSWELL, HAROLD (1902–1978) was an important media scholar from the 1920s to the 1970s. A faculty member at Yale, Lasswell served on the Commission on Freedom of the Press, better known as the Hutchins Commission, and as director of War Communication Research at the Library of Congress. He conducted extensive research in the propaganda of World War I and World War II. *Language of Politics*, which came out of the World War II propaganda analysis work, remains one of the definitive books on content analysis.

In his book *Propaganda Technique in the World War* (1927), Lasswell noted that media messages can serve as magic bullets, swaying the masses toward almost any point of view. Lasswell believed that individuals were extremely vulnerable to messages transmitted by the mass media, which were "the new hammer and anvil of social solidarity." Lasswell believed that for propaganda to be most successful, however, individuals had to be prepared slowly over time to accept new and radical ideas.

Lasswell also provided mass communication scholars with several important models with which to work. He noted that the study of communication aims to answer "who says what to whom through what channel with what effect." Thus, mass communication researchers could analyze the communicator, the content, the audience, and the actual responses by media consumers. He also argued that the study of politics involved the questions of "who gets what, when, how."

Lasswell categorized the three activities of communicators as the surveillance of the environment, the correlation of society's response to the environment, and the transmission of social heritage.

SOURCE: Stanley J. Baran and Dennis K. Davis, *Mass Communication Theory: Foundations, Ferment, and Future*, 1995.

Wayne Wanta

LAZARSFELD, PAUL F. (1901–1976) was perhaps the most influential mass communication scholar during the 1940s and 1950s. Through his Bureau of Applied Social Research at Columbia University, Lazarsfeld and his colleagues researched how people use the mass media to make important decisions. His research gave rise to the "two-step" theory of the flow of mass communication.

Lazarsfeld was born in Austria in 1901. He fled Nazi Germany in 1933, leaving his position at the University of Vienna Psychological Institute. In 1939, he joined the Columbia University faculty.

Though he examined such topics as unemployment, education and psychology, mathematical sociology, and market research, Lazarsfeld likely will be best remembered for his work on two groundbreaking studies of voting behavior. One was in 1940 with Bernard Berelson and Hazel Gaudet in Erie County, Ohio, which led to the book *The People's Choice*. Then, in 1948, he and Berelson and William McPhee did a study in Elmira, New York, called *Voting: A Study of Opinion Formation in a Presidential Campaign*. Both showed limited effects of mass media. In 1955, he collaborated with Elihu Katz on the book *Personal Influence: The Part Played by People in the Flow of Mass Communication*. This was an in-depth analysis of the two-step flow concept, which says that messages pass from the media through opinion leaders to opinion followers. (*See also* The People's Choice.)

SOURCE: Ann K. Pasanella, *The Mind Traveler: A Guide to Paul F. Lazarsfeld's Communication Research Papers*, 1994.

Wayne Wanta

LEAGUE OF WOMEN VOTERS is a group, founded in 1920, that works to educate women and the general public about the political process. Today it aims to present unbiased political information, such as polling locales and information sheets on political candidates, during elections. It has become a major source of political information for the public, especially in local elections. It is a national organization.

SOURCE: Jay M. Shafritz, *The HarperCollins Dictionary of American Government and Politics*, 1992.

Jacqueline Nash Gifford

LEAK is a term used to define the purposeful disclosure of sensitive information to the public, generally through the mass media. Two classic situations involving disclosure of sensitive information are the release of government documents and information in the Pentagon Papers case and in the Watergate affair, both during the Nixon administration. Those cases, as well as the more recent controversy over leaks in the investigation of President Clinton, obscure the fact that leaks are a staple of news coverage and occur every day. Most pieces of information attributed to anonymous sources are probably leaks.

SOURCE: Jay M. Shafritz, *The HarperCollins Dictionary of American Government and Politics*, 1992.

Jacqueline Nash Gifford

LEMMON, WALTER S. (1895–1967) pioneered "educational" radio programming for a worldwide audience. In 1934, he organized and became head of the noncommercial World Wide Broadcasting Foundation, which operated shortwave station W1XAL, located outside Boston. The call letters were changed to WRUL (World Radio University) in 1939. The station at that time did not carry advertising and relied on corporate donations and listener support. WRUL stressed English-language training programs. It also featured aviation, poetry, world affairs, music, astronomy, and natural sciences programs. The station relied heavily on faculty and students at universities in the Boston area for program production. Throughout the 1930s, the Department of State and other government agencies were uneasy about shortwave stations in private hands, seeing them as central to U.S. efforts to counter fascist government propaganda in Europe and Latin America. With the notable exception of WRUL, most international shortwave stations featured entertainment fare. During the war years, WRUL programming supported the Allied cause, and the station was often singled out for criticism in Nazi propaganda. By 1942, WRUL was producing programming in 24 languages. Despite Lemmon's unquestioned loyalty, during late 1942 he and other shortwave broadcasters were pressed to lease their facilities to the government so that government agencies could centralize the war effort. These lease efforts are recognized as the roots of the Voice of America. Lemmon was the only broadcaster who steadfastly refused to arrange lease terms.

On November 5, the Board of War Communications, acting on an executive order, took the drastic step of issuing an order of closure on WRUL. Lemmon reconciled himself to the wartime takeover and continued to operate WRUL with programming furnished by government agencies. He regained WRUL in 1947 and in 1950 accepted commercial advertising. Lemmon relinquished ownership of the station in 1960, selling it to the Metropolitan Broadcasting Corporation.

SOURCES: Andre J. E. Mostert, Jr., "A History of WRUL: The Walter S. Lemmon Years, 1931 to 1960," M.A. thesis, Brigham Young University, 1969; "Nazi Hate and Fear WRUL: Propaganda from the U.S.A.," *Life*, December 15, 1941, p. 43; "Walter Lemmon, Inventor, Is Dead," *New York Times*, March 21, 1967, p. 46.

Michael B. Salwen

LIBEL is written defamation. A plaintiff in a libel case must prove three things:

1. Publication, which covers not only print media but also broadcast media. It also has been held by courts to apply to letters where person A writes to person B about person C.

2. Identification, which means that the plaintiff is clearly identified. This can be by use of the name or a picture or a verbal description.

3. Defamation, which means that the material in question indicates the identified person did something illegal or immoral or contrary to the standards of the community.

Technically, a plaintiff must also prove fault and harm. However, fault is not really an issue because libel results from the deliberate act of publishing, and harm is presumed to result from any libel.

Libel suits are civil cases, and winners collect monetary damages. A series of Supreme Court cases beginning with *New York Times v. Sullivan* (367 U.S. 254) established that a public official or public figure must prove actual malice or reckless disregard of the truth to win a libel suit. If the public official or public figure can prove this, he or she can collect punitive damages, which run into six or seven figures.

SOURCE: Dwight L. Teeter, Jr., and Don R. LeDuc, *Law of Mass Communications*, eighth edition, 1995.

Guido H. Stempel III

LIMITED-EFFECTS MODEL. Early mass communication research showed what came to be termed limited effects. A frequent finding was that communication increased information but did not change attitudes. This perplexed researchers of a half century ago so much that there were journal articles about why information campaigns did not change attitudes.

More recent research has modified the model. Perhaps the groundbreaking study was by Dorothy Douglas, Bruce Westley, and Steven Chaffee in Wisconsin. They found that attitudes about mental retardation could be changed by an information campaign. They concluded this was possible because the topic does not invoke deep-seated personal values and is not controversial. The researchers conceded that the same results probably would not have been obtained if the topic had been sex education or water fluoridation.

So, while an information campaign will not change everybody's attitude, and while information campaigns will work better on some topics than on others, they can and do work under the right conditions.

SOURCES: Dorothy F. Douglas, Bruce H. Westley, and Steven H. Chaffee, "An Information Campaign That Changed Attitudes," *Journalism Quarterly*, Autumn 1970; Werner J. Severin and James W. Tankard, Jr., *Communication Theories*, fourth edition, 1997.

Guido H. Stempel III

LIPPMANN, WALTER (1889–1974) was one of the first political columnists and was believed by many to have been the best. But more important for the field of political communication, he was the author of *Public Opinion* in 1922. It remains the classic statement, and some would date the beginning of the study of political communication from this book.

Lippmann graduated from Harvard and started his graduate work there in philosophy. He left Harvard to work for Lincoln Steffans, a muckracker, at a Boston newspaper. In 1914, he became the editor of *New Republic* magazine, known for its liberal political idealism. He enlisted as the assistant to the secretary of war during World War I. In that position, he wrote propaganda for the government.

He left the government in 1921 to edit *New York World* and later the *New York Herald Tribune*. There he wrote the political column "Today and Tomorrow," which eventually became syndicated.

Lippmann wrote many books on political philosophy. The most prominent besides *Public Opinion* was *The Phantom Public* (1925). In these books he explored a democratic system's successes and failures, using the United States as an example. The press, in his view, could bring the facts to the American public to make decisions about politics (the informed electorate) and other events. However, he cautioned journalists from relying totally on objectivity and suggested that more effort should be made to put news events into perspective.

SOURCES: Erik Barnouw, ed., *International Encyclopedia of Communications*, 1989; William Howard Taft, ed., *Encyclopedia of 20th Century Journalists*, 1986.

Jacqueline Nash Gifford

LITERARY DIGEST **POLL** predicted wrongly that Alfred Landon would defeat Franklin D. Roosevelt in the 1936 presidential election. It was a mail poll sent to people who had telephones or owned automobiles. That obviously was not a representative group, but the larger problem was that the poll had a 23 percent response rate. Roosevelt won in a landslide, and the *Literary Digest* poll, which had correctly predicted the outcome of five previous presidential elections and other elections besides, was dead.

SOURCE: Michael Nelson, ed., *Congressional Quarterly's Guide to the Presidency*, 1989.

Jacqueline Nash Gifford

LOBBYING involves the use of people, representing businesses or minority or other special interest groups, to influence the political process. Lobbying is considered a form of communication because it relies on formal and informal methods of speech or written communication as the expressions of ideas or thoughts. On the most formal level, lobbying is done by representatives sent to a location, such as Washington, D.C., to affect politicians' decision making and national policy. To do their jobs effectively, lobbyists bring the legislature facts to support their representative group's philosophy or position. Lobbyists use various types of communication to influence their groups, such as direct-mail campaigns, media advertising, face-to-face communication, and testimony before special-issue congressional committees. Sometimes lobbyists use money as a way of showing their support for or against a particular issue or person.

Lobbying activities are protected under the First Amendment (the right to freedom of expression and to petition one's government). Some researchers believe lobbyists pollute the political system, leading to stalemates and gridlock, while others believe they provide a voice for the variety of interests of Americans.

SOURCES: Erik Barnouw, ed., *International Encyclopedia of Communications*, 1989; Allan J. Cigler and Burdett A. Loomis, *Interest Group Politics*, 1983; Jack C. Plano and Milton Greenberg, *The American Political Dictionary*, 1993.

Jacqueline Nash Gifford

LONG, HUEY (1893–1935) began as a traveling salesman in the backwoods of Louisiana. In the end he would become a footnote to twentieth-century history as one of two U.S. senators killed while in office. In between, he would challenge the president of the United States during America's depression. Long, "the kingfish" of Louisiana, used his ability to speak directly to the common person with a passion that allowed one to dream that there was someone in government looking out for him or her. Rising in politics from his first elected office as railroad commissioner to governor and then U.S. senator, Long opposed Franklin D. Roosevelt in response to the depression. Long considered the New Deal too slow and too tame for the country and fought New Deal programs in Louisiana. He envisioned a society in which no person would have wealth beyond $3 million and no less than $5,000 salary (the equivalent of $50,000 in today's dollars). He proposed to "make every man a king." His style was personal campaigning from door to door or speaking to small clusters of potential voters. His theme was consistent: attack the rich and powerful.

There was no middle ground about Long. He was either loved or hated. He was the first U.S. senator to employ full-time bodyguards. Although he never graduated from high school or college, Long got free textbooks for all children and built Louisiana State University into a respected institution of higher education.

On September 8, 1935, following a special session of the Louisiana legislature, which Long had called as a U.S. senator—not governor—Long was shot and killed by Dr. Carl A. Weiss in the Louisiana state capitol. Robert Penn Warren's book *All the King's Men*, which was later made into an Academy Award-winning movie, is generally considered biographical about Long.

SOURCES: Harold B. McSween, "Huey Long at His Centenary," *Virginia Quarterly Review*, Summer 1993; David Zinman, "The Meteoric Life and Mysterious Death of Huey Long," *American History Illustrated*, July 1993.

J. Sean McCleneghan

M

MAGAZINES. *See Christianity and Crisis; Christianity Today; National Review; New Republic; Newsweek; Time* Magazine; *U.S. News.*

MASS MEDIA is a term used to describe newspapers, magazines, books, television, radio, movies, on-line services, and Internet. They reach large numbers of people and serve as information gatherers and disseminators in a society. They also serve as entertainers to varying degrees, which many feel interferes with their role in informing the public. Yet, the very nature of mass media means that they will, at least to some extent, be preoccupied with catering to the masses.

SOURCE: Iain McLean, *The Concise Oxford Dictionary of Politics*, 1996.

Guido H. Stempel III

MAYNARD, ROBERT C. (1937–1993) was the first African American publisher of a major metropolitan newspaper, the *Tribune* of Oakland, California. The sixth child of immigrants from Barbados, Maynard dropped out of high school when he was 16. He did freelance writing and became a reporter for the *York (Pennsylvania) Gazette and Daily.* His reporting of the Civil Rights movement in the South led to a Nieman Fellowship at Harvard. In 1967 he became the first black national correspondent at the *Washington Post.* Five years later he and Earl Caldwell, a reporter for the *New York Times*, were named directors of a summer program at Columbia University. The program, for nonwhite journalists, guaranteed placement on newspaper or television staffs for graduates. That year Maynard accepted a part-time position as a senior editor for *Encore*, a monthly magazine for African Americans, and was appointed ombudsman for the *Washington Post.* In 1977 he founded the Institute for Journalism at Berkeley, California. He also established Jobnet to provide a liaison between nonwhite journalists and potential employers. Maynard was soon hired as a consultant for affirmative action with the Gannett Co.

In 1979 Gannett appointed him editor of the *Oakland Tribune*. In 1983 Maynard purchased the newspaper and became the first African American to have a controlling interest in a city daily with general circulation. Moreover, he was the first big city editor in recent times to buy the newspaper for which he worked. Gannett financed the purchase. In 1985 the newspaper's circulation surpassed 150,000, but it suffered from a continuing decrease in display advertising, and Maynard was diagnosed with prostate cancer. As a result, he sold the newspaper to the Alameda Newspaper Group in 1992. He died of cancer in August 1993 at the age of 56.

SOURCE: *Current Biography Yearbook*, 1993.

Will Norton

McCARTHY, JOSEPH (1908–1957). The junior senator from Wisconsin turned U.S. politics upside down in a speech on February 9, 1950, to a small group in Wheeling, West Virginia. He claimed he had a list of 205 communists working in the Department of State, but his numbers almost immediately changed. In the end, McCarthy provided scant specifics of his charges—few names and even less proof. But the allegation led to several years of communist "witch-hunts" at all levels of government, a "red scare" that would come to bear his name: "McCarthyism." Suspected communists lost their jobs, even if their ties to the Communist Party were tenuous and decades old. Guilt by association became the order of the day. Workers in the entertainment industry were especially targeted, and many of them had their careers ruined by being "blacklisted." Loyalty oaths and loyalty review boards became a requirement for public service. The press played a key role in McCarthy's rise as it eagerly reported his allegations but failed to investigate whether there was any substance to them. The McCarthy phenomenon was also fueled by the infant medium of television, which often allowed him to take his charges directly to the public. But television also played a part in McCarthy's demise. Edward R. Murrow, in one of the first television newsmagazine shows, *See It Now*, took McCarthy to task for his smear tactics. McCarthy was given the opportunity to reply by CBS, and he was an implausible buffoon in his response. McCarthy continued to lose credibility until censured by the Senate on December 2, 1954, for improper conduct. He became increasingly alcoholic and died three years later, but he left a legacy. The word "McCarthyism" is still in our political vocabulary as a description of guilt-by-association smearing of a political opponent.

SOURCES: Albert Fried, *McCarthyism: The Great American Red Scare*, 1997; Thomas Rosteck, *See It Now Confronts McCarthyism*, 1994; Jim Tuck, *McCarthyism and New York's Hearst Press*, 1995.

Marc Edge

McCOMBS, MAXWELL (1938–) was coauthor with Donald Shaw of the first agenda-setting study, done in the 1968 presidential election. When it was reported in *Public Opinion Quarterly*, the study sparked interest in the concept of agenda setting, and more than 200 agenda-setting studies have since been done. The basic concept is that the media do not tell people what to think; they tell them what to think about. Correlation between the media agenda and the public agenda has been well demonstrated, but causation has not.

A graduate of Tulane, McCombs received his Ph.D. from Stanford and taught a year at the University of California–Los Angeles (UCLA) before going to North Carolina, where he and Shaw did the first agenda-setting study. He then went to Syracuse as the Jon Ben Snow Professor of Research and also headed the American Newspaper Publishers' Association News Research Center. The center funded and published studies of newspapers, many of them dealing with political topics. From there he went to Texas as chair of the Department of Journalism in 1985. (*See also* Agenda Setting.)

SOURCE: William David Sloan, ed., *Makers of the Media Mind*, 1990.

Guido H. Stempel III

McGINNISS, JOE (1942–). At age 25, this *Philadelphia Inquirer* reporter convinced the advertising agency molding presidential candidate Richard Nixon's television image to give him inside access for a book on the process. He did not reveal he was a card-carrying Democrat and had been rebuffed in an earlier approach to the Humphrey camp. The result was a No. 1 bestseller, *The Selling of the President*, 1968, which was hardly flattering of the winner. In 1976, McGinniss wrote *Heroes*, a personal memoir of his disappointment in meeting various political figures, including George McGovern, who labeled the account "full of inaccurate and fabricated quotations." In 1993, McGinniss wrote *The Last Brother*, a biography of Senator Edward Kennedy, who had refused to cooperate with the project. The book drew criticism not only for its invented dialogue and "ruminations" for its subject but also from the allegations of plagiarism from other writers. To his credit, in 1995 McGinniss returned a $1.75 million advance for a book on the O. J. Simpson trial because he said he felt he could add nothing to the story. Author of several other fiction and non-fiction books and a professor of literature at Colgate, McGinniss has come to symbolize to some the excesses of the "new journalism."

SOURCE: Janet Malcolm, *The Journalist and the Murderer*, 1990.

Marc Edge

THE McLAUGHLIN GROUP, a television political talk show on the air since 1982, broke from the tradition of somber political analysis and instead had journalists as panelists engage in shouting matches, banter, insults, and on-the-air chaos. The program's popularity and ratings success spawned a series of spin-offs, including CNN's *Capital Gang* and *Crossfire*. Host John McLaughlin

berated the panelists with whom he disagreed ("Wronnnnnng!"), addressed the
panelists in an affable ribbing manner (Morton "Mortahn-Salt-when-it-rains-it-
pours" Kendrake and Eleanor-gee-I-think-you-re-swell" Clift), and pressed panelists to assign numerical values to the significance of political issues ("on a
scale of zero to 10, with 10 being metaphysical certitude and zero being metaphysical doubt, how would you rate . . . ?"). The program was criticized for
trivializing political issues, emphasizing entertainment over analysis, and low-
ering the level of political discourse. President Ronald Reagan, a fan of the
program, compared *The McLaughlin Group* to the movie *Animal House*, adding,
"Its nutritional value is somewhere between potato chips and Twinkies." Critics
also claimed that the program treated political issues in a flippant manner, as
when McLaughlin introduced a discussion about Democratic presidential candidate Walter Mondale's selection of Geraldine Ferraro as his vice presidential
choice with "It's a girl!" McLaughlin, however, claimed that politics did not
have to be boring. *The McLaughlin Group* traces its roots to *Agronsky and
Company*, which went on the air over the CBS television affiliate in Washington
in 1969. Unlike other public affairs programs at the time, such as *Meet the
Press, Issues and Answers*, and *Face the Nation, Agronsky and Company* did
not include newsmakers and politicians, only journalists. *Agronsky and Company*, however, was fairly sedate compared to *The McLaughlin Group*. Another
precursor, in 1970, *60 Minutes*, added a "Point/Counterpoint" segment that
pitted liberal Nichola Von Hoffman against conservative James Kilpatrick on a
single issue during each program. The segment was immensely popular, and in
1974 Shana Alexander replaced Hoffman. The segment's tendency to portray
political discussion as verbal one-upmanship had the undesirable tendency that
would be magnified in *The McLaughlin Group* for journalists to engage in spir-
ited personal attacks and put-downs.

SOURCES: Eric Alterman, *Sound and Fury: The Washington Punditocracy and the
Collapse of American Politics*, 1992; Alan Hirsch, *Talking Heads: Political Talk Shows
and Their Star Pundits*, 1991.

Michael B. Salwen

McLEOD, JACK M. (1930–) is Maier-Bascom Professor of Journalism and
Mass Communication at the University of Wisconsin–Madison. He is a leading
authority on the role of media in broadening democratic participation and community integration. He joined the journalism faculty at Wisconsin in 1962 after
earning a Ph.D. in social psychology from the University of Michigan, where
he also served as assistant study director in the Survey Research Center. McLeod
has served for more than 30 years as director of the Mass Communication
Research Center at Wisconsin and as a mentor for countless graduate students
with concentrations in political communication. He and Steve Chaffee developed
the co-orientation concept in communication. The International Communication
Association awarded him the Fisher Mentorship Award in 1991 in recognition

of his service to students and to the field. He was the 1997 recipient of the Paul J. Deutschmann Award for Excellence in Research from the Association for Education in Journalism and Mass Communication. (*See also* Co-orientation; Family Communication Patterns.)

SOURCES: Jay G. Blumler, Jack M. McLeod, and Karl Erik Rosengren, eds., *Comparatively Speaking: Communication and Culture across Space and Time*, 1992; Jack M. McLeod, Katie Daly, and Zhongshi Guo, "Community Integration, Local Media Use, and Democratic Processes," *Communication Research*, April 1996.

Lowndes F. Stephens

MEDIA LEGAL ISSUES. *See* Alien and Sedition Acts of 1798; Censorship; Deregulation of the Federal Communications Commission; Equal Time Rule; Fairness Doctrine; Freedom of Information Act; Freedom of Speech; Freedom of the Press; Joint Operating Agreements; Libel.

MEDIA ORGANIZATIONS. *See* Corporation for Public Broadcasting; C-SPAN; The Freedom Forum; Pew Research Center for the People and the Press.

MEDIA TECHNIQUES. *See* Endorsements; Hoaxes; Leak; Muckraker; National Election Service (NES); Pack Journalism; Political Cartoons; Political Columnists; Political Satirists; Sound Bites.

MIAMI HERALD V. TORNILLO established the First Amendment right of newspapers to refuse to print a reply demanded by a candidate for political office whom it had attacked. The case arose under the 1913 Florida Election Code, which required newspapers to publish such demanded replies. Pat Tornillo, a teachers' union leader, was a Democratic candidate for the state legislature in 1972, when the *Herald* twice criticized him in editorials. Tornillo demanded the opportunity to reply and, when refused, sued the paper. The trial court found the state law unconstitutional, but the Florida Supreme Court reversed that decision, so the *Herald* appealed to the U.S. Supreme Court. In part Tornillo's argument was that since such a right of reply is required for broadcast media, it should be required for all media. The U.S. Supreme Court disagreed, saying that this would violate the First Amendment. The Court said that requiring publication was simply the other side of the coin of censorship, which prohibits publication, and that the First Amendment must leave it to editors to decide what to publish. Most newspapers would, in fact, permit a reply in the form of a letter to the editor, and possibly the *Miami Herald* would have done so, too, if Tornillo had simply sent a letter and not raised the legal issue.

SOURCES: *Miami Herald v. Tornillo* (418 U.S. 441); Wayne Overbeck, *Major Principles of Media Law*, 1996 edition.

Marc Edge

MORAL MAJORITY was founded by Rev. Jerry Falwell to promote the ideology presented by conservative Christians throughout America. While it does not specifically endorse candidates (although it has been historically traced to support Republican ideology), it is very vocal and active in opposing "immoral" activities, such as abortion, pornography, and obscenity. The group's members believe they have the right and duty to vote and promote those political issues that uphold the moral dignity of the country and its citizens.

SOURCE: Leon Hurwitz, *Historical Dictionary of Censorship in the U.S.*, 1985.

Jacqueline Nash Gifford

MOYERS, BILL (1934–) is a journalist whose unique interests in metaphysical topics have shaped an era of intellectual public television. Moyers, whose original name was Billy Don Moyers, was born in Texas to a blue-collar family.

His entry into the world of political communications was as a summer hire for U.S. senator Lyndon B. Johnson's reelection campaign. It was the beginning of a long, yet often troubled, alliance. After completing his journalism degree at the University of Texas, he worked for Johnson as a special assistant and later was director of public affairs of the Peace Corps, a position that combined community affairs, political savvy, and a desire to help others.

In 1963, Johnson's sudden ascension to the presidency found Moyers leaving the Peace Corps position and serving as an adviser to the new president. He was later promoted to White House chief of staff and eventually press secretary. Moyers used his journalism savvy to influence Johnson's reputation, which was failing in the public's eyes and threatening his chances of reelection. Together they faced tough issues, including racial unrest in the South and the country's involvement in Vietnam. Moyers' reputation as a political adviser is best remembered in regard to his involvement with the creation of the "Daisy Commercial," which attacked Senator Barry Goldwater, who had been nominated by the Republican Party as its presidential candidate.

In 1966, Moyers left the White House to work for *Newsday*, despite the president's protests. He turned *Newsday* into the forerunner of today's newsmagazine format—full of sharp analyses and commentaries. Under his direction, *Newsday* won three Pulitzer Prizes.

In 1970, Moyers uprooted again, only this time to reconnect with America. He traveled a bit, interviewing common people, and wrote *Listening to America: A Traveler Rediscovers His Country*, a widely accepted book. In the early 1970s, he joined CBS as a special correspondent and also joined the staff of WNET-TV, a public television station in New York City. There he began to look for ways to differentiate himself from his commercial television personae. His television program, called *Bill Moyers' Journal*, examined political and social topics from a "thinking man's perspective," using interviews from scholars and well-known citizens.

Moyers is one of the few major voices building the case for pluralism in American (and global) thought. An underlying theme of many of his presentations is that a community is built through humility in one's own opinions and willingness to listen to other voices. His gentle interviewing style has been called "acolyte journalism" by his detractors but constructive by his legion of followers. If anything, he stands out as an increasingly solitary voice of calm and reason in the self-righteous and divisive discourse of modern mass media. His television specials have covered such topics as funding of education, *Genesis*, the connection between mind and body, and drug rehabilitation.

SOURCES: *Contemporary Authors*, 1994; *Current Biography*, 1994; David Neff, "Bill Moyers' National Bible Study," *Christianity Today*, October 28, 1996.

Jacqueline Nash Gifford and David C. Perlmutter

MUCKRAKER is the expression used to define a journalist who unearths corruption and wrongdoing in politics and business. The expression was first used by President Theodore Roosevelt when he was accused by media of antibusiness sentiment. The first decade of the twentieth century is frequently referred to as the era of muckraking because of the exposés of government and business, usually in magazines. Prominent muckrakers included Lincoln Steffens, Ida Tarbell, Ray Stannard Baker, and Upton Sinclair. Today, muckrakers are known as "investigative reporters." (*See also* Upton Sinclair; Ida Tarbell.)

SOURCES: William A. Safire, *Safire's New Political Dictionary*, 1993; Arthur Weinberg and Lila Weinberg, eds., *The Muckrakers*, 1961.

Jacqueline Nash Gifford

MURROW, EDWARD R. (1927–1965) set a standard for television journalism that has rarely been attained since. Like most of the television pioneers, he was on radio first, and there he first came to the attention of the American public. During the Munich crisis of 1938 he arranged for the first multiple, live news pickup ever attempted, and his voice was one of those heard. Then in 1940 he made memorable broadcasts from London during the German aerial blitz.

Murrow first appeared on television during the political conventions of 1948, but in 1951 he made his full introduction into the new medium with his program *See It Now*. For the next seven years, Murrow provided excellent political coverage. One widely acclaimed program was the first hour-long *See It Now* entitled "Christmas in Korea," which was reported and shot in Korea. It was a vivid portrayal of the stalemated war.

Murrow was critical of Senator Joseph McCarthy and "McCarthyism," and on March 9, 1954, he took on McCarthy directly in his *See It Now* broadcast. What Murrow did was simply show McCarthy in action and let the facts speak for themselves. The program was widely acclaimed and is still considered perhaps "television's finest hour." The *New York Times* said it was the occasion on which "broadcasting recaptured its soul." There was, however, criticism from sponsors and from some viewers, and concern from within CBS. *See It Now* stayed on the air only four more years.

In 1953, Murrow began an interview show, *Person to Person*, which involved informal interviews with celebrities. He also worked with *CBS Reports*, where he was part of the famous documentary on migrant workers, "Harvest of Shame."

In 1961, he left CBS to take charge of the U.S. Information Agency. Illness forced his retirement in 1963.

SOURCES: Michael Emery and Edwin Emery, *The Press and America*, eighth edition, 1996; Alexander Kendrick, *Prime Time*, 1969.

Guido H. Stempel III

N

NAFZIGER, RALPH O. (1896–1973) was one of the pioneers in mass communication research. While a faculty member at Minnesota in the 1940s, he helped establish the Minnesota Poll, one of the early state opinion polls. During World War II, he was part of the group of researchers who analyzed propaganda for the Office of War Information.

He was coeditor of the first research methods book in mass communication, *Introduction to Journalism Research* (1949) and of the second research methods book in mass communication, *Introduction to Mass Communications Research* (1958, 1963).

He received his bachelor's, master's, and doctoral degrees from the University of Wisconsin and returned there in 1949 as director of the School of Journalism, a position he held until his retirement in 1966. He then served as executive secretary for the Association for Education in Journalism for six years.

SOURCES: Harold L. Nelson, "Ralph Nafziger," *Journalism Quarterly*, Autumn 1973; William David Sloan, *Makers of the Media Mind*, 1990.

Guido H. Stempel III

NATIONAL ASSOCIATION FOR THE ADVANCEMENT OF COLORED PEOPLE (NAACP) is America's largest organization that fights discrimination on the basis of race and color. The NAACP's rise to national prominence hinged upon a single event: the Niagara Movement, a meeting at which several leading African American men, including W.E.B. Du Bois, created a plan to stamp out discrimination. Fueled with energy, this group attracted the attention of white sympathizers, mostly from the media and among lawyers, to aid in the cause. Du Bois was the organization's first director and also its publicist, writing *The Crisis* to chronicle and bring attention to the NAACP's fight against racial injustice. The NAACP's goal has been to seek, protect, and defend equality for all Americans. Through the NAACP's work in the courtroom, many segregation and discrimination laws were overturned. In the 1960s, the group was very instrumental in the success of the Civil Rights movement, along with the Southern Christian Leadership Coalition.

SOURCES: Kathleen Thompson Hill and Gerald N. Hill, *The Real Life Dictionary of American Politics*, 1994; Jack Salzman, David Lionel Smith, and Cornel West, *Encyclopedia of Afro-American Culture and History*, 1990.

Jacqueline Nash Gifford

NATIONAL ELECTION SERVICE (NES). During the 1964 Republican presidential primary, confusion reigned supreme among the media. The Associated Press and United Press International showed Nelson Rockefeller in the lead, while ABC and CBS projected victory for Barry Goldwater, and NBC said the race was too close to call. The five decided to found a cooperative to tally the vote next time and at least get their stories straight. The National Election Service began its biennial tabulation of votes during the 1966 congressional election. Today it utilizes a 100,000-plus army to cover all the voting districts in the country. Volunteers from such groups as the League of Women Voters form the bulk of the NES workers in return for contributions to their organizations. The scrutinizers phone results to regional centers from which figures are sent by computer to NES headquarters in New York City. In addition to providing returns for its members, NES provides results to other media organizations for a fee. In 1990, CNN joined the NES cooperative, replacing UPI, which dropped out due to financial problems. In 1993, NES was merged with Voter Research and Surveys (VRS), which the networks had founded three years earlier to conduct joint exit polls. The move prompted the head of VRS to set up his own exit-polling company, confusingly called Election News Service (ENS). The promise of more in-depth statistical analysis convinced flagship clients the *Washington Post* and the *New York Times* to cast their lot with ENS.

SOURCE: Michael L. Young, *The American Dictionary of Campaigns and Elections*, 1987.

Marc Edge

NATIONAL ORGANIZATION FOR WOMEN (NOW) was founded in 1966 by author Betty Friedan. She wrote *The Feminine Mystique*, a radical book that discusses the women's movement. NOW concentrates its energies on supporting political policies that promote equal rights and equal opportunity for women. The group also works to fight job discrimination on the basis of sex. NOW uses various forms of communication to spread its political philosophy, including pamphlets, lobbying, and demonstrations. It claims to have nearly 300,000 members across America.

SOURCE: Leon Hurowitz, *Historical Dictionary of Censorship in the U.S.*, 1985.

Jacqueline Nash Gifford

NATIONAL REVIEW was founded in 1955 by William F. Buckley, Jr., as the voice of conservatism. By 1960 it had only 32,000 readers and a deficit of $860,000, but by 1970 circulation was 111,000 and by 1997, 218,000. On the 35th anniversary, columnist George Will said of the *National Review*: "It is simply the case that the *National Review* is the most consequential journal of opinion ever. . . . For two generations it has been the beating heart of the movement that has transformed America." On the 40th anniversary, editor John O'Sullivan, called by Will Margaret Thatcher's favorite domestic policy adviser, said the magazine could boast "a world-historical achievement for a journal of opinion: we made a modest profit."

In a 1955 publisher's statement, Buckley, now the editor at large and author of spy novels, wrote that the magazine "stands athwart history yelling stop at a time when no one is inclined to do so, or to have much patience with those who so urge it." Over the years, the masthead has listed such conservatives as James Burnham, Russell Kirk, James Jackson Kilpatrick, John Chamberlain, Joan Didion, and Henry Haslitt.

SOURCE: George Will, Henry Kissinger, Pat Sajak, John O'Sullivan, Jim Talent, and Kate O'Beirne, "National Review Hits 40," *National Review*, December 1995.

Don Ranly

NATIONAL RIFLE ASSOCIATION (NRA) is an organization that seeks to protect private citizens' right to bear arms under the Second Amendment of the Constitution. When it was created in 1871, it promoted marksmanship, but it became politically motivated when Washington began to clamp down on gun ownership as a possible method for deterring crime. Its influence with the U.S. Congress is indicated by the reluctance of Congress to pass gun control legislation that national polls indicate is favored by a vast majority of the American public. The NRA is a major contributor to congressional campaigns.

SOURCE: Kathleen Thompson Hill and Gerald N. Hill, *The Real Life Dictionary of American Politics*, 1994.

Guido H. Stempel III

NEAR V. MINNESOTA was the first case in which the U.S. Supreme Court applied and upheld freedom of the press on the state level. In 1927, a newspaper called the *Saturday Press* was published by Jay M. Near and Howard Guilford. It printed scandalous stories about public figures and bigotry against minority and religious groups. Under Minnesota's Public Nuisance Abatement Law, a gag order was placed on the newspaper until it toned down its coverage. Near and Guilford filed a lawsuit (with prompting from the American Civil Liberties Union) on the grounds that the paper had a right to print as it wished under the First Amendment. The case eventually was decided in the Court, which ruled on the press' behalf, 5–4. The Supreme Court majority believed that under the First Amendment there could be no prior restraint of the press. The minority recognized a First Amendment problem but felt the injunction was an appropriate punishment. This was the first prior restraint case decided by the Supreme Court. In subsequent cases, the First Amendment aspect has become the overriding consideration.

SOURCES: Kermit L. Hall, *Oxford Dictionary Companion to the Supreme Court of the United States*, 1992; Robert Mayer, *The Court and the American Crises, 1930–1953*, 1955; *Near v. Minnesota*, 283 U.S. 697, 1931.

Jacqueline Nash Gifford

THE NEW REPUBLIC is a weekly liberal political magazine that was started in 1914 by Willard Straight. The first editor of the magazine was Herbert Croly. Croly led the paper through some of the early twentieth century's more democratic causes, including labor and women's issues. Throughout its history, however, it has criticized the conservative side of American domestic and foreign politics, economics, and other societal issues.

The magazine has cultivated a strong reputation among its readers and fellow journalists for its insights into the political world. It has won numerous awards, including the National Magazine Award for Excellence in the Public Interest. The magazine also is known for its talented contributors, who have included Walter Lippmann, John Dewey, Margaret Sanger, John Steinbeck, and John Updike.

SOURCES: *The New Republic*'s homepage on the World Wide Web; William Howard Taft, ed., *The Encyclopedia of 20th Century Journalists*, 1986.

Jacqueline Nash Gifford

NEWSPAPER EXECUTIVES. *See* James Gordon Bennett; John and Gardner Cowles; Benjamin Day; Horace Greeley; Roy Wilson Howard; Joseph Pulitzer.

NEWSPAPERS. *See* Black Press; *Chicago Tribune; New York Times*; Spanish-Language Press; *Washington Post*.

NEWSWEEK was founded in 1933 by Thomas J. C. Martyn, an Englishman who had been the first foreign editor of *Time*. It lost more than $2 million in its first four years and then was merged with *Today*. Malcolm Muir, who had been president of McGraw-Hill Publishing Company, became its president and publisher.

It had started out as simply a news digest, but it expanded to include background and interpretation under its new management. Unlike *Time*, it included signed columns. In the 1960s it made a major promotional campaign around the theme ''the magazine that separates fact from opinion,'' an obvious dig at *Time*. Nonetheless, *Newsweek* is generally perceived as the most liberal of the three newsmagazines, and while the columnists are still there, all the opinion is not in the columns.

Ownership changed in 1961, when Philip L. Graham of the *Washington Post* acquired a majority of the stock, and it has remained part of that organization since. Under this ownership it has gained on *Time* in circulation and now trails *Time* by less than 1 million with 3.2 million circulation.

SOURCES: Philip S. Cook, Douglas Gomery, and Lawrence W. Lichty, eds., *The Future of News: Television-Newspapers-Wire Services-Newsmagazines*, 1992; Theodore Peterson, *Magazines in the Twentieth Century*, 1964.

Guido H. Stempel III

NEW WORLD INFORMATION AND COMMUNICATION ORDER. The United Nations Educational, Scientific, and Cultural Organization's (UNESCO) involvement with a new world information and communication order (NWICO) stems from the 1960s, when the organization teamed with international professional bodies to enhance the information and communication capabilities of developing countries. By 1970, developing countries were generally dissatisfied with what they called imbalances in the world's communication order. Two major complaints were at the core of this dissatisfaction—the monopoly of international communication resources by a few developed countries and the poor image of developing countries presented through the world's media.

Six landmark meetings define UNESCO and the NWICO debate: San José, Costa Rica, 1967; Nairobi, 1976; Paris, 1978; Belgrade, 1980; and Paris, 1982 and 1983. Perhaps the most controversial of the meetings were the one at Nairobi, where a declaration on mass media was discussed, and the one in Belgrade, where the MacBride Report was adopted. The report's most contentious recommendations concerned the monopoly issue and freedom of the press that is "inseparable from responsibility." These recommendations were attacked in the West as attempts at government control of the media. UNESCO's retreat from the issues and from notions that the NWICO required immediate restructuring of the world information and communication order was supported by its declaration in 1982 that the NWICO was "an evolving and continuous process." Moreover, the organization began to emphasize international technical cooperation on a model suggested by an earlier U.S. initiative. The International Programme for Development and Communication (IPDC) signified this shift. Nonetheless, the U.S. government withdrew from UNESCO in December 1983, citing concerns for "individual human rights and the free flow of information." The decision caught NWICO observers by surprise. Coming at the height of tensions in U.S.–Soviet relations, the withdrawal made UNESCO one of the major casualties of the Cold War.

SOURCES: Johan Galtung and Richard C. Vincent, *Global Glasnost: Toward a New World Information Order?*, 1992; George Gerbner, Hamid Mowlana, and Kaarle Nordenstreng, eds., *The Global Media Debate: Its Rise, Fall and Renewal*, 1993; UNESCO, *One World: Report by the International Commission for the Study of Communication Problems*, 1980.

Folu Folarin Ogundimu

NEW YORK TIMES. The *Times* is generally considered the best newspaper in the United States. It has been so voted in polls of editors and educators. More important, for our purposes, the *Times* is a major source of political news. With perhaps the largest reporting staff of any medium, it provides extensive coverage of Washington and international coverage that is unmatched. It is read by leaders in government, education, and business. Its influence extends beyond its own readership because the New York Times Service has as subscribers nearly all of the larger newspapers. The *Times'* coverage reaches more than half the newspaper readers in the United States.

The *Times* was founded in 1851 by Henry Raymond, who sought to provide something other than the sensationalism of James Gordon Bennett's *Herald* or the politicized coverage of Horace Greeley's *Tribune.* The emphasis was on news, especially foreign news, and that concept has prevailed.

However, after Raymond's death in 1869, the paper ran into considerable financial difficulty. It was rescued in 1896 by Adolph Ochs, who set the paper on the road to greatness. A major factor in what the paper achieved was its managing editor, Carr Van Anda. He concluded that the *Titanic* must have sunk, and the *Times* beat its competitors on that story. But more important, Van Anda followed up by organizing extensive coverage of the survivors when they landed in New York. The result was a classic in American journalism.

The Ochs family has retained ownership and leadership of the *Times*, and the paper has kept pace with the changes in the newspaper field. To their outstanding national and international coverage they have added exceptional business and science sections. The legendary grayness of the front page has given way to a modern, six-column format with color pictures.

SOURCES: Michael Emery, *America's Leading Daily Newspapers*, 1983; John C. Merrill and Harold A. Fisher, *The World's Great Dailies*, 1980.

Guido H. Stempel III

NEW YORK TIMES V. SULLIVAN was the first libel case ever considered by the U.S. Supreme Court and remains the best known. It happened as a result of an advertisement placed in the *New York Times* by the Committee to Defend Martin Luther King and the Struggle for Freedom in the South. It was critical of southern law enforcement. L. B. Sullivan, city commissioner in charge of police in Montgomery, sued the *Times.* He was not mentioned in the ad, but he claimed the references to law enforcement agencies constituted identification of him. The trial court awarded Sullivan $500,000, and the Alabama Supreme Court upheld that verdict. The U.S. Supreme Court, however, reversed that ruling. In the majority opinion, Justice William Brennan said that a public official could collect libel damages only if he or she could show actual malice. While this was widely viewed as an entirely new approach to libel, it was already in use in 10 states. At stake in the case was more than defining libel. Had the *Times* lost, coverage of the Civil Rights movement by the *Times*, other major newspapers, the news magazines, and network television undoubtedly would have become more subdued.

SOURCES: Anthony Lewis, *Make No Law: The Sullivan Case and the First Amendment*, 1992; Deckle McLean, ''The Origins of the Actual Malice Test,'' *Journalism Quarterly* 62: 750–754 (1985); *New York Times v. Sullivan*, 376 U.S. 254, 1964.

Guido H. Stempel III

NIMMO, DAN (1933–) is the most prolific author on political communication today. He has written, coauthored, or coedited at least 24 books on the subject. A native of Springfield, Missouri, Nimmo studied journalism at the University of Missouri before taking his master's (1956) and Ph.D. (1962) degrees at Vanderbilt.

His first book, *Newsgathering in Washington* (1964) was an extensive study of the relationship between public relations and officials and the press in the capital. His second book, *American Political Patterns: Conflict and Consensus*, written in 1967 with Thomas D. Ungs, was released in revised editions in 1969 and 1973. His third book, *The Political Persuaders: The Techniques of Modern Election Campaigns* (1970) detailed how the modern political consulting industry descended from the public relations profession of the 1920s and how its advocacy techniques have become the mainstay of American politics. His most recent work, coauthored with James E. Combs in 1996, is a lighthearted look at the subject entitled, *The Comedy of Democracy*.

Nimmo has written extensively on the use of political symbols, how they have evolved, and how they are used to formulate public opinion. Complex issues are often reduced to powerful symbols in a single word or phrase, such as abortion, gun control, or busing, he asserts, as can inanimate objects such as the flag. These symbols can be used to arouse public support on issues.

SOURCES: *Contemporary Authors*, CD-ROM; Robert E. Denton, Jr., and Gary C. Woodward, *Political Communication in America*, 1985.

Marc Edge

NIXON, RICHARD M. (1913–1994) was probably more critical of the media than any other president and used criticism of the media as a political issue. He also was criticized a great deal by the press, and that began before he was president. His role as a senator in the investigation of Alger Hiss in 1950 brought criticism. In 1952, when he was running for vice president, his campaign finances were questioned so strongly that there was speculation he might be dropped from the Republican ticket. He rescued himself with the famous ''Checkers'' speech on television.

He continued to be criticized for his actions as vice president. The most notable incident came when, in a speech at the convention of the American Society of Newspaper Editors in 1954, he suggested that American troops might be sent to Indochina. It was a trial balloon by the Eisenhower administration, and few trial balloons have drawn so much flak.

When he ran for president in 1960, he complained that the reporters were biased against him. Yet, he had more than three times as many editorial endorsements as his opponent, John F. Kennedy.

Then, in 1962 he ran for governor of California. It was an election that was seen as having great bearing on who would be the Republican candidate for president in 1964. Nixon was expected to win but lost to Democrat Pat Browne. On the same day, James Rhodes in Ohio and George Romney in Michigan upset incumbent Democratic governors, and Nelson Rockefeller, expected to have a close race for governor of New York, won easily. Two days later Nixon held a press conference announcing that he was retiring from politics and saying to the assembled journalists, "You won't have old Dick Nixon to kick around anymore." What he succeeded in doing was stealing the media play from the three Republicans who had won and thus kept his political career alive.

Nixon was elected president in 1968, and his administration was critical of the media, although the criticism came more from Vice President Spiro Agnew than from Nixon. He left office in 1974 bitter about the Watergate exposé by the *Washington Post* that led to his resignation. (*See also* Spiro Agnew; Kennedy-Nixon Debates.)

SOURCE: Michael Emery and Edwin Emery, *The Press and America*, sixth edition, 1988.

Guido H. Stempel III

O

OMBUDSMEN are internal critics working for U.S. newspapers, primarily from the late 1960s on. Their job is to solicit, investigate, and respond to reader complaints as well as to examine their publications for bias and fairness in reporting. The ombudsmen are generally former reporters, editors, or managers with more than 20 years' experience in journalism. They were selected for the job because of their journalistic experience, concern for press responsibility, and respect from peers. One of the first, if not the first, was John Herchenroeder, assistant to the executive editor at the *Louisville Courier Journal* and the *Times*. He was appointed in June 1967 by Norman Isaacs, then executive editor of the two Louisville newspapers. By the early 1980s there were 22 ombudsmen-type programs in 20 different cities across the United States. The average circulation of papers with ombudsmen was 204,272. By the mid-1980s, there were 29 U.S. dailies with ombudsmen, or about 2 percent of all daily newspapers. Many ombudsmen write regular columns for their newspapers outlining problems, solutions, and suggestions for improved behavior of their own publications as well as for the entire field of journalism. They spend time talking with readers, meeting with community groups, and responding to internal and external complaints about their newspapers. They are part press critic and part public relations person.

SOURCES: William L. Barnett, ''Survey Shows Few Papers Are Using Ombudsmen,'' *Journalism Quarterly*, Spring 1973; James S. Ettema and Theodore L. Glasser, ''Public Accountability or Public Relations: Newspaper Ombudsmen Define Their Role,'' *Journalism Quarterly*, Spring 1987; Suraj Kapoor and Ralph Smith, ''The Newspaper Ombudsman: A Progress Report,'' *Journalism Quarterly*, Autumn 1979; Donald T. Mogavero, ''The American Press Ombudsman,'' *Journalism Quarterly*, Autumn 1982.

Ardyth B. Sohn

ONE-PARTY PRESS became a key issue in the 1948 presidential campaign. President Harry Truman's whistle-stop campaign, which won the election for him, focused on two issues. One was the "do-nothing eightieth Congress." The other was the one-party press. What Truman meant was that the newspapers, which favored his opponent, Republican Thomas E. Dewey, heavily on the editorial pages also favored him in their news coverage. It was a successful campaign tactic, although there is little evidence to support the claim that news coverage was influenced by editorial preference.

The issue was raised again by Democratic candidate Adlai Stevenson after the 1952 presidential election. Two studies of coverage found some support for the charges. In subsequent presidential elections there have been numerous studies, and most have found that the editorial position of a newspaper does not seem to influence the news coverage.

SOURCES: Nathan Blumberg, *One Party Press*, 1954; Guido H. Stempel III and John W. Windhauser, eds., *The Media in the 1984 and 1988 Presidential Campaigns*, 1991.

Guido H. Stempel III

OPINION LEADERS are individuals who, through informal communication, influence public opinion. The concept comes from the work of Paul Lazarsfeld and his associates in studies of elections. They found that communication about campaigns was not one step directly from the media, but two steps from the media to opinion leaders to those whom the opinion leaders influenced. Because of this, political communication strategists recognize that they may need to reach the opinion leaders through the mass media more than they need to reach the general public.

SOURCE: Erik Barnouw, ed., *International Encyclopedia of Communications*, 1989.

Guido H. Stempel III

OPINION MEASUREMENT is the term used to explain the processes of surveying and polling. The major considerations in opinion measurement are:

1. Research design.
2. Research skills of the pollsters.
3. Appropriateness of the measurement techniques used.
4. Competence of interviewers.
5. Representativeness of the sample.
6. Tabulation procedures.
7. Interpretation of the results.

These dimensions influence the results of the survey or poll and the likelihood that the results mean what the researcher says they mean and can be trusted by the group that hopes to use them and by the public.

SOURCE: Erik Barnouw, ed., *International Encyclopedia of Communications*, 1989.
Jacqueline Nash Gifford

O'ROURKE, P. J. A conservative political humorist, O'Rourke is the international affairs editor for *Rolling Stone* and former editor of *National Lampoon*. His books include *Modern Manners* (1981), *The Bachelor Home Companion* (1987), *Republican Party Reptile* (1987), *Holidays in Hell* (1988), *Parliament of Whores* (1991), *Give War a Chance* (1992), and *All the Trouble in the World* (1994). Widely published in leading magazines, O'Rourke uses satire and parody to advance a libertarian viewpoint with humorous style more often associated with writers of the Left. His literary journalism exaggerates his ostensibly innocent bewilderment at the cynical excesses of corrupt and disingenuous officials in the United States and abroad. In *Parliament of Whores*, he writes, ''The whole idea of our government is this: if enough people get together and act in concert, they can take something and not pay for it.'' He affirms individual liberty against almost all forms of collectivism. He argues that liberal politicians foster and cultivate public anxiety in order to expand their personal power. Underlying O'Rourke's contrarian humor are a serious criticism of political corruption and popular culture and a call for public morality and personal responsibility.

SOURCE: *Contemporary Authors*, New Revision Series, vol. 41, 1994.
Paul Ashdown

P

PACK JOURNALISM is a derogatory term used to describe media members who cover the same beats, such as politics, and then report the same perspective on a topic. The term is derogatory because it suggests lack of originality and shallowness in reporting. Two factors motivate a pack journalist: a strong desire to be competitive with peers and the desire to be seen as "on top" of a story in the eyes or ears of the audience. Reporters sometimes are afraid to offer their own perspective because editors will wonder why they reported the story differently. The term was coined by Timothy Crouse, a *Rolling Stone* reporter, who wrote the critically acclaimed book *The Boys on the Bus*. In the book, Crouse reports his observations as part of the 1976 presidential press corps. (*See also* Timothy Crouse.)

SOURCE: Larry J. Sabato, *Feeding Frenzy*, 1991.

Jacqueline Nash Gifford

PAINE, THOMAS (1737–1809) is affectionately known as the "poet of the American Revolution" because of such works as *Common Sense*, which in 1776 articulated the reasons to seek independence from England, and for his *Crisis* papers, the first of which in December 1776 rallied the rebels' cause with such lines as: "These are the times that try men's souls," "Tyranny, like hell, is not easily conquered," "Heaven knows how to put a proper price upon its goods; and it would be strange indeed if so celestial an article as FREEDOM should not be highly rated."

Paine's major contributions to the literature of political philosophy certainly include *The Rights of Man*—his 1791 response to Edmund Burke's *Reflections on the French Revolution*—and *The Age of Reason*, published in 1794.

Less well known is his first significant pamphlet, *The Case of the Officers of Excise*, written in 1772, when Paine was still in his native England, to get

Parliament to increase the wages of tax collectors. Forced to sell his property to escape imprisonment for debt, Paine sailed to America in the fall of 1774. A letter of recommendation from Benjamin Franklin soon earned Paine a position as editor of *Pennsylvania Magazine*. A few weeks after his arrival, he wrote ''African Slavery in America,'' one of the best of the early attacks on slavery.

But as Paine was a giant among the pamphleteers and journalists urging the cause of liberty in America, France, and, indeed, throughout the world, he was among the most tragic victims of the abuse of free expression and of ungrateful political enemies.

Paine spent almost a year in a French prison and came close to being a victim of the guillotine because of the calculated indifference of Gouverneur Morris, the American minister to France, 1792–1794. Afterward, Paine was scorned in America because of the criticisms of institutionalized religion he made in *The Age of Reason* and because he was a chief target for much of the calumny aimed at Jeffersonian Democrats at the turn of the nineteenth century.

Paine, who died in poverty, could not rest in peace. His bones were unearthed by one of those who vilified him while alive—William Cobett—and shipped to England, where they were soon lost.

Astronomer and social commentator Carl Sagan characterized Paine as one who ''courageously opposed monarchy, aristocracy, racism, slavery, superstition, and sexism when all those constituted conventional wisdom.''

SOURCE: Philip S. Foner, *The Life and Major Writings of Thomas Paine*, 1945.

Jacqueline Nash Gifford

PANAMA INVASION. When U.S., troops stormed Panama on December 20, 1989, to depose dictator General Manuel Noriega, the high command wanted to avoid the embarrassment it had encountered in the 1983 invasion of Grenada. Then, hoping to avoid the ''Vietnam Syndrome,'' where unfavorable news damaged domestic support for a foreign war, the military excluded the press from the invasion force. When reporters turned up in chartered boats, they were forced back at gunpoint by U.S. troops. After that, a national media pool was formed by reporters cleared and ready to mobilize with armed forces on short notice. But in return for this concession, the military demanded almost total control over any information obtained. The seven reporters taken to Panama with the invading forces arrived four hours after the operation began, were kept in a windowless room, and were not allowed to file dispatches for another six hours. They were taken only to areas where the fighting was already over. Troops were ordered not to talk to reporters. Some newspapers and television stations demanded to be allowed to land chartered planes, to which the military first agreed but then refused, claiming it could not guarantee the safety of journalists. Consequently, there was no coverage of combat, and coverage instead centered on the aftermath, in which Panamanians were curiously portrayed as being overjoyed at having been left homeless by the destruction. The war was portrayed as a simple contest of wills between President George Bush and the demonized strongman Noriega. Underlying issues were ignored, such as Noriega's increasing resistance to control by U.S. intelligence services and Bush's insistence on renegotiating the 1977 treaty agreed to by then-president Jimmy Carter, which ceded U.S. control of the Panama Canal in 1999. The absence of reporters also meant that there was no accurate account of casualties.

SOURCE: Christian Jacqueline Johns and P. Ward Johnson, *State Crime, the Media and the Invasion of Panama*, 1994.

Marc Edge

THE PARTISAN PRESS (also called the Party Press) referred to an era in American journalism when newspapers were openly partisan organs that espoused the views of the political parties that funded them. The era of the commercial and ostensibly nonpartisan Penny Press, usually attributed to the establishment of Ben Day's *New York Sun* in 1833, eclipsed the Partisan Press. Nevertheless, a partisan press remained active until 1860, when the creation of the Government Printing Office largely did away with the administration's ability to award lucrative printing contracts to sympathetic partisan publishers. The early partisan newspapers in particular carried little, if any, of what today we call "news" and "reporting." Instead, a publisher on the payroll of a candidate or political party edited party documents for inclusion in the newspaper and wrote opinion pieces reflective of party positions. The typical Partisan Press newspaper cost about six cents, more than the average citizen could afford. The readership consisted of a largely elite, politically active audience. The main function of the partisan newspapers was to preach to the converted and furnish them with ammunition for political debates. Many of the founders of the American republic were directly or indirectly involved in the editorial operations of partisan newspapers. Journalism scholar J. Herbert Altschull wrote that "the goal of 'objectivity' was one that did not even occur to the founders, for there did not exist in the press of their era any publisher or editor who did not see his journal as an instrument for spreading good, or truth, and not merely a catalog of point of view." In the Miltonian tradition of "marketplace of ideas," the founders believed the readers became informed about political issues by exposing themselves to all political viewpoints, including partisan viewpoints. The partisan newspapers were not above reporting scurrilous attacks on opposition figures.

SOURCES: Bernard Roshco, *Newsmaking*, 1975; W. D. Sloan, "Scurrility and the Party Press 1789–1816," *American Journalism* 5, No. 2, 1988.

Michael B. Salwen

PENNY PRESS was the nickname for the newspaper revolution in American history. In the first third of the nineteenth century, newspapers were aimed at mercantile and political interests and reached small audiences. The penny press, which began with Benjamin Day's *New York Sun* in 1833, changed that. The penny papers sought wide audiences. They were sensational, and their political coverage was much less partisan than that of their predecessors. The *Sun* was followed by James Gordon Bennett's *Herald* in 1835 and Horace Greeley's *Tribune* in 1841. The penny press revolution gained widespread popularity in America's larger cities, and circulation rose to record levels. (*See also* James Gordon Bennett; Benjamin Day.)

SOURCE: William Howard Taft, ed., *The Encyclopedia of 20th Century Journalism*, 1986.

Guido H. Stempel III

PENTAGON PAPERS. In 1971, the *New York Times* and the *Washington Post* began publishing installments from a government study called "History of United States Decision-Making Process on Vietnam Policy." The study examined the country's policies with Vietnam across three decades. The study's contents were classified as secret but were leaked to the press by Dr. Daniel Ellsberg, formerly a Pentagon analyst. Ellsberg believed that the study's information should be shared with the American public. The Nixon administration sought and obtained an injunction to stop publication. The case went almost immediately to the U.S. Supreme Court.

The Court took the position that the fact that the document was classified did not mean that it involved national security. This was in response to the fact that there were 20 million classified documents. Justice Potter Stewart stated the problem succinctly in his opinion when he said that "when everything is classified, nothing is classified." Only one of the nine justices concluded that national security might be endangered by publication of the papers.

In a 6–3 verdict the Court removed the injunction because it constituted prior restraint, and the government had not offered sufficient justification for doing this.

SOURCE: Leon Hurwitz, *Historical Dictionary of Censorship in the U.S.*, 1985.

Guido H. Stempel III

THE PEOPLE'S CHOICE was the first comprehensive look at how people make voting decisions in a presidential campaign. Paul Lazarsfeld, Bernard Berelson, and Hazel Gaudet, pioneer mass communication researchers, surveyed residents in Erie County, Ohio, during the 1940 presidential campaign, which pitted two-term Democratic incumbent Franklin D. Roosevelt against Republican challenger and businessman Wendell L. Willkie. The county was picked because it had been a bellwether county in recent presidential elections. However, in 1940, it voted for Willkie.

Using an innovative technique called a panel design, the researchers conducted repeated interviews with a sample of 600 residents each month. The major finding of the study, which seemed surprising at the time, was that the mass media had little influence on voting decisions. Voter choice could be best predicted by party affiliation, socioeconomic status, place of residence (rural or urban), and religion (Catholic or Protestant). The media, mainly newspapers, radio, and magazines, played a secondary role, activating latent predispositions and reinforcing prior decisions. More than half the respondents indicated during their first interview that they had already made up their minds. The ones who made up their minds later often were under some type of political cross-pressure. Differences in candidate choice among family members, friends, or coworkers or differences in voter characteristics, such as being poor (a characteristic of many Democratic voters) or Protestant (a characteristic of many Republican voters), had the effect of delaying the voting decision. Lazarsfeld, Berelson, and Gaudet identified three types of persons who delayed their voting decision: crystallizers, who simply waited until the last minute to decide; waverers, who started out with their minds made up, became more indecisive as the campaign progressed, then returned to their initial choice; and party changers, who switched candidates. The latter group consisted of 8 percent of the voters.

Another major finding had to do with personal influence. The researchers found that the majority of voters relied on other people, people who followed the campaign more closely, to provide them with information about the campaign and, in some cases, to influence their voting decision. Lazarsfeld, Berelson, and Gaudet called this process the two-step flow of information. The media furnished information to the most interested voters, and these individuals, whom the researchers called opinion leaders, passed along information to, and presumably influenced, the rest of the elecorate.

SOURCE: Paul F. Lazarsfeld, Bernard Berelson, and Hazel Gaudet, *The People's Choice: How the Voter Makes Up His Mind in a Presidential Election*, 1948.

Churchill L. Roberts

PERSIAN GULF WAR generated charges of government censorship from journalists covering Operation Desert Shield (initial military buildup), Operation Desert Storm (aerial bombardment), and Operation Desert Sabre (ground offensive). The war was triggered when Iraq's Saddam Hussein ordered the invasion of Kuwait on August 12, 1990. On August 12, a U.S. Defense Department National Media Pool was established, but by August 26, the pool had been dissolved after media protests, and individual pools of reporters were assigned to various units. The Pentagon's official policy on reporting was outlined in a 10-page August 14, 1990, memorandum entitled ''Annex Foxtrot'' issued from the U.S. Central Command headquarters. The memo said the news media would be escorted at all times, which was a clear departure from the policy of the Vietnam War, when reporters wandered at will. Of course, they were largely dependent on the military for transportation. A January 7, 1991, memo from Pete Williams, assistant secretary of defense, outlined specific Pentagon Press

Corps Rules about what could and could not be printed or shown on television. The war officially began January 16, 1991, with a U.S.-led air offensive and ended when President George Bush declared a cease-fire February 28, 1991. Restrictions were bent or ignored by journalists, particularly television reporters, who crossed the border and interviewed Saddam Hussein with almost immediate transmission to the United States, provided live coverage of Scud missile attacks, and aired Iraqi government responses. U.S. television coverage included patriotic advertisements and logos framing news reports, and experts were hired to provide analysis and commentary on military strategies, cultural values, and foreign policy. This was the most covered conflict by all U.S. media (United States and world), with an estimated 1,500 reporters (192 in media pools) reporting at the start of the ground war.

SOURCES: *Conduct of the Persian Gulf War: Final Report to Congress, Report by the Department of Defense*, 1992; John R. MacArthur, *Second Front: Censorship and Propaganda in the Gulf War*, 1992; Robert Wiener, *Life from Baghdad: Gathering News at Ground Zero*, 1991.

Ardyth B. Sohn

PEW RESEARCH CENTER FOR THE PEOPLE AND THE PRESS. Formerly known as the Times Mirror Center, this center provides objective information on news that the American electorate follows, attitudes about news media, and use of information technologies. The center conducts public opinion surveys on attitudes of the public about media and how values affect political behavior. The center was founded by the Times Mirror in 1989 and was funded by that corporation until January 1, 1996. The Pew Charitable Trusts are seven charitable funds created between 1948 and 1979. The funds were established by two sons and two daughters of Joseph N. Pew, founder of the Sun Oil Company, and his wife, Mary Anderson Pew. The research center is directed by Andrew Kohut in Washington, D.C. He previously was president of the Gallup Organization and in 1989 he founded Princeton Survey Research Associates.

SOURCES: Internet site: http://www.people-press.org; Telephone interview with staff of the center.

Will Norton

PHOTO OP is jargon for photo opportunity. These are situations created to make it possible for still photographers and video photographers to take pictures of politicians. They are media events and are contrived. The most obvious example is the signing of a popular bill by the president or a state governor. Another frequent example is the picture, usually in the Rose Garden at the White House, of the president with the head of state of another country.

Photo ops are a press secretary's dream because they are completely controlled and almost certain to be positive and favorable.

SOURCE: Jay M. Shafritz, *The HarperCollins Dictionary of American Government and Politics*, 1992.

Guido H. Stempel III

POLITICAL ACTION COMMITTEES (PACs) are groups of private citizens who pool their resources, generally money, to support a candidate's campaign. PACs usually share a common view on an issue. They operate separately from party and candidate committees and therefore are not bound by the election laws, including campaign finance laws.

The history of PACs can be traced back to the labor unions during and after World War II as they sought to prove their ability to influence the political system. Though the political clout of PACs has grown over past years, many groups seek to limit the contributions from PACs to curtail the rising costs of running for political office. At present, though, PACs are not restricted in their spending the way candidates are, and there is more PAC money than candidate and party money in presidential and congressional elections.

SOURCE: Jay M. Shafritz, *The HarperCollins Dictionary of American Government and Politics*, 1992.

Jacqueline Nash Gifford

POLITICAL ACTIVISTS. *See* Hubert Gerold Brown; Stokely Carmichael; Frederick Douglass; Jerry Falwell; Pat Robertson; Gloria Marie Steinem.

POLITICAL CARTOONS appear in newspapers and magazines. The cartoons often take a sarcastic or serious look at current political happenings. They are humorous, but biting. Political cartoonists are among the best-known political communicators. The first famous one was Thomas Nast, who drew for *Harper's* and the *New York Times* in the years after the Civil War. More recent standouts have been Herbert Block (Herblock) of the *Washington Post*, Hugh Haynie of the *Louisville Courier-Journal*, Bill Mauldin of the *St. Louis Post-Dispatch* and the *Chicago Sun Times*, Paul Conrad of the *Los Angeles Times*, and Patrick Oliphant of the *Denver Post*.

SOURCES: Michael Emery and Edwin Emery, *The Press and America*, sixth edition, 1988; Jay M. Shafritz, *The HarperCollins Dictionary of American Government and Politics*, 1992.

Guido H. Stempel III

POLITICAL COLUMNISTS. Newspaper columnists who write almost exclusively about political topics emerged mainly during the 1920s. To be sure, many an earlier columnist had devoted part of his or her attention to politics. Two of the earliest of them, Benjamin Perley Poore and Mary Clemmer Ames, wrote Washington, D.C.–based columns. Poore started in 1854, and Ames started in 1866. However, their focus was not entirely political.

In 1911, contentious liberal Heywood Broun began a column that often dealt with politics, but the true progenitor of political column-writing was David Lawrence, who launched his conservative column in 1921. He is chiefly remembered as the founder of *U.S. News & World Report*, but he continued his syndicated column until 1973.

Other political pundits of the 1920s, with the years their columns ran, include California Progressive Chester Rowell (1920–1947); Frank Kent (1922–1958) of the *Baltimore Sun*, whose syndicated column was entitled "The Great Game of Politics"; the *New York Herald Tribune*'s Mark Sullivan (1923–1952), also remembered for his muckraking magazine articles; black conservative George Schuyler (1924–1977) of the *Pittsburgh Courier*; Edward Price Bell (1927–1931) of the *Chicago Daily News*, whose specialty was world politics and who was once nominated for the Nobel Peace Prize; and the *New York Times'* Olympian conservative Arthur Krock (1927–1966), winner of four Pulitzer Prizes.

Perhaps the most influential of all the early political columnists was two-time Pulitzer Prize winner Walter Lippmann (1931–1971), who was clearly read by world leaders. He was syndicated by the *New York Herald Tribune*.

SOURCE: Charles Fisher, *The Columnists*, 1944.

Sam G. Riley

POLITICAL COMMUNICATORS. *See* Samuel Adams; Roger Ailes; Stephen Tyree Early; Benjamin Franklin; James Campbell Hagerty; Louis Henry Howe.

POLITICAL JOURNALISTS. *See* Joseph and Stewart Alsop; Jack Anderson; Peter Arnett; Timothy Crouse; William Lloyd Garrison; Edwin Lawrence Godkin; Arthur Krock; Walter Lippmann; Robert C. Maynard; Joe McGinniss; P. J. O'Rourke; Thomas Paine; William Safire; Helen Thomas; Hunter S. Thompson; Theodore H. White; Robert U. Woodward and Carl Bernstein.

POLITICAL PERSUADERS is a term coined by political science professor Dan Nimmo in the late 1960s to describe a growing profession of men and women who specialized in managing political campaigns. Modern-day political persuaders are descendants of skilled party politicians like Mark Hanna and James Farley, who acquired national reputations for managing the presidential campaigns of William McKinley and Franklin D. Roosevelt, respectively. Campaigns Inc., formed in 1933 by Clem Whiter and Leone Baxter, was the first full-service agency devoted exclusively to managing political campaigns. The agency won 70 of 75 campaigns in its first 20 years. Although it is not possible to compile a complete list, estimates indicate that political consulting is a growth industry, employing thousands of people in the United States and abroad.

The high financial stakes and complexity of running for offices at all levels of government require consultants skilled in personnel management, media relations, advertising, fund-raising, polling, issue analysis, speechwriting, and television production. Defenders of the profession point out that even talented and highly skilled politicians cannot be elected without the assistance of political persuaders. But critics counter that political consultants have driven up the cost of campaigns, giving wealthy or well-financed candidates and issue groups disproportionate influence in the political process.

SOURCES: Dan Nimmo, *The Political Persuaders: The Techniques of Modern Election Campaigns*, 1970; Dan Nimmo and Robert L. Savage, *Candidates and Their Images: Concepts, Methods, and Findings*, 1976.

Kim A. Smith and Milena Karagyazova

POLITICAL SATIRISTS. Prior to the Civil War, much of the satire appearing in U.S. newspapers and magazines was more social than political. Exceptions included the work of Maine's Seba Smith, who satirized the Jackson administration via his literary character Major Jack Downing (1833—years shown in parentheses indicate the character's first appearance in book form), and in Boston, James Russell Lowell's Hosea Bigelow (1848) needled Manifest Destiny and U.S. involvement in the Mexican War.

Civil War-era humorists who often satirized politics include the North's Charles Farrar Browne, whose Artemus Ward (1862) went after copperheads, bureaucrats, and draft dodgers, and Robert Henry Newell, who satirized the Confederacy through his Orpheus C. Kerr (1862), a Lincoln administration office seeker. A contribution from Ohio was David Ross Locke's copperhead character Petroleum Vesuvius Nasby (1864), who was the ignorant, loudmouthed Archie Bunker of his day. In the South, Charles Henry Smith satirized the North via Georgia cracker Bill Arp (1866).

Both Chicago and national politics were satirized by Finley Peter Dunne's literary character Mr. Dooley (1898), the spirit of whom was revived in the late 1950s by that city's formidable columnist Mike Royko. In like manner, Philander Johnson began in 1906 to satirize Congress "from the inside" through his Senator Sorghum, a technique Kansas City columnist Bill Vaughan revived in the 1960s with his character Congressman Sludgepump.

The most popular political satirist in the 1920s and 1930s was the folksy Will Rogers, and 1949 marked the start of the career of columnist Art Buchwald, who is still writing and whose satire usually depends on purposeful exaggeration. From 1951 to 1964, Fletcher Knebel's "Potomac Fever" column poked fun at Washington politics, as does "Potomac Junction," written by Robert Haught since 1989. Entertainer/columnist Mark Russell writes and sings songs that satirize D.C. politicians—from 1961 to 1981 in Washington's Shoreham Hotel and thereafter on television. He has also written a syndicated humor column since 1975. Calvin Trillion has combined political and social satire in both newspapers and magazines since 1978. The "Bob Leavy's Washington" column has appeared in the *Washington Post* since 1981, and talented newcomer James Lileks has appeared in syndication since 1990.

A great many other talented humorists have written political satire on an occasional basis but in the main have been more oriented toward social satire. The list includes Mark Twain, C. B. Lewis, Kin Hubbard, George Ade, Don Marquis, James Thurber, Robert Benchley, and Dave Barry.

SOURCES: *Dictionary of Literary Biography*, vol. 11: *American Humorists, 1800–1950*, 1982. Norris Yates, *The American Humorist: Conscience of the Twentieth Century*, 1964.

Sam G. Riley

POLITICAL TECHNIQUES. *See* Backlash; Black Power; Concession Speech; Debates; Demonstration; Diplomacy; Disinformation; Leak; Politicalization; Rhetoric.

POLITICALIZATION is the process by which social issues become political issues. Generally, this is done by political communication strategists and politicians who find a social issue, such as abortion, and take possession of it, denying that it is anything other than political. They bring it up for discussion during an election or other key times in the political process. Lobbyists, special interest groups, and the mass media aides greatly control the politicalization of an issue. Lobbyist and special interest groups are the ones that bring the issue to the politicians for consideration and debate in political decision making. The mass media, however, have the greatest control because the success of politicalization of an issue depends on wide distribution or diffusion of the issue in society. The degree to which the mass media discuss or ignore an issue influences public opinion on the issue.

SOURCE: Erik Barnouw, ed., *International Encyclopedia of Communications*, 1989.

Jacqueline Nash Gifford

POLITICALLY ACTIVE ORGANIZATIONS. *See* American Association of Retired Persons; American Civil Liberties Union; American Federation of Labor–Congress of Industrial Organizations; Black Panthers; Christian Coalition; Congressional Black Caucus; John Birch Society; Ku Klux Klan; League of Women Voters; Moral Majority; National Association for the Advancement of Colored People; National Organization for Women.

POLK, JAMES KNOX (1795–1849), 11th president of the United States, was a leading Jacksonian who narrowly defeated Henry Clay in the election of 1844. The rise of the penny press in the 1830s had oriented newspapers more toward mass politics, making charisma more important than ever. Polk wanted his own administration organ and replaced Francis Blair of the *Globe* with Thomas Ritchie, editor of the *Richmond Enquirer*. The *Globe* was renamed the *Union*. The Senate attempted to banish the *Union* editor and reporters because the paper criticized Congress for failing to support the administration during the Mexican

War. A Senate resolution condemning Ritchie for libeling the Senate failed, 27–21. Polk called the resolution a ''foul deed,'' but he was motivated by politics, not concern for freedom of expression. He condemned other newspapers for not supporting his policies and said a protracted war would be the fault of Whig editors and their ''treasonable course.''

SOURCES: Charles A. McCoy, *Polk and the Presidency*, 1960; James K. Polk, *The Diary of James K. Polk*, 1910.

Charles Caudill

POLLS are used to measure political attitudes, beliefs, and actions of a sample representing some percentage or aspect of the population. Samples of the population are interviewed. Historically, straw polls were conducted by newspapers and magazines to measure, unscientifically, voting preferences among the public. However, in the 1930s, three men from the advertising profession found ways to apply scientific techniques to polling for better measurement of attitudes. Those men were George Gallup, Elmo Roper, and Archibald Crossley. Through demographics, the pollsters could reach broader ranges of varied groups and thereby project more accurately.

Polling became an important part of the political communication process when in 1936 a poll conducted by the magazine *Literary Digest* incorrectly predicted that Franklin Delano Roosevelt would be defeated by Alfred Landon for the presidency. The new, scientific polling techniques from Gallup and others predicted that Roosevelt would win. The *Literary Digest*'s error paved the way for the acceptance of scientific polling techniques to be used by the press to accurately measure public opinion. Polling used to be done by personal interview, but today nearly all polls are done by telephone.

More important than the use of polls to predict who will win an election is their use to develop campaign strategy. Candidates rarely offer untested ideas or policies. Instead, they tell the voters what polls indicate the voters would like to hear.

SOURCE: Erik Barnouw, ed., *International Encyclopedia of Communication*, 1989.

Jacqueline Nash Gifford and Guido H. Stempel III

POLLS AND POLLSTERS. *See* Gallup Poll; *Literary Digest* Poll; Elmo Roper.

PRESIDENTIAL MEDIA MANIPULATION. The president has a clear interest in media content. The media define presidential success or failure, and it is therefore in the president's political interest to ensure that media coverage is as favorable as possible. Appropriate coverage can help sway the public agenda, give impetus to the presidential agenda, and create a favorable climate of opinion toward the incumbent. To this end recent presidents have used three interrelated strategies to influence and manipulate media coverage—news conferences, personal relations with journalists, and the White House Office of Communication—as well as a host of other elements such as using public opinion polls to determine executive policy and presidential statements, controlling journalist accreditation, using satellite technology, and providing prepackaged audio and visual material to local stations.

There is, of course, mutual dependency at work here. The media need the president, and the president needs the media. The president is dependent on the media to get his policy across to the public, to present his relationship with Congress, and to establish himself in the eyes of the public as a satisfactory leader. From the media's point of view, the president is the most newsworthy individual in the country. Coverage of the president, his policy, and his administration is essential to the perceived quality of the media product. There is a symbiotic relationship between the president and the media, and each uses the relationship to extract maximum advantage.

SOURCES: Congressional Quarterly, *The President, the Public and the Press*, 1997; John Anthony Maltse, *Spin Control: The White House Office of Communications and the Management of Presidential News*, 1992.

Pamela J. Shoemaker and Michael J. Breen

PRESIDENTIAL NEWS CONFERENCES have been a key element in presidential media manipulation. They are called at the president's request alone, and the interval between conferences is purely a matter of the president's discretion. Presidents frequently open a news conference with an announcement, thus setting the agenda for the news conference and diverting attention from matters less favorable. However, in recent years, the news conference has fallen out of favor and become infrequent.

William Howard Taft was the first president to hold news conferences, but he aborted them after an unfortunate session. Woodrow Wilson resumed them, but he, too, abandoned them. Presidents Warren Harding, Calvin Coolidge, and Herbert Hoover continued them, but Franklin D. Roosevelt made them significant political communication. He had 998 news conferences, an average of 83 a year. Harry S Truman had half that many, and Dwight Eisenhower, John F. Kennedy, Lyndon Johnson, and Jimmy Carter all had about two dozen a year. Richard Nixon averaged 7 a year and Gerald Ford 16. Ronald Reagan set the pattern for the years ahead, averaging only 6 a year, a number that was not equaled by either George Bush or Bill Clinton.

One reason for the decline was that scheduled televised news conferences are likely to draw 500 journalists, some of whom seem to be there to be seen more than for any other reason. That is obviously too many people to engage in a meaningful dialogue, and recent presidents have turned over much of the responsibility for meeting the press to the White House director of communication or the press secretary.

SOURCES: Michael Emery and Edwin Emery, *The Press and America*, eighth edition, 1996; John Tebbel and Sarah Miles Watts, *The Press and the Presidency*, 1985.

Guido H. Stempel III

PRESIDENTS AND THE PRESS. *See* FDR and Radio; Thomas Jefferson; Kennedy-Nixon Debates; Richard M. Nixon; One-Party Press; James Knox Polk; Presidential Media Manipulation; Presidential News Conferences; Ronald Reagan; Franklin D. Roosevelt.

PRESIDENTS' WIVES AND PRESS. *See* Hillary Clinton; Anna Eleanor Roosevelt.

PRESS COUNCILS. Media in the United States generally have been reluctant to cooperate with independent groups set up to hear complaints about the press. The National News Council was created in 1973 but disbanded after 10 years because it lacked financial support and was unable to persuade major news organizations, including the *New York Times*, to participate in its hearings. It investigated 242 complaints. The council, with membership from the public and the media, had no power of enforcement other than the persuasiveness of its decisions. Persons with complaints had to agree not to pursue legal action before the council would agree to investigate. Supporters of the press council concept contend that most persons aggrieved by the press are seeking vindication, not compensation.

The Minnesota News Council probably has been the most successful in providing a noncourtroom forum for hearing complaints about media accuracy, accessibility, and ethics. The Minnesota Newspaper Association and some of the state's major dailies supported creation of the council in 1971. The council's views on what is ethical have sometimes differed from court decisions on what is legal. For example, the U.S. Supreme Court has ruled that newspapers are under no legal obligation to print a letter from a person criticized in the paper, but the Minnesota News Council has taken the view that a newspaper has an ethical obligation to publish a response. On the other hand, the Supreme Court has ruled the press has no legal right to keep sources confidential, but the press council has recognized it is ethical to do so.

The Northwest News Council, funded in 1992 by Washington and Oregon chapters of the Society of Professional Journalists, also has run into opposition from some major media, including the *Portland Oregonian* and the *Seattle Times*.

SOURCES: Sandra Braman, "Public Expectations of Media versus Standards of Codes of Ethics," *Journalism Quarterly*, Spring 1988; Robert Shafer, "The Minnesota News Council: Developing Standards for Press Ethics," *Journalism Quarterly*, Summer 1981.

Daniel J. Foley

PRESS PERFORMANCE. *See* Hutchins Commission; Kerner Commission; New World Information and Communication Order; Ombudsmen; Press Councils.

PRESSURE GROUPS. *See* Lobbying; National Rifle Association; Political Action Committees; Southern Christian Leadership Conference.

PRIMING is a specific kind of agenda setting that has implications for political campaigns. The media in their coverage create an agenda for a political campaign, and that agenda, rather than the candidate's own agenda or campaign platform, may be the basis on which the voter evaluates the candidate.

One study found that during the Persian Gulf crisis, President George Bush's overall rating depended more on opinions of his foreign policy than on opinions about his economic policy. Before the Gulf crisis, economic policy carried more weight, as it apparently did after the crisis.

SOURCES: Shanto Iyengar and Adam Simon, "News Coverage of the Gulf Crisis and Public Opinion: A Study of Agenda Setting, Priming and Framing," *Communication Research*, June 1993; Werner J. Severin and James W. Tankard, Jr., *Communication Theories*, fourth edition, 1997.

Guido H. Stempel III

***PROGRESSIVE* CASE.** This rare court order of "prior restraint" preventing publication of information in 1979 never made it to the U.S. Supreme Court for a ruling under the First Amendment. The Justice Department, claiming national security was at risk, obtained an injunction in federal district court against *Progressive* magazine, which planned to publish information on how to build a hydrogen bomb. The *Progressive*, a left-wing magazine published in Madison, Wisconsin, since 1909, said the "secret" information about the H-bomb had been obtained from unclassified sources and was thus available to anyone. The magazine sought to publish the article to demonstrate how badly the classification system was working. The government, however, cited provisions of the 1954 Atomic Energy Act as justifying prior restraint. Federal judge Robert Warren granted the injunction, ruling the act allowed prior restraint. He did not consider the Pentagon Papers case, in which the U.S. Supreme Court had ruled against prior restraint, to be a clear precedent. Before an appeal could be heard, however, articles containing the same information were published in two other periodicals. The government dropped the case against the *Progressive* immediately, and the magazine published the article six months after the original planned date. The extent to which national security concerns might override the Pentagon Papers decision against prior restraint thus was never clarified by the U.S. Supreme Court.

SOURCES: Ellen Alderman and Caroline Kennedy, *In Our Defense: The Bill of Rights in Action*, 1991; Wayne Overbeck, *Major Principles of Media Law*, 1997–1998.

Marc Edge

PROPAGANDA is written, oral, or visual communication used to influence the attitudes, beliefs, and actions of an audience. Many political groups and governments use propaganda to further their causes and interests to sway public opinion. Communication that is considered propaganda is biased, intentional, and motivated by personal gain on the part of the person or group that initiates the communication process. It is not necessarily false, but it does not have to be true.

Propaganda is loosely tied to advertising and public relations techniques. Communicators who use propaganda do so mostly through formal methods of communicating, generally through the mass media. (*See also* Creel Commission; Elmer Davis.)

SOURCE: Erik Barnouw, ed., *International Encyclopedia of Communications*, 1989.

Jacqueline Nash Gifford

PUBLIC OPINION is one of the most studied concepts, yet there is much disagreement over what it is. Pollsters often are content to define it as the distribution of individual opinions on a public issue, as determined by a scientific poll. In this view, the "public" is a collection of individuals, each of whom has an opinion of equal weight. The study of public opinion therefore involves descriptions of the direction, intensity, and stability of public opinion, as well as changes over time. Public opinion is akin to the "general will" of the people (V. O. Key), the "pictures inside the heads of human beings, the picture of themselves" (Walter Lippmann), the "climate of opinion" (Elizabeth Noelle-Neumann), or the "mood of the populace" (Gabriel Almond). Others, however, have suggested that such focus on the end product distracts study from the more important aspects of public opinion, the social processes that form it. Rather than treating public opinion as the "opinion of the public," some regard public opinion as those "opinions that are public." In this view, "public" is an adjective, not a noun. As Vincent Price and Donald F. Roberts put it, public opinion is "a dynamic process of social organization via discursive communication." The emphasis is upon communication and social action, rather than on a summary of the most popular cognitions held by a group. By viewing public opinion as a process of social organization through public communication, proponents of this view emphasize the importance of understanding the processes through which public opinion is formed, rather than the results of these processes. While this view of public opinion is gaining wider acceptance, it is not a new idea (see Cooley). Its development, however, was hampered by midcentury advancements in scientific polling, which encourage the view of public opinion as the opinions of the public, with its subsequent focus on describing the results of surveys. (*See also* Opinion Leaders; Polls.)

SOURCES: Charles Horton Cooley, *Social Organization: A Study of the Larger Mind*, 1909; Vincent Price and Donald F. Roberts, "Public Opinion Processes," in Charles R. Berger and Steven H. Chaffee, eds., *Handbook of Communication Science*, 1987.

Dominic L. Lasorsa

PUBLIC RELATIONS is a term used to define the informational activities used by corporations, governments, or groups to create attitudes or beliefs that place that entity in a favorable light in the public's eye. Public relations activities are varied; they include information management, attitude surveys, advertising, media planning, event planning, and counseling.

Public relations has its roots in puffery or publicity. P. T. Barnum is considered one of the first to use publicity to entice audiences and gain exposure from the media. Two influential figures in public relations history altered that perception of the profession and lent it a professional air—Ivy Lee and Edward Bernays. Both men used public relations techniques, especially interpersonal communication and media events, to create positive images and communication between a client and its audiences (stockholders, government officials, customers, employees, or competitors).

Public relations practitioners may be hired by a corporation or group directly or work in a public relations firm that handles many different types of clients. Government agencies usually have their own public relations staffs. However, political candidates frequently use the services of a public relations firm during a campaign. (*See also* Damage Control; Photo Op; Political Persuaders; Spin; Strategic Political Communication; White House Office of Communication.)

SOURCES: Erik Barnouw, ed., *International Encyclopedia of Communications*, 1989; Dennis L. Wilcox, Phillip H. Ault, and Warren A. Agee, *Public Relations Strategies and Tactics*, 1992.

Jacqueline Nash Gifford

PULITZER, JOSEPH (1847–1911) was the newspaper publisher who set in motion the yellow journalism of the late nineteenth and early twentieth centuries. Born in Hungary, he came to this country during the Civil War as a military recruit. Under the Civil War draft system, a draftee could hire a substitute, and that's how Pulitzer got his chance to come to this country. He served in the army for a year and then went to St. Louis to become a reporter for a German-language newspaper. Legend has it that he chose St. Louis because a practical joker told him that this would be the best place to learn English; in fact, it was a city with one of the largest German populations.

Pulitzer bought his first newspaper, the *St. Louis Dispatch*, in 1878 and then combined it with another failing newspaper, the *St. Louis Post*, thus forming the *Post Dispatch*. He also was active in St. Louis politics. He was one of the city's three police commissioners. He worked hard for the liberal Republican movement and helped nominate Horace Greeley for president in 1872. Both Greeley and the liberal Republican movement failed, and Pulitzer turned to the Democratic Party.

He bought the *New York World* in 1883 and turned it into a vehicle to promote his political party's rhetoric. Looking to make itself more interesting to readers, the *World* was something of a paradox with sensational news coverage and a solid, serious editorial page. It crusaded against corruption in government and took the side of the common man. The result was a highly profitable newspaper, and in 1887 Pulitzer started the *Evening World* in New York.

Pulitzer's technique was soon emulated by William Randolph Hearst, who imitated the *World* with his *New York Journal* and lured staffers away from the *World* at higher salaries. The *World–Journal* competition became known as yellow journalism after a cartoon character called ''the Yellow Kid.'' It was drawn by Richard F. Outcault, and he was one of those whom Hearst lured away from Pulitzer. Pulitzer, however, found someone else to draw ''the Yellow Kid.'' The competitiveness between the two men for sensationalistic stories coined the phrase ''yellow journalism.'' Part of yellow journalism was sensational reporting of events in Cuba and of the Spanish-American War. Both papers gained circulation, but Pulitzer and the *World* were highly criticized and lost prestige.

The Pulitzer legacy includes the Graduate School of Journalism at Columbia and the prizes that bear his name. His will provided the funding that made both possible. (*See also* William Randolph Hearst; Yellow Journalism.)

SOURCES: George Juergens, *Joseph Pulitzer and the New York World*, 1966; William McGuire and Leslie Wheeler, *American Social Leaders*, 1993; Donald Paneth, *The Encyclopedia of American Journalism*, 1983.

Guido H. Stempel III

Q

Q SORT METHOD was devised by William Stephenson. The procedure begins by having individuals respond to items. Usually, respondents are asked to rate items from 1 to 10, but on a forced normal distribution. So, for example, if you had 60 items, you might give respondents a forced distribution with 1 1, 2 2s, 3 3s, 8 4s, 15 5s, 15 6s, 8 7s, 4 8s, 2 9s, and 1 10. You would correlate respondents with each other rather than correlating questions or items with each other. You then factor analyze, and your factors are groups of people whose responses are similar. You then compare the groups' responses, usually using z scores, to find out which responses set each group apart from the other groups and thus define each group. Stephenson maintained that you could do this with small, purposive samples because the purpose is to determine what the factors are, not what percentage of the population is in each one. Meaningful results have been produced by Q studies with samples of no more than 25. (*See also* William Stephenson.)

SOURCE: William Stephenson, *The Study of Behavior*, 1953.

Guido H. Stempel III

R

RADIO. *See* Elmer Davis; Walter S. Lemmon.

REAGAN, RONALD (1911–) was the 40th U.S. president. He was nicknamed the Great Communicator for his polished political communication style, one he learned as a movie star and as a public speaker.

Reagan grew up in Illinois in a working-class family. He went to Eureka College, a small Christian school. In 1937, he took a Hollywood screen test and signed a contract with Warner Brothers. His film career flourished, although he often played in Grade B movies.

After World War II, he became the president of the Screen Actors Guild. He held this position for six years, including the time of investigations of communist activities by the House Un-American Activities Committee. Although Reagan was known to be a Democrat and very liberal, as president of the guild he worked with the government to unearth communist activities in Hollywood. This eventually led to the blackballing of several actors, actresses, writers, producers, and others.

Reagan secured a job as the host of *General Electric Theater*, a national television program. This engagement led him to doing motivational appearances as well. Here he developed a rhetoric that appealed to business and audience alike. It was full of imagery reminiscent of a time when America was strong. Also during this time he switched party affiliations and became a Republican.

Perhaps more than any other event, a fund-raising speech on behalf of presidential candidate Senator Barry Goldwater pushed Reagan into the national limelight. In one evening, he raised nearly $1 million on behalf of the party's efforts. Reagan then ran for governor of California and won the race and was reelected. Again, voters liked his appeal as a common man sharing his dream of a strong America.

In 1980 he won the Republican Party nomination to run against President

Jimmy Carter, whose term was dogged by inflation, unemployment, and the Iran hostage situation. Reagan won the race by attacking Carter's losing record. A few days after his inauguration, the hostages were freed. It was later reported that Reagan, advised by key military personnel, had given permission for the hostages to be traded in exchange for arms.

Reagan's movie savvy and speaking talents helped him impress the nation. He was at ease in front of the camera and often sought it out. Also his ability to put the nation at ease during times of crisis, such as the National Aeronautics and Space Administration (NASA) spaceship disaster of the Challenger, won him praise from Americans.

He became known as the "Teflon President" because of his ability to communicate in a reassuring way, no matter what the circumstances, and any blame and criticism did not last long. He was easily reelected in 1984.

The event that Reagan is most likely to be remembered for was his work with former Soviet Union leader Mikhail Gorbachev to negotiate the Intermediate-Range Nuclear Forces Treaty, designed to reduce the nuclear war arsenals of both nations.

SOURCES: Leonard Levy and Louis Fisher, *Encyclopedia of the American Presidency*, 1994; Peter B. Levy, *Encyclopedia of the Reagan-Bush Years*, 1996.

Jacqueline Nash Gifford

REHNQUIST, WILLIAM H. (1924–) served as associate justice of the U.S. Supreme Court from 1971 until 1986, when he was appointed the nation's 16th chief justice. A conservative, Rehnquist generally took an unsympathetic view of press freedoms. In the years he was associate justice, he voted for the First Amendment only 21 percent of the time, which is one of the lowest figures for any justice who ever served on the Court. He has become more supportive of the amendment, but only slightly so, in his years as chief justice.

He was the lone dissenter in *Richmond Newspapers v. Virginia* (448 U.S. 555), in which the Supreme Court ruled that the public and the press have the right to attend trials. Neither the First nor the Sixth Amendment requires public access to courts, he said, although the guarantee of the Sixth Amendment is to "a speedy and public trial."

Rehnquist wrote for the majority in *Time v. Firestone* (424 U.S. 448), in which the Court decided *Time* magazine was not entitled to protection under the "actual malice" standards by *New York Times v. Sullivan* and subsequent cases. The Court held that Mary Alice Firestone was not a public figure, even though she held several press conferences during her divorce trial.

An exception to Rehnquist's rulings against the press came in *Hustler Magazine v. Falwell* (485 U.S. 46). Rehnquist wrote for a unanimous Court that Rev. Jerry Falwell was not entitled to damages for emotional distress for a parody that portrayed the nationally known minister as having his first sexual experience with his mother in an outhouse while drunk. "At the heart of the

First Amendment is the recognition of the fundamental importance of the free flow of ideas and opinions on matters of public interest and concern,'' Rehnquist wrote.

SOURCE: Melvin I. Urofsky, ed., *The Supreme Court Justices: A Biographical Dictionary*, 1994.

Daniel J. Foley

RELIANCE VERSUS USE. Where do people get most of their news? Various polls have been asking that for more than half a century. The best known of these were the ones done by the Roper Organization that ask ''First, I'd like to ask you where you usually get most of your information about what's going on in the world today—from newspapers, radio or television or magazines or talking to people or where?'' When that question was first asked in 1959, newspapers came out slightly ahead, but television soon moved ahead and in recent years has led by 20 percent.

Yet other studies that have asked people about local news or state news or specific kinds of news have found that newspapers were the main source. More important, the answers to this type of question, which is really about reliance, do not correlate with answers to knowledge questions or media use questions. Media use is related to news knowledge.

It is important to recognize that most people get news from more than one source. For political communicators this is an important point because it means that they should not focus just on one medium. Furthermore, effective political communication means striving for different messages in print media from those in television. Otherwise, you are not using the capability of each medium to the maximum.

SOURCES: Joey K. Reagan and Richard V. Ducey, ''Effects of News Measures on Selection of State Government News Sources,'' *Journalism Quarterly*, Summer 1983; John P. Robinson and Mark R. Levy, with Dennis K. Davis, *The Main Source: Learning from Television News*, 1986; Guido H. Stempel III, ''Where People Really Get Most of Their News,'' *Newspaper Research Journal*, Fall 1991.

Guido H. Stempel III

RESEARCH FINDINGS AND TECHNIQUES. *See* Opinion Measurement; The People's Choice; Q Sort Method; Tracking Polls.

RHETORIC defines the study of persuasive communications. The philosophy behind the study of rhetoric is that persuasive communications can be analyzed on three levels:

1. Message conception.

2. Message composition.

3. Message presentation.

The study of persuasive communications has historic ties to debates between the great Greek philosophers about the variables that affect the writer–reader, speaker–listener relationship. Over the course of human time, the study of rhetoric has become more and more scientific as researchers try to quantify the variables to improve the quality of the communication relationships.

It is obvious why political communicators are interested in the study of rhetoric: they want to create written and oral messages that have the best chance to be understood and to be persuasive in the vast mix of multiple messages in the mass media and in society.

SOURCE: Erik Barnouw, ed., *International Encyclopedia of Communications*, 1989.

Jacqueline Nash Gifford

RICHMOND NEWSPAPERS V. VIRGINIA. In a 7–1 decision written by Chief Justice Warren Burger, the U.S. Supreme Court ruled that the public (and by extension, the press) has a right to attend criminal trials. Throughout the 1970s, the Court ruled that if the media could obtain information, then that information could be published. Even if the material was obtained by possibly illegal means (*see* Pentagon Papers), the press had a right to publish what it knew. The question in *Richmond Newspapers*, however, concerned the right of the press to obtain the information in the first place.

The case involved the fourth trial of a defendant whose previous three trials had been reversed or declared mistrials. The trial judge, who had presided over two of the three previous trials, closed the fourth trial, with no objection from either the prosecution or the press. Late in the day, however, two reporters argued that the trial could not be closed without a hearing to determine if the defendant's rights could be protected in some way other than closing the courtroom. The judge refused to vacate his order, and the Virginia Supreme Court upheld the order.

In overruling the state court, Burger said that under the First, Sixth, and Fourteenth Amendments there is a presumptive right of the public and the press to attend criminal trials. In a concurring opinion, however, Justice Potter Stewart stressed that the right of access is not absolute. Yet the Court's ruling in the subsequent *Globe Newspaper Co. v. Superior Court, County of Norfolk* seems to indicate that it is unlikely that closing of a trial is acceptable.

SOURCE: *Richmond Newspapers v. Virginia*, 448 U.S. 555, 1980.

Larry L. Burriss

ROBERTSON, PAT (1930–) is credited for moving America's conservative Christians into a powerful political force. He also founded the Christian Broadcasting Network, which he uses as a vehicle for spreading his political and religious views. Robertson is well educated and comes from a successful family. His father was a congressman for nearly 34 years, and his mother was a zealous Christian and a homemaker. This combination shaped his future.

He obtained his law degree from Yale University Law School yet did not pass New York's bar exam. Instead, he decided to work in the financial and communications industries. A fateful dinner at his mother's home led to his changing professional direction and becoming "born again" in Christianity.

In 1961, he put the Christian Broadcasting Network (CBN) on the air, with religious music and programming. To raise money to continue the station, Robertson asked for pledges from 700 people to give $10 monthly. In exchange, he gave prayer and guidance. The "700 Club" was born. Over time, nearly 200 radio and television stations became part of his network. However, his decision to join cable television catapulted his ventures nationally.

CBN uses its airwaves not only to promote Christianity but to comment on political, social, and economic issues from a Christian perspective. Through the network, Robertson and his followers created the Committee for Freedom, a religious special interest group that gives financial support to candidates who espouse ideas in line with conservative Christianity.

Robertson ran for the 1988 Republican presidential nomination but backed out amid scandal about his marriage. Robertson's actions demonstrate that there is a strong block of American voters who see a desire to instill morality into government. However, Robertson and his followers have not been embraced by many conservative voters who do not like the idea of church and state blending together in citizens' lives.

SOURCES: *Current Biography Yearbook*, 1987; Charles H. Lippy, ed., *Twentieth Century Shapers of American Popular Religion*, 1989.

Jacqueline Nash Gifford

ROOSEVELT, ANNA ELEANOR, the first president's wife to extensively engage in mass communication, pioneered in techniques of reaching the nation's women during the administration of Franklin D. Roosevelt. Overcoming the shyness she had shown as a young wife and mother, Roosevelt made a role for herself as First Lady from 1933 to 1945 that has yet to be matched by any successor. In carving out her public career, she was mentored by Louis Howe, her husband's political adviser, and Loren Hickok, a close friend who was a reporter for the Associated Press. Eleanor Roosevelt projected her own humanitarian interests through the mass media, although she also traveled widely and spoke to innumerable audiences. Her activities, which centered on liberal causes and urged women to become politically active, helped to humanize the New Deal during the depression. During World War II they helped build support for the war effort. Roosevelt reached out to the public through weekly White House press conferences for women reporters only and a syndicated column, "My Day," that provided a diarylike account of her daily experiences. She also gave sponsored radio broadcasts on topics aimed at women, such as descriptions of White House life. She was a prolific contributor to women's magazines, writing advice columns that dealt with women's social roles. While she emphasized the importance of women's traditional responsibilities, she encouraged women to involve themselves in a world outside the home and promoted the Democratic Party.

SOURCE: Maurine H. Beasley, *Eleanor Roosevelt and the Media: A Public Quest for Self-Fulfillment*, 1987.

Maurine H. Beasley

ROOSEVELT, FRANKLIN D. (1882–1945) was probably the most effective political communicator ever to occupy the White House. He presided at a time of great national crisis, first from the depression and then from World War II. His policies were often controversial, but he prevailed and was reelected three times.

Two things stand out in his communication efforts. One was that he held more press conferences than any other president—a total of 998 during the slightly more than 12 years he was in office. That's more than the total for all his successors in the White House. It was one reason he had good relations with the reporters, despite the fact that the majority of newspapers opposed him editorially. Despite the frequency of press conferences, they almost always yielded real news.

The other thing was his "fireside chats"—his radio talks to the American public. Few have had a better radio voice than Roosevelt, and few, if any, presidents have offered more substance in their radio talks to the public. He used the relatively new medium of radio to great advantage. (*See also* FDR and Radio; Louis Henry Howe.)

SOURCE: James E. Pollard, *The Presidents and the Press*, 1947.

Guido H. Stempel III

ROPER, ELMO (1900–1971) was one of the major pioneers in polling. He was educated at the University of Minnesota and the University of Edinburgh. Upon leaving college, he went into sales and management and developed a penchant for measuring consumer tastes and preferences, using forecasting and survey sampling techniques. Unlike others, he used scientific techniques for polling. Because of his uncanny ability for accuracy, he was approached to write a public opinion column for *Fortune* magazine, a position he held for 15 years. In 1933, he established Roper Research Associates. Roper was one of those who correctly predicted Franklin D. Roosevelt's victory in the 1936 presidential race. The *Literary Digest*, which had correctly predicted the outcome in five previous presidential elections, incorrectly predicted Alfred Landon would win.

Roper was best known for the work he did for the Television Information Office beginning in 1959. Those polls concluded that "most Americans get most of their news from television,'' and that was perhaps the most widely quoted poll finding of that era.

SOURCES: Erik Barnouw, ed., *International Encyclopedia of Communications*, 1989; Edward Vernoff, *International Dictionary of 20th Century Biographies*, 1987.

Jacqueline Nash Gifford

S

SABATO, LARRY (1952–) is a researcher and scholar in the area of American government and politics, particularly elections. He is perhaps the leading scholar on the work of political consultants. Sabato has a Ph.D. from Queen's College in Oxford. There he was a political lecturer. He then came back to the United States to teach at the University of Virginia, where he had obtained his bachelor's degree. His books include *The Rise of Political Consultants, New Ways of Winning Elections*, and *PAC Power: Inside the World of Political Action Committees*.

The Rise of Political Consultants is considered the foremost source on the use of mass media and consultants in political campaigns. His recent interests involve looking at the use of technology and advertising in political campaigns.

SOURCE: *Contemporary Authors*, New Revision Series, vol. 27, 1989.

Jacqueline Nash Gifford

SAFIRE, WILLIAM (1929–). Safire served in the Nixon White House as an idea man and speechwriter. He is currently known as the influential, conservative columnist for the *New York Times* and a self-styled "language maven."

Safire's life and work have several areas of relevance for students of political communication. First, despite his emphasis on word craft, he was an early creator of the for-the-camera pseudoevent. He staged-managed the "kitchen debate" between Vice President Richard Nixon and Russian premier Nikita Khrushchev.

Second, Safire's columns and books, such as *The New Language of Politics* and *Political Dictionary*, provide well-researched, lucid, and often humorous insights into the construction of political phraseology, often tweaking the tortured syntax of the powerful. Academic linguists, however, have called him a "language shaman" for perpetuating a myth that one standard form of English can be practiced.

Third, Safire is known as the king of "source wedging." Seizing one bit of information about, for example, a closed policy meeting, he uses it to pry more bits from others present until a coherent, if not necessarily completely accurate, rendition of the "secret" proceedings is revealed. He is thus one of the most powerful Washington columnists because he is able to disclose policy plans and discussions that are inaccessible to other journalists.

Safire augments his persuasive vigor with sly self-depreciation. He is perhaps the only citizen of the Beltway to admit that "sometimes everybody can be wrong."

SOURCES: Steven Pinker, *The Language Instinct*, 1994; William Safire, "Pundit Bashing," *New York Times Magazine*, May 27, 1990; William Safire, *Safire's Political Dictionary*, 1993.

David C. Perlmutter

SARNOFF, DAVID (1891–1971) is respected as the father of American television, starting the National Broadcasting Company (NBC) in 1926. Sarnoff, born of Russian descent, started his broadcast career in the predecessor of broadcasting—the telegraph. He was a messenger boy at the Commercial Cable Co. and later worked for Marconi Wireless Telegraph Company.

But then a tragic event changed his life forever, as it did the rest of America. He was the person who received the first news that the *Titanic* was sinking. His smart, fast thinking and use of technology helped America and the rest of the world gather information on the accident.

Sarnoff had his own ideas for the future of radio. He wanted to create the first radio receiver and got his chance when he started to work for the Radio Corporation of America (RCA) in 1928. He then led the company in creating the first radio receivers, making millions of dollars. He later led efforts to create radio programming, starting the National Broadcasting Company. Later he toyed with television technology, even starting a small television station, but World War II interrupted his plans. In the war, he was a communications consultant. After the war, he returned to his idea of a television station, and once again RCA led the revolution in new communications technology, creating television receivers. He was instrumental in efforts to standardize color television technology in America.

SOURCES: Les Brown, *Encyclopedia of Television*, 1992; *Contemporary Authors*, vol. 113, 1985.

Jacqueline Nash Gifford

SCHENCK. The decision in *Schenck v. U.S.* (1919) includes probably the most widely quoted (and misquoted) statement from a Supreme Court decision. It is the statement of Justice Oliver Wendell Holmes that "the most stringent protection of free speech would not protect a man in falsely shouting fire in a theater and causing a panic." What is frequently left out is the word "falsely."

That is interesting because falseness had nothing to do with the case. The case involved the distribution of an antidraft pamphlet during World War I. Schenck was the secretary of the Socialist Party, the distributor of the pamphlet. Holmes ruled that although there was no evidence that the pamphlet had had any effect, it was intended to interfere with military conscription during wartime. This endangered the nation's security and thus constituted what Holmes called "a clear and present danger." Subsequently, Holmes modified his position on this issue. The *Yates* decision nearly 40 years later at least changed the meaning of clear and present danger in that there had to be a clear result of the speech in question. Many who refer to *Schenck* apparently are unaware of this.

SOURCE: *Schenck v. U.S.*, 249 U.S. 47, 1919.

Guido H. Stempel III

SCHRAMM, WILBUR (1907–1987) was one of the leading pioneers in mass communication research. His career started as a journalist for the *Boston Herald* and then the Associated Press in the mid-1920s through the mid-1930s. In 1935, he became an assistant professor at the University of Iowa, Iowa City. He later taught at the University of Illinois (Champaign-Urbana), Stanford University, and the East-West Institute in Hawaii. He was the first director of the Illinois Institute of Communication Research and was director of Stanford's Institute for Communication Research. His long career in mass education research and communication research included work with the U.S. Office of Education and the United Nations.

As a researcher, Schramm devised communication models that were among the first to look at how human communication varied from technical communications (technology). Specifically, his models looked at the experiences of the encoder and the decoder, or the speaker and the listener, and how those experiences shaped what was actually communicated. His models proposed that human communication be analyzed in terms of unique characteristics of the encoder and decoder and their shared experiences as humans.

His books include the pioneering *Process and Effects of Mass Communication* (1954) and *Men, Messages and Media: A Look at Human Communication* (1973). He was coauthor with Daniel Lerner of *Communication and Change in the Developing Countries* (1967) and with William L. Rivers of *Responsibility in Mass Communication* (1969).

SOURCES: *Current Biography* (1994); Edwin Emery and Joseph P. McKerns, "AEJMC: 75 Years in the Making," *Journalism Monographs*, No. 104, November 1987; Donald Paneth, *Encyclopedia of American Journalism*; Donna Straub, Werner J. Severin, and James W. Tankard, Jr., *Communication Theories: Origins, Methods, and Uses in the Mass Media*, fourth edition, 1997.

Jacqueline Nash Gifford

SCOPES MONKEY TRIAL. This trial in a small town in Tennessee became a national political event because it pitted Clarence Darrow against William

Jennings Bryan. It came about because in 1925 the state of Tennessee passed the Butler Act, which made it illegal to teach Charles Darwin's evolution theory in any of the state's classrooms, including colleges and universities.

The American Civil Liberties Union (ACLU) jumped on the chance to test the constitutionality of the new law and sought an opportunity for a test case of the law. It sent out press releases looking for suitable candidates, hopefully, teachers, who would be willing to participate in the test case. Farther away, in a small town called Dayton, Tennessee, two men—George Washington Rappleyea, a citizen, and school board president F. E. Robinson—read about the ACLU's plan. They decided they wanted to take part in the ACLU's "experiment" and put the small city on the map. Dayton would be an ideal location, in their opinion, because the town's residents were known for their fundamentalist belief that the Bible was literal. In addition, the pair had the perfect "defendant": Dayton high school teacher John Thomas Scopes. Scopes, 25 years old, taught evolution in a science course and was known to be a supporter of Darwin's theories. Rappleyea and Robinson approached Scopes, who agreed with their plan. The ACLU agreed to use Scopes as the defendant in the case. Both groups felt confident of their ability to have the law ruled unconstitutional of the separation of church and state.

The case finally went to trial on July 10, 1925. However, events did not go as smoothly as the ACLU had anticipated. The press flocked to the little town and dubbed the case the "monkey trial," lending a mocking tone to the case. Judge John T. Raulston forbade the case from becoming an issue of the law's constitutionality. The question was solely whether Scopes had committed a crime in light of the law. Scopes was not permitted to testify about his actions.

Darrow's and Bryan's oratory and legal skills went head-to-head as Darrow used scientists to support his defendant, and Bryan used biblical Scriptures and rhetoric to support his position. At one point, he even went to the witness chair himself to defend the Bible! Twelve days later, on July 21, Scopes was found guilty by jury of violating the law and fined $100. The case was appealed, and the lower court's opinion was overturned, but not on the basis of the constitutionality of the law. Instead, it found that the $100 fine was excessive for the crime committed. It was not until 1967, more than 40 years later, that Tennessee repealed the act.

SOURCES: Leon Hurvitz, *Historical Dictionary of Censorship in the United States*, 1985; George C. Kohn, *Encyclopedia of American Scandal*, 1989.

Jacqueline Nash Gifford

SEDITIOUS LIBEL seems clear enough in Black's *Law Dictionary*: "A communication . . . with the intent to incite the people to change the government otherwise than by lawful means, or to advocate the violent overthrow of the government by force of violence." But from the onset of the printing press in the sixteenth century and through much of seventeenth- and eighteenth-century

America and England, seditious libel law was frequently used to punish virtually any expression that challenged or criticized government or the crown. Such a view of seditious libel survives in many twentieth-century nations, even though it is unconstitutional in the United States.

A mere seven years after the First Amendment was ratified in 1791, Congress passed the Alien and Sedition Laws. Those measures, which expired in 1800, punished by fine, imprisonment, or deportation persons who defamed the federal government or brought it into disrepute. While contemporary laws such as the Smith Act (U.S.C.A. #2385A) may punish advocacy of the overthrow of the government by force or violence, they are stopped short of punishing persons for abstract discussion of overthrow of the government.

In 1964, in the landmark free expression case of *New York Times v. Sullivan*, the U.S. Supreme Court said, "Although the Sedition Act was never tested in this Court, the attack upon its validity has carried the day in the court of history." Further, Justice William Brennan's opinion said citizens not only had the right to criticize government but had the *duty* to criticize.

SOURCE: Donald M. Gillmor and Jerome A. Barron, *Mass Communication Law*, third edition, 1979.

Herb Strentz

SELECTIVITY. Among the earliest findings of communication research was that many people remained unmoved by persuasive and propagandistic efforts, with some people going to great length to protect their belief systems from information that might threaten them. One researcher even referred to media audiences as "obstinate." Selective exposure, selective perception, selective attention, and selective retention were identified as processes through which people may maintain currently held beliefs and attitudes in the face of potentially contradictory evidence.

Conclusions about the audience and the persuasive process have been considerably modified given more recent research and changes in the media environment. Yet, the idea that people approach media messages with motivations to accept, avoid, or modify the messages based on the content of their currently held belief systems remains important.

Briefly, selective exposure is a process by which individuals will avoid exposure to media messages they expect will disagree with their currently held beliefs. An example would be newspaper readers who avoid the newspaper's editorial page because they expect it to be offensive to their political view.

Selective attention and perception occur once exposure has taken place and may be more important than selective exposure because the content of media may be difficult to predict. Selective perception occurs when a receiver perceives a message in a way that supports a previously held position. For example, viewers of presidential debates with different political leanings may perceive the same candidate's performance in very different ways. Selective attention means that in a media message, viewers or readers may focus on those aspects that are most congenial with their belief systems and largely ignore other aspects. Selective retention means that congenial information is more likely to be remembered than discrepant information.

Selectivity is derived, at least in part, from cognitive dissonance theory, which says that holding two or more discrepant cognitions in one's mind creates a psychological discomfort that will be avoided if possible.

That people do learn, change, and grow is evidence that selectivity is not absolute. Research has indicated that if discrepant information is particularly interesting, useful, or salient, it will be attended to and absorbed into belief systems. Fundamentally, of course, all the selectivity processes are predicated on the existence of well-organized belief systems concerning the issue or topic in question. Obviously, this is not the case for every person on every issue, leaving considerable room for media messages to shape the beliefs and attitudes of the receivers.

SOURCES: Maxwell E. McCombs and Lee B. Becker, *Using Mass Communication Theory*, 1979; Werner J. Severin and James W. Tankard, Jr., *Communication Theories: Origins, Methods and Uses in the Mass Media*, fourth edition, 1997.

David Kennamer

"SELLING OF THE PENTAGON" was an installment of *CBS Reports*. Broadcast in February 1971, it was a hard-hitting documentary on how much the Pentagon spent on public relations and marketing. The Nixon administration and congressional conservatives characterized the program as a hatchet job and demanded an investigation. A House committee subpoenaed CBS president Frank Stanton for the network's "outtakes." Stanton refused, accusing the government of attempted censorship.

In fact, CBS had at least somewhat distorted an interview by editing together answers to different questions while making it appear the interview subject was answering a single question. The Pentagon accused CBS of distortion, and an internal network inquiry confirmed this. Still, CBS held firm publicly, maintaining its First Amendment footing. In spite of the House Judiciary Committee's recommendation to cite Stanton for contempt of Congress, the entire House voted 226–181 to reject the citation. In the wake of the investigation, the network sought to avoid future embarrassments by clarifying its standards. Amendments to the network's standards and practices manual were written and distributed to CBS news employees with specific guidelines that pertained to editing, including a section that all interviews be spontaneous and unrehearsed.

SOURCE: Sally Bedell Smith, *In All His Glory: The Life of William S. Paley*, 1990.

Joseph A. Russomanno

SENSATIONALISM. *See* Penny Press; Yellow Journalism.

SHAW, BERNARD (1940–) is the principal Washington anchor for the Cable News Network (CNN). He handles much of the network's special events coverage. He has been with CNN since its inception in 1980, having made the move from ABC because of the opportunity to anchor newscasts there. Before that, Shaw served as Latin American correspondent and bureau chief for ABC News (he is fluent in Spanish) and later as senior Capitol Hill correspondent for ABC News. Prior to that, he was with CBS News and an anchor/reporter for WNUS in Chicago. He has received extensive recognition and awards for his work, including George Foster Peabody and Emmy Awards. He acquired perhaps his greatest recognition for his coverage of the outbreak of the Persian Gulf War in January 1991. As cameras captured the image of bombs and antiaircraft fire, Shaw and CNN reporters Peter Arnett and John Holliman described what they saw and felt from their vantage point in Baghdad, Iraq, by means of a high-tech satellite telephone. Shaw's work not only from Baghdad but from other locations as well is thought to have greatly enhanced the reputation and credibility of CNN as a news source. CNN vice president Ed Turner calls Shaw "today's Walter Cronkite." Cronkite, Shaw's idol and mentor, compliments the CNN anchor in words similar to those he used to hear during his days at CBS: "He sounds authoritative and believable." A journalist first and foremost, Shaw says, "I'm not here to entertain anyone."

SOURCE: Judy Flander, "Sizing Up Shaw," *USA Today*, March 4, 1991, p. 4.

Joseph A. Russomanno

SHAW, DONALD L. (1936–) was coauthor with Max McCombs of the first agenda-setting study, done in the 1968 presidential election. When it was published in *Public Opinion Quarterly*, it stimulated interest in the topic, and there have been more than 200 agenda-setting studies since.

Shaw received his bachelor's and master's degrees from the University of North Carolina and returned there as a faculty member after completing his doctorate at Wisconsin. He was associate editor of *Journalism Quarterly* from 1983 to 1987 and then editor from 1989 to 1992. He was also coeditor with Robert Stevenson of *Foreign News and the New World Information Order*, published in 1984. It is one of the more extensive studies of foreign news coverage. (*See also* Agenda Setting.)

SOURCE: William David Sloan, *Makers of the Media Mind*, 1990.

Guido H. Stempel III

SINCLAIR, UPTON (1878–1968), novelist, social activist, and political candidate, was one of the turn-of-the-century writers to whom President Theodore Roosevelt gave the name "muckrakers." Sinclair is best remembered for his novel *The Jungle* (1906), an account of horrors in the Chicago meatpacking industry. He also wrote *Oil!* (1927), an examination of the Teapot Dome Scandal; *Boston* (1928), about the controversial Sacco-Vanzetti case; and *The Brass Check* (1919), a press criticism.

But Sinclair's most enduring legacy is the 1934 gubernatorial race in California, a campaign Heywood Broun called the dirtiest in American history. Sinclair had run for governor twice before as a socialist and lost. But in August 1934, he won the Democratic primary in a landslide, and most political analysts believed he would easily defeat his Republican opponent, Governor Frank F. Merriam, in November.

But the Republicans soon conceived a winning strategy. Sinclair had used his fame and skill as an author to launch his campaign. His opponents now turned his reckless career as a muckraker against him. He had attacked some of the most powerful interests in California—the press, the movie studios, the oil industry, the churches, and the bankers.

Advertising pioneer Albert D. Lasker directed the most sophisticated direct-mail campaign of its day, and his agency also created a series of radio dramas that predicted California under Governor Sinclair would be a kind of Siberia with palms.

The *Los Angeles Times* published an embarrassing Sinclair quote on its front page every day. Some were from his novels and were merely what a character was saying, but they were passed off as reflections of the author's beliefs.

While Sinclair got 900,000 votes, more than any previous Democratic candidate for governor, he lost by 200,000 votes. He immediately wrote another book, *I, Candidate for Governor: And How I Got Licked*. Curiously, some of the newspapers that had attacked him during the campaign paid substantial sums to publish excerpts of the book.

SOURCE: Greg Mitchell, *The Campaign of the Century—Upton Sinclair's Race for Governor of California and the Birth of Media Politics*, 1992.

Larry L. Burriss

60 MINUTES raised the curtain on a new sort of program format—the television newsmagazine. The CBS program debuted in 1968 with correspondents Mike Wallace and Harry Reasoner. It was the first to regularly devote itself to addressing only a few topics in each program, but in depth. With executive producer Don Hewitt in command, *60 Minutes* now produces 120 segments annually. Each requires an average of 6 to 10 weeks to produce. In addition to the correspondents whom the public sees each week reporting the stories, the staff consists of about 70 producers, editors, and reporters. Other *60 Minutes* alumni include Dan Rather and Diane Sawyer.

Now a ratings success in its familiar Sunday evening time slot, *60 Minutes* was not always so prosperous. It initially struggled to find an audience as well as a regular time slot. Now it is not only one of the most watched news programs but one of the most watched of *all* television programs. It built its reputation not only by producing quality journalism but also by adding a sense of drama to many of its segments. Correspondent Mike Wallace acquired a reputation of conducting "ambush interviews"—presenting evidence of wrongdoing to people and grilling them relentlessly. Visually, extreme close-ups of interviewees often add to the drama.

SOURCE: Sydney W. Head, Christopher Sterling, and Lemuel B. Schofield, *Broadcasting in America: A Survey of Electronic Media*, seventh edition, 1994.

Joseph A. Russomanno

SOUND BITES. The use of video or film clips of news subjects speaking in a segment of a television news story. In radio, the equivalent audio quotation is known as an "actuality." Studies have shown that the length of television sound bites in election campaign coverage fell from an average of more than 40 seconds in the 1960s to less than 10 seconds in the 1990s. One study of sound bites in the 1992 presidential campaign concluded that the 20-year trend of shrinking sound bites had stopped, adding "but then, due to a floor effect, it probably couldn't have shrunk much more anyway." The same study found that almost 30 percent of total story time was devoted to sound bites. Reasons for the reduction in average sound bite length can be found in the increasing sophistication of both television journalism and political campaigning. Television has become much more mediated than in its early years. Then, a journalist's role was passive; the words of news subjects dominated reports. Technical advances allowed easier editing and increasingly made the journalist the primary communicator. In the 1970s, journalism became more interpretive, and statements of politicians and candidates for public office were accepted less often at face value. Modern campaign techniques, on the other hand, have been increasingly oriented to exploiting the superficiality of television, stressing pacing and visual imagery. The result has been that political candidates package their messages in quotable bites designed for television news. Yet the television sound bites often are emphasized by the print media as well.

SOURCES: Daniel C. Hallin, "Sound Bite News: Television Coverage of Elections," *Journal of Communication*, Spring 1992; Dennis T. Lowry and Jon A. Shidler, "The Sound Bites, the Biters, and the Bitten: An Analysis of Network TV News Bias in Campaign '92," *Journalism and Mass Communication Quarterly*, Spring 1993.

Marc Edge

SOUTHERN CHRISTIAN LEADERSHIP CONFERENCE was started by Dr. Martin Luther King, Jr., during the late 1950s to organize southern black ministers for the Civil Rights movement. The SCLC, as it is commonly called, organized the protest campaigns throughout the South, including the famous marches and bus boycotts in Birmingham and Selma that drew national attention to the plight of African Americans.

These events catapulted King to the national forefront along with the Civil

Rights movement. Specifically, the SCLC looked to increase black voting, end segregation, and outlaw job discrimination based on race or culture.

Perhaps the best-known demonstration organized by the SCLC was the 1963 March on Washington at which Dr. King gave his famous "I Have a Dream" speech to thousands of Americans at the Lincoln Memorial and millions who watched at home on their televisions or listened on their radios.

After King's assassination, the SCLC suffered an identity crisis and organizational turmoil, despite the diligent efforts of Rev. Ralph D. Abernathy, King's successor. The organization is still active today but has failed to recapture its momentum of earlier years.

SOURCE: Jack Salzman, David Lionel Smith, and Cornel West, eds., *Encyclopedia of African-American Culture and History*, 1990.

Jacqueline Nash Gifford

SPANISH-LANGUAGE PRESS. The first Spanish-language newspaper, *El Misisipi*, was founded in New Orleans in 1808. Much of its content focused on international issues, and many articles were translated into English. Other Spanish-language papers were soon established elsewhere around the country, reflecting immigration from Mexico, Cuba, and Puerto Rico. This early Spanish-language press often mixed news and editorial opinion. Today, Spanish-language newspapers range from dailies to community-based weeklies. Papers circulating in the United States include some published in Latin America. A recent count lists 450 Hispanic dailies, 86 percent of which are published in Spanish. The two oldest in the continental United States are *El Diario-La Prensa*, which was established in 1913 in New York, and *La Opinion*, which was founded in 1926 in Los Angeles. The Spanish-language press emphasizes news from Latin America and local Latino issues and events. While its readers share a common language, their ethnic origins still vary geographically. Major metropolitan newspapers have delved into the Hispanic market, with special Spanish-language editions. One current example is the daily *El Neuvo Herald*, a supplement of the *Miami Herald*. In addition, Spanish-language magazines are flourishing as advertisers target the growing Latino population. In 1996, there were 222 Spanish-language magazines.

SOURCES: Rafael Chabran and Richard Chabran, "The Spanish-Language and Latino Press of the United States: Newspapers and Periodicals," in *Handbook of Hispanic Cultures in the United States: Literature and Art; The 1997 Hispanic Media Directory*.

Carol M. Liebler and B. Carol Eaton

SPIN is the word used to characterize the deliberate actions of political consultants and commentators to influence public opinion. "Spin doctors," as they are commonly called, offer their own analysis of a political event to the media. Their purpose is to interpret and offer reasons for statements and actions by political candidates or incumbents. Good spin doctors are adept at spinning the reality of an event so that the political candidate or incumbent is seen in a positive light.

SOURCE: Jay M. Shafritz, *The HarperCollins Dictionary of American Government and Politics*, 1988.

Jacqueline Nash Gifford

SPIRAL OF SILENCE. In the early 1970s, Elisabeth Noelle-Neumann coined the term ''spiral of silence'' to describe her theory of the formation of public opinion. Based on the notion that humans strive to avoid social isolation, the theory maintains that humans observe the ''climate of opinion'' by sensing whether their position on an important issue is gaining or losing favor. Willingness to speak out, the theory holds, depends on the popularity of one's position. Those sensing that their position is weakening will clam up, encouraging others to take the same view, resulting in a spiral of silence, regardless of the merits or real strength of the position. According to Noelle-Neumann, much of a person's information about public opinion comes from the mass media, thereby giving them a powerful role in the formation of public opinion. Besides being a readily available and convenient source of information about the climate of public opinion, the media are said to share three important characteristics that contribute to their influence: cumulation, ubiquity, and consonance. The media are everywhere, reinforcing the same message, day after day. Noelle-Neumann, a professor of communication research at the University of Mainz, Germany, has used her theory to predict successfully the outcome of elections in Germany since 1972.

SOURCE: Elisabeth Noelle-Neumann, *The Spiral of Silence: Public Opinion—Our Social Skin*, 1984.

Dominic L. Lasorsa

STEINEM, GLORIA MARIE (1934–) cofounded *Ms* magazine in 1972. She edited it and considered it her primary commitment for 17 years. *Ms* brought a feminist perspective to contemporary issues and events and set a trend for similar emerging magazines. The magazine offered a large ''letters to the editor'' section, which served as a public forum for those who felt they had no other outlet for commentary. The magazine was bought by Australian feminists, who then sold it to Lang Communications, which agreed to publish it as an advertising-free (reader-supported) magazine. Steinem also helped to found *New York* magazine, where she was a political columnist.

Following her graduation (magna cum laude, Phi Beta Kappa) from Smith College in 1956, she worked as a freelance writer publishing articles in newspapers. In the 1960s she was active in the women's liberation movement and was frequently chosen by the media to be its spokesperson, which earned her some resentment from the radical members of the movement because they did not regard her as representative. In the early 1970s, she was one of the founders of the National Women's Political Caucus, which encouraged women to run for political office. Through the 1970s and 1980s she continued to be active in founding other politically active women's organizations. Her books include *Moving beyond Words* (1994), *Revolution from Within* (1992), and *Outrageous Acts and Everyday Rebellions* (1983).

SOURCES: The books mentioned and Gloria Steinem, "Sex, Lies, and Advertising," *Ms*, July/August 1990.

Ardyth B. Sohn

STEPHENSON, WILLIAM (1902–1976) developed Q methodology, a quantitative approach for the scientific study of human subjectivity, with the individual as well as with populations. He devised a method of using factor analysis to assign people into attitude factor arrays that can be described and analyzed. Q methodology continues to be used in the study of attitudes toward politics and politicians, the communication processes and effects, the media, advertising, and the health care system. Stephenson described himself as "neither journalist nor creative writer . . . but just a social scientist who lets neither psychology nor sociology nor statistics get in the way of insights into [the] complex matters at issue." His long and active career took him from physics, to psychology, to communication and journalism. Born in 1902 in Durham, England, he attended the University of Durham, earning a bachelor's, master's, and Ph.D. in physics in 1927. He received a second Ph.D. in psychology in 1929. He worked in clinical psychology before joining the staff of the Institute of Experimental Psychology at Oxford, first as assistant director and later as director. Stephenson emerged from World War II with the rank of brigadier general after serving as a consultant to the Central Trade Test Board, Royal Air Force, and the British Army War Office. In 1948, Stephenson joined the psychology faculty at the University of Chicago, where he worked with Carl Rogers. He became distinguished research professor of journalism and professor of psychology at the University of Missouri in 1957, where he remained until his retirement in 1974. His landmark books include *The Study of Behavior* (1953) and *The Play Theory of Mass Communication* (1967). The Stephenson Research Center, founded in his memory at the University of Missouri, annually hosts the International Society for the Scientific Study of Subjectivity Conference to present Q methodology research from many disciplines. (*See also* Q Sort Method.)

SOURCES: Stephen R. Brown and Donald J. Brenner, *Science, Psychology, and Communication: Essays Honoring William Stephenson*, 1972; Keith Sanders, "William Stephenson: The Study of (His) Behavior," *Mass Comm Review*, December 1974.

Judith Sylvester

STEREOTYPING. The tendency to categorize or group people and to perceive or respond to people as possessing those traits and qualities that are associated with a particular category of people. Stereotypes are learned, relatively fixed, and often negative impressions of a group of people based on easily identified characteristics such as ethnicity, race, gender, or religion. The noun "stereotype" originally denoted a metal printer's mold that could exactly reproduce a printed page. Walter Lippmann used the term "stereotypes" in his 1922 book *Public Opinion* to describe "the pictures in our heads." Lippmann's concern was with the influence of stereotypes to create "pictures of groups of people that were distorted or unjustified." Lippmann wrote about the nature of language and meaning in terms of how the press shapes public opinion by portraying the "world" outside the reader's experience.

SOURCES: Melvin DeFleur, Patricia Kearney, and Timothy Plax, *Fundamentals of Human Communication*, 1991; Walter Lippmann, *Public Opinion*, 1922.

Kathleen B. Watters

STRATEGIC POLITICAL COMMUNICATION. Political communication encompasses the creation, distribution, control, use, processing, and effects of information as a political resource, whether by governments, organizations, groups, or individuals. Strategic political communication incorporates the use of sophisticated knowledge of such attributes of human behavior as attitude and preference structures, cultural tendencies, and media-use patterns. This involves knowledge of such relevant organizational behaviors as how news organizations make decisions regarding news content and how congressional committees schedule and structure hearings. The objective of strategic political communication is to shape and target messages so as to maximize their desired impact while minimizing undesired collateral effects. Social scientists have been gathering knowledge and generating theories about the nature and effects of political communication for more than half a century. Since at least the 1960s, professional practitioners of political communication have been applying this knowledge for the benefit of their clients. Initially, those clients were mostly political candidates interested in election, and the advice they received guided their decisions on advertising content, debate strategy, and the like. Beginning in 1981 with the selling of the Reagan administration's tax policy and continuing to the present, the clients have come to include advocates of special interests who seek to influence voters in referenda or to mobilize "grassroots" pressure on legislators and even governments themselves. In the 1980s, for example, the British government employed such techniques to sway public opinion in favor of maintaining American missile bases in England, and in 1990 the Bush administration used strategic communication to build popular support for an American military response following Saddam Hussein's invasion of Kuwait.

Strategic political communication is intensely research-driven. Its practitioners use content analysis of the media, demographic analysis, focus groups, and survey research to determine the precise nature of the informational environment in which they are working. Then they shape and direct their clients' messages to appeal to the desired audience and to mobilize it to take the desired action. Because of the observed effectiveness of emotional appeals, these messages have been increasingly oriented away from reason and toward emotion, a fact that, over time, produced a new style of political dialogue in countries like the United States, where strategic communication is widely practiced. Elements of this new style of dialogue include high expectations for action, a short political attention span, and a tendency to see political issues in oversimplified terms, none of which bodes especially well for sustaining a meaningful democratic political culture.

SOURCE: Jarol B. Manheim, *Strategic Public Diplomacy and American Foreign Policy,* 1993.

Jarol B. Manheim

SUPREME COURT JUSTICES. *See* Hugo Black; Louis Brandeis; William J. Brennan, Jr.; Warren Burger; William O. Douglas; William H. Rehnquist.

SYMBOLIC SPEECH. Recent U.S. Supreme Court decisions have extended First Amendment protection to ''expressive conduct''—conduct involving actions rather than words—used in such a way as to make political/social statements. In a 5–4 ruling in *Texas v. Johnson* (410 U.S. 397), the Court overturned the guilty verdict on a flag-burning case. Congress immediately answered this unpopular ruling by passing a federal law that criminalized physical mutilation of the U.S. flag. Protesters in New York and Seattle tested this law by burning flags and were arrested. In 1990 the same 5–4 majority that had overturned the conviction in *Texas v. Johnson* declared the law unconstitutional. Subsequent efforts to adopt a constitutional amendment to ban flag burning fell short in both the House and the Senate.

The opposite result had occurred in *U.S. v. O'Brien* (391 U.S. 367) two decades earlier in a case involving draft card burning. Here, the Court ruled that substantial non-First Amendment government interests were at stake, specifically, the need for speedy military induction in wartime. Using this reasoning, the Court considered this symbolic speech case content neutral, whereas *Texas v. Johnson* was content-based and hence less susceptible to government prohibition. A similar decision in *Tinker v. Des Moines* (393 U.S. 503) upheld the right of schoolchildren to wear black armbands to protest U.S. involvement in Vietnam.

Another form of symbolic speech is the protest march or peaceful demonstration, which is specifically protected under the First Amendment.

Symbolic speech thus enjoys considerable protection but is far from absolute as a right. To strike a police officer might be an expression of political protest, but it would not likely be ruled protectable symbolic speech. A number of court cases suggest that violent acts or physically preventing people from entering a building go beyond First Amendment protection.

SOURCE: Lee Bollinger, *The Tolerant Society: Freedom of Speech and Extremist Speech in America*, 1986.

Sam G. Riley

T

TARBELL, IDA (1857–1944), literary journalist, adventurer, and lecturer, was one of the late nineteenth- and early twentieth-century investigative reporters to whom President Theodore Roosevelt gave the name "muckrakers."

A founder of investigative reporting, Tarbell is best known for her 19-part series (1902–1904) in *McClure's* in which she laid out the monopolistic practices of Standard Oil. The series was later published as a book (*The History of the Standard Oil Company*) that remains a model of hard-nosed, in-depth reporting that stakes out a moral position and then provides the documentation to support that position.

The History of the Standard Oil Company also illustrated the "watchdog" role of the press because the book incensed the nation, and that led the Supreme Court later to break up the petroleum giant.

Never married herself, Tarbell nonetheless advocated that women stay home and care for their families, but she also defended the notion of equal pay for equal work. She herself attended college, worked 14 to 16 hours a day as a newspaper managing editor, and went to Paris. She also wrote a series of articles for newspapers and magazines such as *McClure's* and *American Magazine* (which she also coedited and co-owned) on such diverse topics as mining safety, child raising, and women inventors. She also wrote popular books on Napoleon and eight books on Abraham Lincoln. *All in a Day's Work*, her autobiography, was published in 1939.

SOURCES: Kathleen Brady, *Ida Tarbell: Portrait of a Muckraker*, 1984; Ida Tarbell, *All in a Day's Work*, 1939.

Larry L. Burriss

TELEVISION JOURNALISM. *See* David Brinkley; Walter Cronkite; Fred Friendly; Ted Koppel; *The McLaughlin Group*; Bill Moyers; Edward R. Mur-

row; David Sarnoff; "Selling of the Pentagon"; Bernard Shaw; *60 Minutes*;
Television's Initial Handling of Politics.

TELEVISION'S INITIAL HANDLING OF POLITICS. From the start of
regular network telecasts in 1947, television largely defined itself as an entertainment medium. Coverage of current events, including politics, absorbed relatively little of the daily schedule. The national networks had only 15-minute,
early evening newscasts and relegated other news programs to less popular time
slots. NBC and CBS waited until 1963 to expand their evening news programs
to 30 minutes. ABC did not do so until 1967.

One exception was the national party convention. Beginning in 1948, the
networks telecast most of the convention proceedings. Altruism did not explain
the networks' behavior. Advertiser demand for time was soft in the summer,
when audiences were relatively small. Furthermore, televising the conventions
spared the networks the cost of airing entertainment programming.

Television's early coverage of politics had two important characteristics. First,
it was relatively unmediated. That is, more of a politician's speech was actually
aired, uninterrupted and uncommented upon. Network news personnel were
strikingly uncritical of those they covered. Two factors explain television news'
deference to political leaders. One was a fear of the Federal Communications
Commission (FCC), which oversaw the broadcast industry. Although the FCC
rarely involved itself in the networks' operations, individual members of Congress or the executive branch could pressure the commission to do so. Then,
too, television's first generation of newscasters prized "objective" news presentations as the ultimate measure of journalistic professionalism. Many had
worked for newspapers and wire services with traditions of neutral presentation.
Moreover, critical reports invited comparisons to the more partisan newspapers
or strident radio commentators of the 1930s.

Over time, television news adopted a more detached stance toward politics.
Correspondents began assessing politicians' remarks, often in a cutting final
remark at the end of a report. Relatedly, the networks increased their mediation
of political news, greatly curtailing their coverage of national party conventions
and reducing the length of sound bites or direct quotes from individual speeches.
Comparing network coverage of presidential campaigns, Kiku Adatto found that
the average sound bite from a candidate dropped from 42.3 seconds in 1968 to
9.8 seconds 20 years later.

The shift from unmediated, deferential coverage had several explanations.
One was technological. The introduction of videotape and high-speed editing
equipment allowed television news personnel to edit and greatly increase the
tempo of individual sequences. Faster pacing, producers argued, appealed to
viewers. Then, too, the failure of America's intervention in Vietnam and the
Nixon administration scandals seemed to justify skeptical reportage; most journalists had come to regard strictly objective coverage as serving the needs of
those in power. The emergence of campaign efforts to manipulate television

news features similarly invited jaded presentations. Finally, as prominent network anchors and correspondents became celebrities, narcissism enveloped presentation. Network anchors and correspondents made themselves the center of stories.

SOURCES: Kiku Adatto, *Picture Perfect: The Art and Artifice of Public Image Making*, 1993; Edward Bliss, Jr., *Now the News: The Story of Broadcast Journalism*, 1991.

James L. Baughman

THIRD-PERSON EFFECT is an increasingly popular theory of public opinion enunciated by sociologist W. Philips Davison in 1983. The effect consists of two components: (1) a perceptual component that predicts people perceive the mass media to be more effective in influencing other people than themselves and (2) an action component that predicts people act on this perception to support restrictions (i.e., censorship) on the media to ''protect'' vulnerable others from harmful consequences. The perceptual component was summarized in an oft-cited quotation by Davison that ''in the view of those trying to evaluate the effects of a communication, its greatest impact will not be on 'me' or 'you,' but on 'them'—the third person.'' The perceptual component enjoys a good deal of empirical support. Only recently, however, have researchers begun to investigate the action component. Two possible political consequences of the third-person effect are that policymakers, elites, and even the general public will support media restrictions to ''protect'' the public from perceived harmful messages (e.g., sex and violence) and that policymakers will take political action in response to media reports of social ills that they anticipate will mobilize the public to demand that the ills be corrected. Few empirical studies have extended the third-person effect to elections. One such study by Rucinski and Salmon during the 1988 presidential campaign found support for the perceptual component. They reported that people perceived five types of media content about the election (news, political ads, negative political ads, debates, and polls) to exert greater influence on other people's voting decisions than on their own. The researchers, however, did not find the predicted support for media restrictions.

SOURCES: W. Phillips Davison, ''The Third-Person Effect in Communication,'' *Public Opinion Quarterly*, Spring 1983; Richard Perloff, ''Third-Person Effect Research, 1983–1992: A Review and Synthesis,'' *International Journal of Public Opinion Research* 5, 1993; Dianne Rucinski and Charles T. Salmon, ''The 'Other' as the Vulnerable Voter: A Study of the Third-Person Effect in the 1988 U.S. Presidential Campaign,'' *International Journal of Public Opinion Research* 2, 1990.

Michael B. Salwen and Paul D. Driscoll

THOMAS, CLARENCE is the second black justice of the U.S. Supreme Court. Hearings on his nomination concluded October 15, 1991, with the closest U.S. Senate vote (52–48) for a U.S. Supreme Court justice in the twentieth century.

Thomas, the 106th U.S. Supreme Court justice, replaced Thurgood Marshall. When President George Bush's nominee began Senate Judiciary Committee hearings on September 10, he was pressed by the committee and news media for his views on abortion, minority preference programs, and the concept of natural law. However, he appeared headed for easy confirmation until a former female aide, Anita F. Hill, publicly accused him on October 6 of sexual harassment from 1981 to 1983. According to reports that day in the *New York Times* and on National Public Radio, the Senate Judiciary Committee staff first heard of the charges in an affidavit submitted to them September 10 by Hill (and later leaked to the press). Hill, a University of Oklahoma law professor, said Thomas had asked her out when she worked for him at the Department of Education and at the Equal Employment Opportunity Commission. When she refused to date him, she said he began talking about sexual acts he had seen in pornographic movies. A political mud fight erupted after the Hill charges were made public. Republican legislators accused the Democrats of leaking the affidavit to the press, seven female Democratic members of the House lobbied male colleagues in the Senate to delay confirmation, and the all-male Senate Judiciary Committee was pressured by women's groups and female legislators to postpone its October 8 vote. At 8 P.M. on October 8, the Senate agreed to delay the vote. The October 11–14 Senate Judiciary Committee hearings featuring testimony by both Hill and Thomas were broadcast over radio and television and earned high ratings. An October 13 poll by CBS and the *New York Times* showed that 45 percent favored Thomas' confirmation but that 58 percent believed his version of the events discussed in the hearings.

SOURCES: *Facts on File, World News Digest* 51, 1991; *New York Times*, selected stories, September 10 to October 15, 1991.

Ardyth B. Sohn

THOMAS, HELEN (1920–) has covered the White House beat for more than 40 years and paved the way for female journalists in a traditional man's-only world. She was born in Kentucky to Lebanese parents who owned a grocery store. They uprooted the family and moved to Detroit. Thomas credits her parents' encouragement of all the children to be successful in helping her seek out her career. She took a strong interest in journalism in high school and graduated with a degree in English from Wayne State University.

Her break into professional journalism came when she landed the position of copy girl at the *Washington Daily News*. She was quickly promoted to junior reporter only to lose her job. This proved to be a lucky break because she landed a job as copy writer for the radio wire of United Press International. She covered women's topics and soon was permitted to write a column about Washington's influential people. In 1955, she began to cover the Department of Justice.

As she gained experience and confidence, she boldly followed Washington's elite, including the presidents, always looking for the rare opportunity to ask a question when they least expected it. She built a reputation for asking tough, fair questions, demanding clarification in common language. She felt compelled to capture and report with accuracy the real personalities and beliefs of some of Washington's most influential people.

She has covered eight presidents and has received numerous journalism awards and honorary degrees. A self-described feminist, she works hard to reach out to young women journalists.

SOURCES: *Current Biography*, 1994; William A. Taft, *Encyclopedia of 20th Century Journalists*, 1984.

Jacqueline Nash Gifford

THOMPSON, HUNTER S. (1937–). The originator of gonzo journalism, Thompson influenced a generation of political writers with his participatory, high-intensity, spontaneous reporting. It abandoned objectivity and placed the reporter at the center of the story, usually in an extreme situation and adversarial to the subject. Thompson's literary persona is that of a hyperstimulated outlaw prophet in the vanguard of the Apocalypse. His theme is the meaninglessness of American life, especially as it is reflected in the political subculture. "I have a fatal compulsion to find a higher sense in things that make no sense at all," he writes.

After working for several newspapers, including the *New York Herald Tribune* and the *National Observer*, Thompson joined *Rolling Stone* in 1970 and stayed for five years. Political corruption, according to Kaul, "operates as a metaphor in Thompson's works for the degradation of American culture. Deception, fraud, greed, hubris, lying, and relentless perjury, among many others—all are indicted and condemned in an explosively prophetic moral rhetoric."

His best-known books are *Fear and Loathing: On the Campaign Trail '72* and *The Great Shark Hunt: Strange Tales from a Strange Time*, but he wrote six other books. His work has also appeared in leading magazines.

SOURCES: Robert Draper, *Rolling Stone Magazine: The Uncensored History*, 1990; Arthur J. Kaul, "Hunter S. Thompson," in Thomas B. Connery, ed., *A Sourcebook of American Literary Journalism: Representative Writers in an Emerging Genre*, 1992.

Paul Ashdown

TIME **MAGAZINE** was the first successful newsmagazine in America. It was founded in February 1923 by Briton Hadden and Henry R. Luce, two young Yale graduates with modest journalistic experience, but no absence of self-confidence. Hadden and Luce sought a unique publication, a weekly synthesis of the news. *Time* would present "a final report on a whole world of news," organized into different entries each containing no more than 400 words. These, in turn, were written with a distinctive style and omniscient point of view. Presentation was all-important. *Time* initially had no reporters—only staff members who based their entries on newspaper clippings.

Over the next 15 years, *Time* became one of the most influential publications in America, despite competition from two rival news weeklies, *Newsweek* and *U.S. News*, both of which were established in 1933. Journalists in particular admired and started to imitate *Time*'s knowing style. Washington-based correspondents in the mid-1930s, one survey found, read *Time* more than any other periodical. "*Time* has made itself indispensable," one magazine editor confessed in 1937.

Time's circulation rose from 243,000 in 1929 to slightly more than 700,000 in 1938. Readers tended to be cosmopolitan members of the middle and upper class in medium-size communities who sought a master summary of the week's news. Many turned to *Time* because their local newspapers, defining news as an endless series of individual events, resisted carrying news analyses or weekly news summaries. The complications of 1930s America—the Great Depression, the subsequent expansion of federal government, and the crises in Europe and Asia—created a need, particularly among the middle class, for new types of news presentation. Some began turning to the analytical news columns, pioneered by Walter Lippmann, and the weekly news reviews many larger newspapers began in their Sunday editions, partly because of *Time*'s success.

Time's politics eventually undermined its credibility with many readers. At first, the periodical was more smart-alecky than partisan. Any bias seemed slight when compared to the stridency of many dailies. But in the late 1930s, Luce, who had assumed effective control of the magazine following Hadden's death in 1929, started to insist that his publication echo his internationalist, liberal Republican views. *Time* gradually became an extension of Luce's politics. By 1960, *Newsweek* began to compete effectively for readers and influence by positioning itself somewhat to the left of *Time*. By then, however, television news had begun to undermine the position of all newsmagazines. Readers no longer had to rely on them for an understanding of an ever-complex world; network television newscasts appeared to present the same synthesis, every day.

SOURCE: James L. Baughman, *Henry R. Luce and the Rise of the American News Media*, 1987.

James L. Baughman

TIMES MIRROR CENTER. *See* Pew Research Center for the People and the Press.

TRACKING POLLS. This refers to a series of polls over a period of time to see how effective a candidate's campaign is, how the public is responding on various issues, and the impact of events during the campaign. Results of tracking polls become a major basis for changing the campaign, abandoning some issues, and raising other new issues. They are done by the candidate or the party, and results are released to the public on a limited and selective basis.

SOURCE: Erik Barnouw, *International Encyclopedia of Communications*, 1989.

Guido H. Stempel III

TRUMAN, HARRY S. *See* "Dewey Defeats Truman"; One-Party Press.

TRUMAN FIRING OF MacARTHUR. In America's 200-plus years of military history, it has not been uncommon during wartime for military commanders to be relieved from duty. The most famous case of a general's being relieved of his command is President Harry S Truman's firing of General Douglas MacArthur, the supreme commander of United Nations forces during the Korean War. There are several theories about why MacArthur was fired. The most widely accepted is that MacArthur was sacked because of his arrogant and insubordinate attitude. Truman's policy was to contain the war, and despite the presence of large numbers of communist Chinese troops in Korea, he ruled out bombing China. MacArthur disagreed and was very vocal about it.

Another theory is that Truman's decisions about MacArthur and the Korean War strategy were made with significant consideration of the United States' diplomatic relations with Great Britain. After World War II, Britain was physically and economically devastated. It was dependent on the United States for defense from the communist bloc. This officially began with the creation of the North Atlantic Treaty Organization (NATO) in 1949. Britain hoped that the United States would deploy a large force in Western Europe. Britain was afraid that if the Korean War expanded, the United States would decrease its troops in Western Europe. The possibility of war between the United States and China also concerned Britain because Britain had commercial interests in China. Britain had, in fact, recognized the government of communist China, which the United States had not done, and was pushing for communist China to be in the United Nations, which the United States opposed. All this led to intense anti-MacArthur sentiment in Britain. MacArthur criticized Britain's policies and advocated use of nuclear weapons against the communist Chinese and the use of Nationalist Chinese troops to invade the China mainland.

SOURCES: Laura Belmonte, "Anglo-American Relations and the Dismissal of MacArthur," *Diplomatic History*, Fall 1995; Roy K. Flint, *Korean War*, 1995.

J. Sean McCleneghan

U

USES AND GRATIFICATIONS. *See* Elihu Katz.

U.S. NEWS was started by David Lawrence in 1933, 10 years after the start of *Time*. Lawrence was already a well-known political reporter and columnist. In 1926 he had started *U.S. Daily*, which carried full texts of government announcements, court decisions, and documents. He dropped that when he started *U.S. News*. Because he thought there was a need for a magazine devoted entirely to world news, he started *World Report* in 1946. The two publications were combined into *U.S. News and World Report* in 1948.

Lawrence's focus always was on political and economic news, and *U.S. News* has never dealt with entertainment or human interest. It thus is a more serious magazine than either *Time* or *Newsweek*. It has always lagged behind those two in circulation, but currently it has 2.3 million subscribers. That is slightly more than half of *Time*'s circulation and about a million less than *Newsweek*'s.

While the magazine is generally viewed as conservative, it has always sought to be objective. Studies of its coverage of presidential elections have found it to be in the middle between *Time* and *Newsweek* in favorability to the Republican candidate.

SOURCES: Philip S. Cook, Douglas Gomery, and Lawrence W. Lichty, eds., *The Future of News: Television-Newspapers-Wire Services-News Magazines*, 1992; Theodore Peterson, *Magazines in the Twentieth Century*, 1964.

Guido H. Stempel III

V

VOTER NEED FOR ORIENTATION. Partisan orientation has consistently been demonstrated to be the major factor that structures voting decisions. However, the increasing shift toward more independent voting habits among the American electorate since the 1950s has resulted in higher levels of uncertainty about voter decisions during election campaigns. Research by David Weaver and Maxwell McCombs has indicated that the media have considerable influence on the decisions of independent voters because of their greater "need for orientation," as they termed it, during election campaigns.

Weaver and McCombs conceptualized the need for orientation as a multidimensional variable related to voters' interest in an election campaign and how uncertain they are about how they will vote. Those with high interest in a campaign coupled with a high degree of uncertainty about their vote choice are classified as having a high need for orientation. Moderate need for orientation is indicated by either high interest or low uncertainty or low interest and high uncertainty. Voters with low interest and uncertainty are rated as low in need for orientation.

Weaver and McCombs have found that voters with a high need for orientation tend to discuss more often and consider important campaign issues receiving the heaviest coverage in the media, especially in the later stages of campaigns. Furthermore, voters high in need for orientation are more likely than other voters to claim the issues are more important than candidate image or party affiliation in determining how they vote.

SOURCES: David H. Weaver, "Political Issues and Voter Need for Orientation," in Donald L. Shaw and Maxwell E. McCombs, eds., *The Emergence of Political Issues: The Agenda-Setting Function of the Press*, 1973; David H. Weaver, Doris Graber, Maxwell E. McCombs, and Chaim H. Eyal, *Media Agenda-Setting in a Presidential Election: Issues, Images and Interest*, 1981.

Kim A. Smith and Milena Karagyazova

W

WASHINGTON POST. As befits the major newspaper in the country's capital, the *Post* is recognized as providing perhaps the best coverage of the federal government. It was not always so. The *Post*, founded in 1877 as a partisan Democratic newspaper, did not achieve eminence in its first 70 years. It was not a great newspaper when Philip Graham took over as publisher in 1946, but he started it on its way with the help of a great managing editor, Russell Wiggins. Graham created the paper's first foreign bureaus, one in London and the other in New Delhi. He encouraged investigative reporting and fought Senator Joseph McCarthy's smear campaign.

When Graham committed suicide in 1963, his wife Katharine took over the paper. She brought in Ben Bradlee, and he rose to the position of executive editor. He made major contributions to both the appearance and the coverage of the paper.

The *Post* is undoubtedly best known for its Watergate coverage. The story was in their town, and their coverage kept it alive to the point that Richard Nixon was forced to resign as president.

SOURCES: Michael Emery, *America's Leading Daily Newspapers*, 1983; John C. Merrill and Harold A. Fisher, *The World's Great Dailies*, 1980.

Guido H. Stempel III

WATERGATE. This upscale Washington, D.C., apartment complex will forever be linked by name to the scandal that toppled the presidency of Richard Nixon in 1974. A break-in interrupted at Democratic National Committee headquarters in the complex on June 17, 1972, led to the sequence of events that ended in Nixon's resignation slightly more than two years later. The five burglars, arrested with electronic "bugs," were tried and convicted in early 1973 after Nixon had been reelected in a landslide over Democratic challenger George

McGovern. Also found guilty of wiretapping and conspiracy were G. Gordon Liddy, chief lawyer for the Committee to Re-Elect the President (CREEP), and former White House consultant E. Howard Hunt, Jr. A series of investigative reports by *Washington Post* reporters Carl Bernstein and Bob Woodward detailed links between the burglars and Nixon's reelection bid as well other "dirty tricks" by CREEP. Revelations led to the resignations of Nixon's chief of staff, H. R. Haldeman, and domestic affairs adviser John Erlichman. A special prosecutor was named, and a Senate Select Committee on Presidential Campaign Activities began televised hearings. The testimony of White House counsel John Dean implicated Nixon in a cover-up of the Watergate burglary, and tape recordings of conversations in the Oval Office were revealed. The tapes proved Nixon's knowledge and complicity in the cover-up. His resignation August 9, 1974, came after impeachment motions were instituted in the House of Representatives.

SOURCES: Sam Ervin, Jr., *The Whole Truth: The Watergate Conspiracy*, 1980; Michael Schudson, *Watergate in American Memory*, 1992.

Marc Edge

WEAVER, DAVID H. (1946–) is the Roy W. Howard Professor of Journalism at Indiana University, where he has been on the faculty since 1974. A graduate of Indiana, he received his master's and doctorate from the University of North Carolina.

He has done important work in the role of agenda setting and who sets the agenda in presidential campaigns. He and Indiana colleague G. C. Wilhoit have done the definitive study of newspeople in the United States. The study deals with political leaning of newspeople as well as their perspective of their role.

Weaver and Wilhoit also coauthored *Newsroom Guide to Polls and Surveys*, an important reference source for newspeople who deal with surveys.

SOURCES: David H. Weaver and G. C. Wilhoit, *The American Journalist in the 1990s: U.S. News People at the End of an Era*, 1996; *Who's Who in America*, 1997–1998.

Guido H. Stempel III

WESTLEY, BRUCE H. (1915–1990) was coauthor of the Westley-MacLean model, which first appeared in *Journalism Quarterly* in the Winter 1957 issue. The model emphasizes purposive communication or the notion that communication decisions are not random but are made for a reason. He also was the founding editor of *Journalism Monographs*, which first appeared in 1966. He remained editor until 1982. He also served as associate editor of *Journalism Quarterly* with responsibility for theory and methodology articles from 1963 to 1973. Part of his contribution to communication research was his copyediting skill exercised on behalf of both those publications. He also wrote the most successful editing textbook of his era.

Westley played a major part in the two leading communication research texts. He wrote a chapter and did much of the editing in *Introduction to Mass Communications Research* (1958), edited by Ralph O. Nafziger and David Manning White. He was coeditor and had a chapter in *Research Methods in Mass Communication* (1981). He received the Paul J. Deutschmann Award for contributions to research from the Association for Education in Journalism and Mass Communication in 1985.

Westley was a faculty member in journalism at the University of Wisconsin from 1946 to 1969 and chair of the Department of Journalism and a faculty member at Kentucky from 1969 to 1983.

SOURCE: Edwin Emery and Joseph P. McKerns, "AEJMC: 75 Years in the Making," *Journalism Monograph* 104, November 1987.

Guido H. Stempel III

WHITE, THEODORE H. (1915–1986) created a genre of political "insider" reporting with his series of books *The Making of the President*, which chronicled four successive presidential campaigns, beginning with John F. Kennedy's victory over Richard Nixon in 1960. But while his Pulitzer Prize-winning *The Making of the President: 1960* was a revelation for its style and insight, rumblings about his lack of objectivity and patriotic sentimentality grew through his 1964 and 1968 books into criticisms of hero-worship and undisguised sympathy for the Establishment. Rather than write the fifth such book in 1976, White instead penned his autobiography, *In Search of History*, which was hailed as a minor classic. In it, White recalled his humble beginnings in Boston, his coverage of the China front in World War II for *Time* magazine, and his coverage of postwar Europe, first for the Overseas News Agency and later for *Reporter* magazine. White's last book, *America in Search of Itself: The Making of the President, 1956–1980*, examined the administrations of U.S. presidents from Eisenhower to Reagan.

SOURCE: *Contemporary Authors* (CD-ROM).

Marc Edge

WHITE HOUSE OFFICE OF COMMUNICATION was established by President Richard Nixon. It serves as a tool of presidential policy by promoting the presidential agenda in every way possible. The office replaced the press secretary as the main link of the White House to the media. It is a public relations arm of the White House, with the aim of setting the public agenda in line with executive policy. The office oversees the dissemination of policy and tries to ensure that the entire presidential team follows the same policy. The public agenda is used to fashion presidential statements. That public agenda is determined by means of focus groups and opinion polls. The office generates sound bites for presidential use to maximize every public occasion to further policy.

SOURCE: John Anthony Maltse, *Spin Control, The White House Office of Communication and the Management of Presidential News,* 1992.

Pamela J. Shoemaker and Michael J. Breen

WOODWARD, ROBERT U. (1943), **AND BERNSTEIN, CARL** (1944). In an age when national television anchors and reporters are the media stars, Carl Bernstein and Bob Woodward were a throwback to the turn of the century, when newspaper reporters' names were household words. They were little-known local reporters for the *Washington Post* when a burglary was foiled at Democratic National Committee headquarters one night in June 1972. Woodward, a Yale graduate, had turned to reporting after a five-year stint as a navy officer and turned down a Harvard Law School admission opportunity. Bernstein was a University of Maryland dropout when he started reporting. They teamed up in what must be one of the most persistent examples of reporting in modern journalism history. The tentacles of the break-in were tracked relentlessly. They were the first to reveal that the Watergate burglars were connected to Howard Hunt, an ex-Central Intelligence Agency (CIA) operative. Their reporting tactics weren't new, it is generally agreed, but their persistence and doggedness were matchless. When the story began to lead to the White House, *Post* executive editor Ben Bradlee made the decision to keep the Woodward-Bernstein team on the story rather than turning it over to the national reporters. Although no one credits them with single-handedly toppling President Richard Nixon, most observers credit their stories with keeping the pressure on the White House that led to the revelations by one of the burglars, James McCord, of the high-level involvement. The movie version of the book *All the President's Men,* which followed the articles, further ensured the team a place in the American consciousness for decades to come. This book was followed by one on the period before Nixon's resignation, *The Final Days.* Of this work, Nixon said, ''I respect [some members of the press]; but for those who write history as fiction on third-hand knowledge, I have nothing but contempt. And I will never forgive them. Never.''

The sourcing of these two books, as well as others that have followed from the pens of Woodward and Bernstein, has sometimes stirred journalistic controversy. For example, Woodward's solo work, *Veil: The Secret Wars of the CIA, 1981–1987,* often lacks direct clear attribution, leading to nonfiction that reads like fiction, in a now-you-are-in-the-room-with-the-political-greats approach.

The two have gone their separate, but productive, ways. Woodward is still on the *Post* staff, now as an editor. Bernstein works primarily as an independent author.

SOURCE: Bob Woodward and Carl Berstein, *All the President's Men,* 1974.

Wallace B. Eberhard

Y

YELLOW JOURNALISM is a name for sensational journalism with heavy emphasis on human interest and relatively little on political, social, or economic issues. The term was coined to describe the journalism of Joseph Pulitzer and William Randolph Hearst at the turn of the century, during their heated competition in New York City. The word "yellow" was borrowed from a popular cartoon character called the "Yellow Kid," which was originated by Putlizer in the *New York World* and copied by Hearst. (*See also* William Randolph Hearst; Joseph Pulitzer.)

SOURCE: Kathleen Thompson Hill and Gerald N. Hill, *Real Life Dictionary of American Politics*, 1994.

Guido H. Stempel III

Z

ZENGER, JOHN PETER (1697–1748). In today's terms, a media event earned John Peter Zenger a place in history. He was a 13-year-old, fatherless German immigrant when he arrived in New York with others from the Palatines in 1710, part of a group sent by Queen Anne. Indentured as an apprentice to William Bradford, he learned the printing trade. He settled in New York in 1722, married, and in 1725 began a partnership with Bradford, before becoming independent within a short time. A middle-class revolt against the British administration led to Zenger's being set up as editor of an antigovernment journal, the *New York Weekly Journal.* The content was undoubtedly penned by his supporters, irritated by the arbitrary removal of Lewis Morris from a chief justiceship by Governor William Cosby. Although his own writing lacked the quality of his better-educated backers, it was full of spirit. More important, as publisher of the newspaper, he was legally responsible for its contents. In April 1735 he was charged with libel, specifically for his articles attacking the opinions and actions of the governor. He was jailed, and his supporters could have made bail but didn't. He communicated with his wife and others through the jail door. A prominent Philadelphia lawyer, Andrew Hamilton, mounted a brilliant and effective challenge to prevailing law that eventually freed Zenger. Despite the orders of the judge, Hamilton urged the jury to consider the truth of Zenger's statements as a defense against the libel charge. The jury did just that, despite the lack of legal precedent, and found for Zenger. Zenger became a celebrated figure in colonial America and was named public printer for both New York and New Jersey.

SOURCES: Cathy Covert, " 'Passion Is Ye Prevailing Motive': The Feud behind the Zenger Case," *Journalism Quarterly,* Spring 1973; Livingston Rutherford, *John Peter Zenger, His Press, His Trial, and Bibliography of Zenger Imprints,* 1968.

Wallace B. Eberhard

Selected Bibliography

Rather than offering the usual lengthy bibliography consisting of items of unequal importance, we decided to offer a short, guided tour through selected literature of political communication. Taken together, the items we discuss here offer a reasonable overview of the field. They cover the major areas and include the more profound and succinct thought of the field and offer the reader a useful perspective on the field. Individually, they all have something important to say, and each will increase the reader's understanding of the field.

While we recognize that journal articles are on the cutting edge of knowledge in a field, we have focused on books because books bring together various studies into a single context. The result is a better overall perspective because the connection between studies is made clearer.

Serious study of political communication should begin with reading Walter Lippmann's *Public Opinion*. Written three-quarters of a century ago in the context of World War I, it deals with the basics of political communication, which have not changed. Lippmann tells us that reality is the "pictures in our heads," and he warns that we don't believe what we see; we see what we believe. His discussion of stereotypes is essential for anyone who wants to understand political communication. He is not talking simply about racial, ethnic, or sexual stereotypes, but rather the wide range of beliefs we have and hold as stereotypes. The public, the media, and the politicians all traffic in stereotypes, and consequently the truth suffers.

Another important book about basics involved in political communication is *Four Theories of the Press* by Fred Siebert, Theodore Peterson, and Wilbur Schramm. It explains the relationship between the media and the political system. The four theories are authoritarian, communist, libertarian, and social responsibility. Authoritarian governments control the media by censorship and licensing. Communist governments control the media by putting them in the hands of party members, thus infiltrating the media. A libertarian government does not control or license the media but depends on truth emerging from the marketplace of ideas. Social responsibility theory says that the media must operate in the best interest of society. Note that it is society, not the party in power, as many politicians would have it. That's what distinguishes the social responsibility from the communist theory. Others have suggested that there should be more than four theories, but we feel that every press system fits into one of these four theories.

These two books provide a basis for understanding what political communication is all about. Several others come to mind, first, because they describe the system in action, and second, because they are the most widely read books about political communication. One is Theodore White's *The Making of the President, 1960*. It was the first of four books that White wrote about presidential campaigns, and he then wrote something of a wrap-up entitled *America in Search of Itself: The Making of the President, 1956–1980*. However, the 1960 campaign book received the most favorable critical acclaim. The feeling was that it told more, perhaps because the candidates and their staffs were not aware how closely White was watching in 1960. After that book, however, they had to expect that he would be watching.

Another best-seller was Joe McGinniss' *The Selling of the President*. McGinniss observed the 1968 campaign of Richard Nixon from inside the campaign staff. He described how the staff sold Nixon to the American public by manipulating his image and creating the illusion that rehearsed events were spontaneous. It is a case study; all candidates and all campaigns are not like this. Yet McGinniss has provided an inside view of the process that no one else has provided.

Nearly as popular was *The Boys on the Bus*, by Timothy Crouse. He was with the press during the 1972 presidential primary. His theme was that the reporters practiced pack journalism, writing the same stories with the same leads and the same emphasis. His argument is compelling, but anyone who reads this book also should read Carolyn Martindale's article in the summer 1984 *Journalism Quarterly*. In a study of coverage of 14 events by two wire services and five major newspapers in the 1980 campaign, she found little evidence of pack journalism.

The claim of one-party press by Democratic candidate Adlai Stevenson in 1952 and similar claims by other losing candidates have inspired numerous studies of campaign coverage. Many are limited in time frame and media studied, but few have found evidence of bias in coverage. Two extensive studies became books. Richard Hofstetter's *Bias in the News* is a study of coverage of the 1972 campaign by the Associated Press, the *Chicago Tribune*, the *Washington Post*, and the three television networks. He found little evidence of partisan bias.

The Media in the 1984 and 1988 Presidential Campaigns, by Guido H. Stempel III and John W. Windhauser, reports on studies of 17 major newspapers, the newsmagazines, and the three television networks in those two elections. It also includes analysis of editorials and public opinion polls in Louisville and Chicago to assess the impact of editorial endorsements. That study found issue coverage meager but did not conclude that the coverage was biased in either campaign in any of these media.

Advertising is part of presidential campaigns, too, and Kathleen Hall Jamieson has contributed two important books in this area—*Packaging the Presidency* and *Dirty Politics*. The former deals with criticism of presidential campaign advertising. The latter is notable in that it offers some hope for the voter in learning how to cope with the distortion created by campaign ads.

Sidney Kraus has compiled two important books about another aspect of presidential campaigns—debates. The first was *The Great Debates: Background, Perspectives, Effects*. It includes background about the staging of the debates, but, more important, it reports on studies of the effects of the Kennedy-Nixon debates. It is thus probably the largest collection of data on debate effects. *Televised Political Debates* provides an overview of debates at a later date after they have become established in the campaign routine.

There are, of course, political campaigns besides those for the presidency. Not a great deal of research has been done on such campaigns, however. The best is *Covering Campaigns*, by Peter Clarke and Susan H. Evans. It analyzes newspaper coverage of 82 congressional races in the 1978 election and documents the advantage that incumbents have in such races.

Two books that look at aspects of campaigns other than coverage are *The Rise of Political Consultants*, by Larry Sabato, and *Candidates, Consultants and Campaigns*, by Frank I. Luntz. Both deal with the proliferation of consultants in the last two decades and the implications of this for campaigns.

Political communication is about more than elections, and coverage of presidents is a continuing process. *The Press and the Presidency*, by John W. Tebbel and Sarah Miles Watts, traces presidential coverage through the years, showing what happened in each presidency and how coverage has evolved.

In addition to books on media coverage, there are some important ones on theory and research in the field. An early classic is *The People's Choice*, by Paul F. Lazarsfeld, Bernard Berelson, and Hazel Gaudet. Better known as the "Erie County study," this dealt with voter decision making in a bellwether Ohio county in the 1940 presidential election. It concluded that media have little effect on voters' choices. More recent works in the field have concluded otherwise, and the reader might find it useful to consult the chapter by Steven H. Chaffee and John L. Hochheimer in *Mass Communication Review Yearbook*, volume 5, which places this study in the larger perspective of 40 years of research.

The Effects of Mass Communication, by Joseph Klapper, important as a major compilation of early research in the field, also offered the conclusion that media effects were minimal.

Agenda-setting research successfully challenged that point of view, and there are several books we would suggest on that topic. One is *Agenda Setting: Read-*

ings on Media, Public Opinion, and Policymaking, edited by Maxwell Mc-Combs and David Protess. It includes the original study of McCombs and Donald Shaw that touched off the interest in agenda setting a quarter of a century ago. It also has a number of other studies that have appeared in communication journals and thus offers a substantial run of data about agenda setting.

If you would rather read a series of syntheses looking into varied aspects of agenda setting, then you should read *Communication and Democracy: Exploring the Intellectual Frontiers in Agenda-Setting Theory*, edited by McCombs, Shaw, and David Weaver.

Agenda setting assumed at the outset that media set the agenda. Other research suggested politicians may set it. Yet, on reflection, the public may set it and apparently has set it in some instances. This aspect of agenda setting is dealt with in *The Public and the National Agenda*, by Wayne Wanta.

Another area of research is covered in *The Main Source: Learning from Television News*, by John Robinson and Mark Levy. While surveys show television as the most frequently named medium as the main source, this book makes it clear that television is not an effective source of political information. Its contribution apparently has to do with images.

The theory of cognitive dissonance has generated a great deal of empirical data. It begins with Leon Festinger's book, *Theory of Cognitive Dissonance*. Brief and readable, it makes a lot of things that happen in political communication make sense.

For an overall view of theory and research, we would suggest *Communication Theories*, by Werner J. Severin and James W. Tankard. It deals with more than political communication, but the book is organized in a way that makes issues related to political communication easy to find.

Beyond this list is the frontier of political communication found in such journals as *Journalism and Mass Communication Quarterly, Journal of Communication, Political Communication*, and *Public Opinion Quarterly*.

REFERENCES

Steven H. Chaffee and John L. Hochheimer, "The Beginnings of Political Communication Research in the United States: Origins of the Limited Effects Model," in Michael Gurevitch and Mark R. Levy, eds., *Mass Communication Review Yearbook*, Vol. 5 (Beverly Hills, Calif.: Sage, 1985).

Peter Clarke and Susan H. Evans, *Covering Campaigns: Journalism in Congressional Elections* (Stanford, Calif.: Stanford University Press, 1983).

Timothy Crouse, *The Boys on the Bus* (New York: Random House, 1973).

Leon Festinger, *Theory of Cognitive Dissonance* (Stanford, Calif.: Stanford University Press, 1957).

Richard Hofstetter, *Bias in the News* (Columbus: Ohio State University Press, 1976).

Kathleen Hall Jamieson, *Dirty Politics: Deception, Distraction, and Democracy* (New York: Oxford University Press, 1992).

Kathleen Hall Jamieson, *Packaging the Presidency: A History and Criticism of Campaign Advertising*, third edition (New York: Oxford University Press, 1996).

Joseph T. Klapper, *The Effects of Mass Communication* (New York: Free Press, 1960).

Sidney Kraus, *Televised Political Debates and Public Policy* (Hillsdale, N.J.: Erlbaum, 1988).

Sidney Kraus, *The Great Debates: Background, Perspective, Effects* (Bloomington: Indiana University Press, 1962).

Paul F. Lazarsfeld, Bernard Berelson, and Hazel Gaudet, *The People's Choice* (New York: Columbia University Press, 1948).

Walter Lippmann, *Public Opinion* (New York: Macmillan, 1922).

Frank I. Luntz, *Candidates, Consultants and Campaigns* (Oxford, England: Basil Blackwell, 1988).

Carolyn Martindale, ''Newspaper and Wire Service Leads in Coverage of the 1980 Campaign,'' *Journalism Quarterly*, Summer 1984.

Maxwell E. McCombs, Donald L. Shaw, and David Weaver, eds., *Communication and Democracy: Exploring the Intellectual Frontiers in Agenda-Setting Theory* (Mahwah, N.J.: Erlbaum, 1997).

Joe McGinniss, *The Selling of the President* (New York: Pocket Books, 1970).

David L. Protess and Maxwell McCombs, eds., *Agenda Setting: Readings on Media, Public Opinion, and Policymaking* (Hillsdale, N.J.: Erlbaum, 1991).

John P. Robinson and Mark Levy, *The Main Source: Learning from Television News* (Newbury Park, Calif.: Sage, 1986).

Larry Sabato, *The Rise of Political Consultants* (New York: Basic Books, 1981).

Werner J. Severin and James W. Tankard, Jr., *Communication Theories*, fourth edition (White Plains, N.Y.: Longman, 1997).

Fred S. Siebert, Theodore Peterson, and Wilbur Schramm, *Four Theories of the Press* (Urbana: University of Illinois Press, 1956).

Guido H. Stempel III and John W. Windhauser, eds., *The Media in the 1984 and 1988 Presidential Campaigns* (Westport, Conn.: Greenwood Press, 1991).

John W. Tebbel and Sarah Miles Watts, *The Press and the Presidents* (New York: Oxford University Press, 1985).

Wayne Wanta, *The Public and the National Agenda* (Mahwah N.J.: Erlbaum, 1997).

Theodore H. White, *America in Search of Itself: The Making of the President 1956–1980* (New York: Harper and Row, 1982).

Theodore H. White, *The Making of the President, 1960* (New York: Atheneum, 1962).

Index

Page numbers in **boldface** type refer to main entries in the dictionary.

Abrams v. United States, **3**
Adams, John, 6
Adams, Samuel, **3–4**
Agenda-setting, **4**. *See also* Lippmann,
  Walter; McCombs, Maxwell; Shaw,
  Donald
Agnew, Spiro, **4**
Ailes, Roger, **5**
Al-Amin, Jamil Abdullah, 15–16
Alien and Sedition Acts of 1798, **5–6**,
  131
Alsop, Joseph and Stewart, **6**
American Association of Retired Persons
  (AARP), **6**
American Civil Liberties Union (ACLU),
  7
American Federation of Labor–Congress
  of Industrial Organizations (AFL–CIO),
  7
Anderson, Jack, **7**
Armstrong, Bess Furman, **7–8**
Arnett, Peter, **8–9**. *See also* Cable News
  Network (CNN)

Backlash, **10**
Bennett, James Gordon, **10–11**
Berelson, Bernard, 159
Bernstein, Carl, **154**
Black, Hugo, **11**
Black Panthers, **11**, 20

Black power, **11–12**, 20
Black press, **12**
Blumler, Jay, **12–13**
Boorstin, Daniel, **13**
Boston Tea Party, 4
Brandeis, Louis, **13–14**. *See also Schenck
  v. United States*
Brennan, William J., Jr., **14**. *See also
  New York Times v. Sullivan*
Brinkley, David, **14–15**
Brown, Hubert Gerold, **15–16**
Burger, Warren, **16**. *See also New York
  Times v. Sullivan*
Bush, George, 5, 104
Bush-Rather interview, 5, **16–17**

Cable News Network (CNN), 8, **18**. *See
  also* Arnett, Peter
Cantril, Albert Hadley, **18–19**
Cantril, Hadley, **19**
Carmichael, Stokely, 11–12, **20**
Censorship, **20**
Chaffee, Steven H., **20–21**, 27, 47, 80,
  159
Chandler v. Florida, 16
Chicago Defender, 12
Chicago Tribune, **21**, 38
Christian Broadcasting Network, 124
Christian Coalition, **21–22**, 23
Christianity and Crisis, **22**

Christianity and politics, 21, **22–23**, 88
Christianity Today, **23–24**
Clarke, Peter, 159
Clear and present danger, **24**. *See also*
   Schenck v. United States
Cleaver, Eldridge, 11
Clinton, Bill, 26
Clinton, Hillary, **24–25**
Cognitive dissonance. *See* Festinger,
   Leon
Cohen, Akiba, 25
Communications researchers. *See* Blum-
   ler, Jay; Boorstin, Daniel; Cantril, Al-
   bert Hadley; Cantril, Hadley; Chaffee,
   Steven H.; Cohen, Akiba; Donohue,
   George; Dennis, Jack; Festinger, Leon;
   Galtung, Johan; Gans, Herbert; Gerb-
   ner, George; Graber, Doris; Jamieson,
   Kathleen Hall; Katz, Elihu; Kraus, Sid-
   ney; Lasswell, Harold; Lazarsfeld, Paul;
   McCombs, Maxwell; McLeod, Jack;
   Nafziger, Ralph; Nimmo, Dan; Olien,
   Clarice; Sabato, Larry; Schramm, Wil-
   bur; Stephenson, William; Tickenor,
   Philip; Weaver, David H.; Westley,
   Bruce
Communication theory. *See* Agenda-
   setting; Congruity; Co-orientation; Cul-
   tivation; Diffusion; Family
   communication patterns; Framing; Ga-
   tekeeping; Generation X; Hypodermic
   effect; Indexing; Knowledge gap;
   Limited-effects model; Priming; Reli-
   ance versus use; Selectivity; Spiral of
   silence; Third-person effect; Voter need
   for orientation
Concession speech, **26**
Congressional Black Caucus, **26**
Congruity, **26–27**
Co-orientation, **27**
Corporation for Public Broadcasting
   (CPB), **27–28**
Cowles, John and Gardner, **28–29**
Creel Commission, **29**
Cronkite, Walter, **29–30**, 36
Crouse, Timothy, **30–31**, 102, 158
C-SPAN, **31**
Cultivation, **31–32**, 58

Daisy commerical, **33**
Damage control, **33–34**. *See also* Public
   relations
Davis, Elmer, **34**
Day, Benjamin, **35**
Debates, **35**, 73
Democratic Convention of 1968, **36**
Demonstration, **36**
Dennis, Jack, **36–37**
Deregulation of the Federal Communica-
   tions Commission, **37–38**
"Dewey Defeats Truman," **38**
Diffusion, **38–39**
Diplomacy, **39**
Disinformation, **39**
Donohue, George, **39–40**, 74
Douglas, William O., 11, **40**
Douglass, Frederick, 12, **40–41**

Early, Stephen Tyree, **42**
Eichman case (*United States v. Eichman*),
   42–43
Endorsements, **43–44**
Equal Time Rule, **44–45**
Evans, Susan H., 159

Fairness Doctrine, **46**
Falwell, Jerry, 23, **47**, 88
Family communication patterns, **47–48**
Famous Episodes. *See* Agnew, Spiro;
   Bush-Rather interview; Daisy Commer-
   cial; Democratic Convention of 1968;
   "Dewey Defeats Truman"; Grenada
   invasion; Hart, Gary; Long, Huey; Mc-
   Carthy, Joseph; Panama invasion;
   Persian Gulf War; Scopes Monkey
   Trial; Thomas, Clarence; Truman firing
   of MacArthur; Watergate
FDR (Franklin Delano Roosevelt) and
   Radio, **48**, 125
Federal Communications Commission
   (FCC), 37
Festinger, Leon, **48–49**, 160
First Amendment. *See Abrams v. United
   States*; Clear and present danger; Eich-
   man Case (*United States v. Eichman*);
   Hustler v. Falwell; *Miami Herald v.*

Tornillo; Near v. Minnesota; New York Times v. Sullivan; Pentagon Papers; *Progressive* Case; *Richmond Newspapers v. Virginia; Schenck v. United States;* Seditious Libel; Symbolic Speech; Zenger, John Peter
Framing, **49**
Franklin, Benjamin, **49–50**
Freedom Forum, **50–51**
Freedom of Information Act (FOI), **51**
Freedom of speech, **51–52**
Freedom of the press, **52**
Freedom's Journal, 12
Friendly, Fred, **52–53**

Gallup, George, 29
Gallup Poll, **54**, 112
Galtung, Johan, **55**
Gans, Herbert, **55**
Garrison, William Lloyd, 40–41, **56**
Gatekeeping, **56–57**
Gaudet, Hazel, 159
Generation X, **57**
Gerbner, George, 31, **57–58**
Godkin, Edwin Lawrence, **58**
Goldwater, Barry, 33
Graber, Doris, **58–59**
Graham, Billy, 23–24
Greeley, Horace, 58, **59**
Grenada invasion, **60**

Hagerty, James Campbell, **61**
Hart, Gary, **62**
Hearst, William Randolph, **62–63**, 118, 155
Hoaxes, **63**
Hochheimer, John L., 159
Hofstetter, Richard, 158
Holmes, Oliver Wendell, 3, 128–29
Horton, Willie, 5
Howard, Roy Wilson, **63–64**
Howe, Louis Henry, **64**, 125
Huntley, Chet, 15
Hustler v. Falwell, **64–65**
Hutchins Commission, **65**
Hypodermic effect (magic bullet theory), **66**

Indexing, **67**

Jamieson, Kathleen Hall, **68**, 159
Jefferson, Thomas, 6, **68–69**
JFK and television, **69–70**
John Birch Society, **70**
Johnson, Lyndon, 33, 36
Joint operating agreements, **70–71**

Katz, Elihu, **72–73**, 78
Kennedy, John, 69–70, 73
Kennedy-Nixon debates, 69, **73**
Kerner Commission, **73–74**
Kirkpatrick, Clayton, 21
Klapper, Joseph, 159
Knowledge gap, 40, **74**
Koppel, Ted, **74–75**
Kraus, Sidney, **75**, 159
Krock, Arthur, **75–76**
Ku Klux Klan, **76**

Lamb, Brian, 31
Lasswell, Harold, **77**
Lazarsfeld, Paul F., 72, **78**, 100, 105–6, 159
League of Women Voters, **78**
Leak, **78–79**
Lemmon, Walter S., **79**
Levy, Mark, 160
Libel, **79–80**
Limited-effects model, **80**
Lippmann, Walter, 4, **80–81**, 157
Literary Digest Poll, **81**, 112
Lobbying, **81–82**
Long, Huey, **82**
Luntz, Frank, 159

Magazines. *See Christianity and Crisis; Christianity Today; National Review; New Republic; Newsweek; Time* Magazine; *U.S. News (and World Report)*
Martindale, Carolyn, 158
Mass media, **83**
Maynard, Robert C., **83–84**
McCarthy, Joseph, 34, 52, 84, 89–90
McCombs, Maxwell, 4, **85**, 160
McCormick, Robert R., 21, 29
McGinniss, Joe, **85**, 158

The McLaughlin Group, **85–86**
McLeod, Jack M., 27, 47–48, **86–87**
Media legal issues. *See* Alien and Sedition Acts of 1798; Censorship; Deregulation of the Federal Communications Commission; Equal Time Rule; Fairness Doctrine; Freedom of Information Act; Freedom of the press; Freedom of speech; Joint operating agreements; Libel
Media Organizations. *See* Corporation for Public Broadcasting; C-SPAN; Freedom Forum; Pew Research Center for the People & the Press
Media Techniques. *See* Endorsements; Hoaxes; Leak; Muckraker; National Election Service (NES); Pack journalism; Political cartoons; Political columnist; Political satirists; Sound bites
Medill, Joseph, 21
Miami Herald v. Tornillo, 16, **87**
Modern Maturity, 6
The Moral Majority, 23, **88**
Moyers, Bill, **88–89**
Muckraker, **89**
Murrow, Edward R., 52, 84, **89–90**

Nafziger, Ralph O., **91**
National Association for the Advancement of Colored People (NAACP), **91–92**
National Election Service (NES), **92**
National Organization of Women (NOW), **92**
National Review, **93**
National Rifle Association (NRA), **93**
Near v. Minnesota, **93–94**
New Republic, 58, **94**
Newspaper executives, 94. *See also* Bennett, James Gordon; Cowles, John and Gardner; Day, Benjamin; Greeley, Horace; Hearst, William Randolph; Howard, Roy Wilson; Pulitzer, Joseph
Newspapers. *See* Black press; *Chicago Tribune*; *New York Times*; Spanish-language press; *Washington Post*
Newsweek, **94–95**
Newton, Huey, 11

New World Information and Communication Order, **95**
New York Herald, 10, 105
New York Sun, 35, 63, 104, 105
New York Times, **96**, 105
New York Times v. Sullivan, 14, **96–97**, 131
New York Tribune, 59, 105
Niebuhr, Reinhold, 22
Nimmo, Dan, **97**, 109
Nixon, Richard M., 4, 5, 26, 36, 69, 73, 85, **97–98**

Office of War Information, 34
Olien, Clarice N., **39–40**, 74
Ombudsmen, **99**
One-Party Press, **100**
Opinion leaders, **100**, 106
Opinion measurement, **100–101**
O'Rourke, P. J., **101**

Pack journalism, 31, **102**, 158
Paine, Thomas, **102–3**
Panama invasion, **103–4**
Partisan press, **104**
Penny press, 35, **104–5**. *See* Day, Benjamin
Pentagon Papers, **105**
The People's Choice, 78, **105–6**
Persian Gulf War, **106–7**
Peterson, Theodore, 157
Pew Research Center for the People & the Press, **107**
Philadelphia Defender, 12
Photo op, **107–8**
Political action committees (PACs), **108**
Political activists. *See* Brown, Hubert Gerold; Carmichael, Stokely; Douglass, Frederick; Falwell, Jerry; Robertson, Pat; Steinem, Gloria Marie
Political cartoons, **108**
Political columnist, **108–9**
Political communicators. *See* Adams, Samuel; Ailes, Roger; Early, Stephen Tyree; Franklin, Benjamin; Hagerty, James Campbell; Howe, Louis Henry
Political journalists. *See* Alsop, Joseph and Stewart; Anderson, Jack; Arnett,

Peter; Bernstein, Carl; Crouse, Timothy; Krock, Arthur; Garrison, William Lloyd; Godkin, Edwin Lawrence; Lippmann, Walter; Maynard, Robert; McGinniss, Joe; O'Rourke, P. J.; Paine, Thomas; Safire, William; Thomas, Helen; Thompson, Hunter S.; White, Theodore H.; Woodward, Robert
Political persuaders, **109–10**. *See also* Dan Nimmo
Political satirists, **110–11**
Political techniques. *See* Backlash; Black power; Concession speech; Debates; Demonstration; Diplomacy; Disinformation; Leak; Politicalization; Rhetoric
Politicalization, **111**
Politically active organizations. *See* American Association of Retired Persons; American Civil Liberties Union; American Federation of Labor–Congress of Industrial Organizations; Black Panthers; Christian Coalition; Congressional Black Caucus; John Birch Society; Ku Klux Klan; League of Women Voters; Moral Majority; National Association for the Advancement of Colored People; National Organization of Women
Polk, James Knox, **111–12**
Polls, **112**
Polls and pollsters, 54, 81, 125–26
Presidential media manipulation, **112–13**
Presidential news conferences, **113**
Presidents and the press. *See* FDR and Radio; Jefferson, Thomas; JFK and television; Kennedy-Nixon Debates; Nixon, Richard M.; One-party press; Polk, James Knox; Presidential media manipulation; Presidential news conference; Reagan, Ronald; Roosevelt, Franklin D.
Presidents' wives and the press. *See* Clinton, Hillary; Roosevelt, Anna Eleanor
Press councils, **114**
Press performance. *See* Hutchins Commission; Kerner Commisson; New

World Information and Communication Order; Ombudsmen; Press councils
Pressure groups. *See* Lobbying; National Rifle Association; Political action committees; Southern Christian Leadership Conference
Priming, **115**. *See also* Agenda-setting
Progressive Case, **115**
Propaganda, **115–16**. *See also* Creel Commission; Elmer Davis
Protess, David, 160
Public opinion, **116**. *See also* Opinion leaders; Polls
Public relations, **116–17**. *See also* Damage control; Photo op; Political persuaders; Spin; Strategic political communicators; White House Office of Communication
Pulitzer, Joseph, 62–63, **117–18**, 155

Q sort method, **119**, 138

Radio, 34, 79, 120
Reagan, Ronald, 5, 46, **120–21**
Rehnquist, William H., **121–22**
Reliance versus use, **122**
Research findings and techniques, 100–101, 105–6, 119, 122, 138, 147
Rhetoric, **122–23**
Richmond Newspapers v. Virginia, **123**
Robertson, Pat, 22, 23, **123–24**
Robinson, John, 160
Roosevelt, Anna Eleanor, 7–8, **124–25**
Roosevelt, Franklin D., 11, 34, 42, 64, **125**
Roper, Elmo, **125–26**

Sabato, Larry, **127**, 159
Safire, William, **127–28**
Sarnoff, David, **128**
Schenck v. United States, 3, 13, 24, **128–29**
Schramm, Wilbur, **129**, 157
Scopes Monkey Trial, **129–30**
Seale, Bobby, 11
Seditious libel, **130–31**
Selectivity, **131–32**
Selling of the Pentagon, **132**

Sensationalism. *See* Penny press; Yellow journalism
Severin, Werner J., 160
Shaw, Bernard, **133**
Shaw, Donald, 4, 85, **133**, 160
Siebert, Fred, 157
Sinclair, Upton, **133–34**
60 Minutes, **134–35**
Sound bites, **135**
Southern Christian Leadership Conference, **135–36**
Spanish-language press, **136**
Spin, **136–37**
Spiral of silence, **137**
Stamp Act, 4
Steinem, Gloria Marie, **137–38**
Stempel, Guido, 158
Stephenson, William, **138**
Stereotyping, **138–39**
Strategic political communication, **139–40**
Supreme Court justices. *See* Black, Hugo; Brandeis, Louis; Brennan, William; Burger, Warren; Douglas, William O.; Rehnquist, William H.
Symbolic speech, **140–41**

Tankard, James W., 160
Tarbell, Ida, **142**
Tebbel, John, 159
Television journalism. *See* Brinkley, David; Cronkite, Walter; Friendly, Fred; Koppel, Ted; The McLaughlin Group; Moyers, Bill; Murrow, Edward R.; Sarnoff, David; Selling of the Pentagon; Shaw, Bernard; *60 Minutes*; Television's initial handling of politics.
Televison's initial handling of politics, **143–44**

Third-person effect, **144**
Thomas, Clarence, **144–45**
Thomas, Helen, **145–46**
Thompson, Hunter S., **146**
Tichenor, Philip, **39–40**, 74
Time Magazine, **146–47**
Times Mirror Center, 107, 147
Toure, Kwame, 20
Tracking polls, **147**
Truman, Harry S, 38, 76, 100, 148
Truman firing of MacArthur, **148**
Turner, Ted, 18
Two-step flow, 72, 78, 106

Uses and gratifications, 72. *See also* Katz, Elihu
U.S. News (and World Report), **149**

Voter need for orientation, **150**

Wanta, Wayne, 160
Washington Post, 105, **151**
Watergate, 98, **151–52**
Watts, Sarah Miles, 159
Weaver, David H., **152**, 160
Wells, Ida B., 12
Westley, Bruce H., 80, **152–53**
White, David Manning, 57
White, Theodore H., **153**, 158
White House Office of Communication, **153**
Whitney v. California, 13
Windhauser, John, 158
Woodward, Robert U., **154**

Yates v. U.S., 24, 129
Yellow journalism, 63, 118, **155**

Zenger, John Peter, **156**

About the Editors and Contributors

PAUL ASHDOWN is Professor in the School of Journalism at the University of Tennessee.

JAMES L. BAUGHMAN is Professor in the School of Journalism and Mass Communication at the University of Wisconsin-Madison.

MAURINE H. BEASLEY is Professor in the College of Journalism at the University of Maryland.

MICHAEL J. BREEN is Head, Department of Communication Studies at Mary Immaculate College in the University of Limerick in Ireland.

JUDITH M. BUDDENBAUM is Professor in the Department of Journalism and Technical Communication at Colorado State University.

LARRY L. BURRISS is Professor in the School of Journalism at Middle Tennessee State University.

CHARLES CAUDILL is Professor in the School of Journalism at the University of Tennessee.

ANJU G. CHAUDHARY is Associate Professor in the Department of Journalism at Howard University.

LEANNE DANIELS is Assistant Professor in the Manship School of Mass Communication at Louisiana State University.

PAUL D. DRISCOLL is Associate Professor in the School of Communications at the University of Miami.

B. CAROL EATON is research manager of programming for National Public Radio.

WALLACE B. EBERHARD is Professor in the Henry W. Grady College of Journalism and Mass Communication at the University of Georgia.

MARC EDGE is a doctoral student in the E. W. Scripps School of Journalism at Ohio University.

DANIEL J. FOLEY is Associate Professor in the School of Journalism at the University of Tennessee.

JACQUELINE NASH GIFFORD is a doctoral student in the E. W. Scripps School of Journalism at Ohio University.

MILENA KARAGYAZOVA, is a freelance writer in Bulgaria, her native country.

DAVID KENNAMER is Associate Professor in the School of Mass Communications at Virginia Commonwealth University.

STEPHEN LACY is Professor in the School of Journalism at Michigan State University.

EDWARD LEE LAMOUREUX is Associate Professor in the Department of Communication at Bradley University.

DOMINIC L. LASORSA is Associate Professor in the Department of Journalism at the University of Texas.

CAROL M. LIEBLER is Associate Professor in the S. I. Newhouse School of Public Communications at Syracuse University.

JAROL B. MANHEIM is Professor in the School of Media and Public Affairs at George Washington University.

J. SEAN McCLENEGHAN is Professor in the School of Journalism and Mass Communications at New Mexico State University.

WILL NORTON is Dean of the College of Journalism and Mass Communications at the University of Nebraska.

FOLU FOLARIN OGUNDIMU is Associate Professor in the School of Journalism at Michigan State University.

DAVID C. PERLMUTTER is Assistant Professor in the Manship School of Journalism and Mass Communication at Louisiana State University.

DON RANLY is Professor in the School of Journalism at the University of Missouri.

SAM G. RILEY is Professor in the Department of Communication Studies at Virginia Polytechnic Institute and State University.

CHURCHILL L. ROBERTS is Professor in the College of Journalism and Communications at the University of Florida.

JOSEPH A. RUSSOMANNO is Assistant Professor in the Walter Cronkite School of Journalism and Telecommunication at Arizona State University.

MICHAEL B. SALWEN is Professor in the School of Communications at the University of Miami.

PAMELA J. SHOEMAKER is the Jon Ben Snow Professor at the S. I. Newhouse School of Public Communications at Syracuse University.

MICHAEL W. SINGLETARY is Assistant Dean, Graduate School, at the University of Tennessee.

KIM A. SMITH is Professor in the Greenlee School of Journalism and Communication at Iowa State University.

ARDYTH B. SOHN is Professor in the Department of Journalism at Butler University.

GUIDO H. STEMPEL III is Distinguished Professor Emeritus in the E. W. Scripps School of Journalism at Ohio University.

LOWNDES F. STEPHENS is Professor in the College of Journalism and Mass Communications at the University of South Carolina.

HERB STRENTZ is Professor in the School of Journalism and Mass Communication at Drake University.

JUDITH SYLVESTER is Assistant Professor in the Manship School of Journalism at Louisiana State University.

WAYNE WANTA is Associate Professor in the School of Journalism and Communication at the University of Oregon.

KATHLEEN B. WATTERS is Associate Professor in the Department of Communication at the University of Dayton.

LIZ WATTS is Assistant Professor in the School of Mass Communications at Texas Tech University.

DAVID H. WEAVER is the Roy W. Howard Professor in the School of Journalism at Indiana University.